AT HOME

Historic Houses of Eastern Massachusetts

# AT HOME

BETH LUEY

**BRIGHT LEAF**
AMHERST AND BOSTON
An imprint of University of Massachusetts Press

ISBN 978-1-62534-419-9 (paper); 418-2 (hardcover)

Designed by Sally Nichols
Set in Adobe Garamond
Printed and bound by Integrated Books International, Inc.

Cover design by Kristina Kachele Design, llc
Cover photo: *Louisa May Alcott seated at a desk in her
bedchamber at Orchard House* (ca. 1872). Used by permission
of Louisa May Alcott's Orchard House.

Library of Congress Cataloging-in-Publication Data

Names: Luey, Beth, author.
Title: At home : historic houses of eastern Massachusetts / Beth Luey.
Description: Amherst : Bright Leaf, [2019] | Includes bibliographical
    references and index.
Identifiers: LCCN 2018051742 (print) | LCCN 2018058013 (ebook) | ISBN
    9781613766668 (ebook) | ISBN 9781613766675 (ebook) | ISBN
9781625344182 (hardcover) | ISBN 9781625344199 (pbk.)
Subjects: LCSH: Dwellings—Massachusetts—Guidebooks. | Architecture,
    Domestic—Massachusetts—Guidebooks. | Historic
    buildings—Massachusetts—Guidebooks. | Massachusetts—Biography.
Classification: LCC F65 (ebook) | LCC F65 .L84 2019 (print) | DDC
    974.4—dc23 LC record available at https://lccn.loc.gov/2018051742

British Library Cataloguing in Publication Data
A catalog record for this book is available from the British Library.

# Contents

# Preface and Acknowledgments

As I walked through the houses in this book, I often thought of the poem "Haunted Houses" by Henry Wadsworth Longfellow:

> All houses wherein men have lived and died
> Are haunted houses. Through the open doors
> The harmless phantoms on their errands glide,
> With feet that make no sound upon the floors.

Although the houses in this book harbor no ghosts, they evoke the spirits of those who lived in them. Knowing their stories, I did sometimes imagine people gliding through doors and along passageways. At Mary Baker Eddy's last house, I felt her assistants tiptoe silently along the thickly carpeted halls to avoid disturbing her during her work and devotions. I sensed the cats at the Gorey House padding along without a sound before jumping onto the artist's desk.

> We meet them at the door-way, on the stair,
> Along the passages they come and go,
> Impalpable impressions on the air,
> A sense of something moving to and fro.

The halls and narrow stairs of the Fairbanks House are well worn, and it was easy to sense Miss Rebecca and her aunts passing by as they performed their daily chores. The Alcott daughters are constantly running from room to room. I almost hoped I might bump into them on the stairs.

> There are more guests at table than the hosts
> invited; the illuminated hall
> Is thronged with quiet, inoffensive ghosts,
> As silent as the pictures on the wall.

In the Otis House, dinner guests from past centuries converse quietly, and throngs of elegantly dressed ladies and gentlemen laugh in the parlor. In the Rotch-Jones-Duff House, the guests are dressed in the plainer clothes of Quakers, and they ascend a less ornate staircase. John and Abigail Adams are not merely portraits on the walls of their house; they are real presences. Beauport is teeming with guests—in the hall, in the dining rooms, on the terrace, in constant conversation and celebration.

> The stranger at my fireside cannot see
> The forms I see, nor hear the sounds I hear;
> He but perceives what is; while unto me
> all that has been is visible and clear.

Before learning the stories of these houses, I would not have noticed these people gliding from room to room or sitting at the hearth, at their desks, or in their parlors. Now I am very much aware of their forms and their voices and the adventures that brought them to their homes. *What has been* is almost as real as *what is.*

> We have no title-deeds to house or lands;
> Owners and occupants of earlier dates
> From graves forgotten stretch their dusty hands,
> And hold in mortmain still their old estates.

We come to these houses as visitors. They are owned by people who are committed to their care and preservation— and by those who lived there in times past. *Mortmain* is a legal term meaning "perpetual, inalienable ownership of real estate"; literally, it means "dead hand." The hands of the dead of these houses—if they do reach out—do so in greeting and welcome, happy to share their lives and stories.

Of the many historic houses in Massachusetts, I chose those whose stories reached out to me. Each visit was an adventure, and talking with the people who lovingly maintain the houses always enriched the experience. The last thing I want is for this book to be a substitute for a visit. Rather, I hope it will inspire you to get into your car—or onto your bicycle—and see for yourself. At the end of each chapter are suggestions for other houses to visit, either nearby or in some way similar.

The houses in this book are all in the eastern half of the state. A forthcoming volume will cover the center and the west. All are open to the public. They charge reasonable admission fees and are free to members of the organizations that own them. All have websites that provide photographs and up-to-date information about hours, admission, accessibility, and special events.

I have had a great deal of fun writing this book, and I have many people to thank for that. The idea came from Matt Becker, executive editor at the University of Massachusetts Press, and he has been a harmonious sounding board throughout its development. My companions on visits to the houses—Priscilla Coit Murphy, Mary and Richard Utt, and my husband, Mike—have offered insights and ideas. And as always, libraries and their staffs made the research possible. I acquired many books through the efforts of the librarians at Fairhaven's Millicent Library and the SAILS Library Network; the Arizona State University Library enabled access to journal and dissertation databases; the Isabella Stewart

Gardner Museum provided transcripts of correspondence; and the Massachusetts Historical Society continues to create extraordinary online resources on the Adams family available to all. The librarians and archivists at Historic New England, the Trustees of the Reservation, the New Bedford Whaling Museum, and the Mary Baker Eddy Library provided guidance as well as documents and photographs. The curators, docents, and guides at the houses were all gracious, knowledgeable, and helpful. Special thanks go to those who read my drafts for accuracy: Daniel Neff at the Fairbanks House; Martha Van Koevering at Beauport; Rick Jones at the Gorey House Museum; the permissions staff at the Mary Baker Eddy Library; Lorna Condon at Historic New England; and Rebecca Clower and Melinda Huff at the Otis House. Thanks as well to Judith Graham, Susan Gray, Suzanne Guiod, Sara Martin, and Liz Bennett for various acts of inspiration, insight, and friendship.

Most of all, thank you to the generations of family members, preservationists, and philanthropists who have kept these houses alive and welcoming to visitors.

# AT HOME

# Over the River and through the Woods

## *The Fairbanks House, Dedham*

EVERY summer since 1902, descendants of Jonathan Fairbanks have gathered for a reunion in Dedham, at the family homestead, America's oldest surviving frame house. Jonathan and his family arrived in Boston in 1633 and began building the house four years later. Family members lived there continuously for nearly three centuries, but it has been a museum during the lifetimes of the living descendants. In some way, though, it is still their home—the site of collective memories that include prosperity, poverty, eccentricity, and murder.

### The Progenitor

Jonathan Fairbanks was born in Sowerby, in the West Riding of Yorkshire, toward the end of the sixteenth century. By the time he came to America he was a man of means. He sailed with his wife, Grace Smith, whom he had married in 1617; their six children, born between 1618 and 1629; and probably some servants. Jonathan's brother Richard and his wife, Elizabeth, settled in Boston in 1633. By 1637 Jonathan had been granted a twelve-acre lot in Dedham, southwest of Boston on the Charles River, and eight acres of swamp to clear. Over the next ten years, he acquired additional land

and hired a professional builder to construct a two-story house that the family genealogist describes as large for its time and "of more than ordinary pretensions." By modern standards, though, the house was modest: two rooms on each floor, an attic room, and a single central chimney.[1]

Jonathan was well respected and active in town affairs. However, church records show that he joined only in 1646, "not withstanding he had long stood off fro' the church upon some scruples about publike profession of faith & the covenant." His brother Richard had more serious disagreements with the church. Lorenzo Sayles Fairbanks, the family genealogist, wrote that in 1637 Richard was "disarmed, with many others, for holding and expressing 'opinions' with regard to the creeds and dogmas of the church." His beliefs made him too dangerous to own, buy, or borrow guns, pistols, swords, powder, shot, or matches. He nevertheless prospered in Boston: he owned a large amount of land and later became Boston's first postmaster.[2]

Jonathan Fairbanks cleared his swamplands and farmed, raising enough food to feed his family and to sell. The sheep and flax they raised enabled the family to spin wool and linen thread. Jonathan made spinning wheels and looms, and other members of the household may have engaged in woodworking, spinning, and weaving. Jonathan added to the house: cellars, a lean-to used as workspace and a dairy, and additional living space at the western end of the building. His oldest son, John, and his family lived in the western addition. By the time of his death in 1668, Jonathan had amassed a considerable estate. Following the English custom, he left the house and land to his oldest son, who was already living there. His wife, Grace, received the movable property and an annuity, while small bequests went to the other children. He had probably made his plans clear to his children before his death, because two of the younger sons had established themselves elsewhere: George in Medfield and Jonas in Lancaster. Jonathan, the youngest, lived in another house in Dedham.[3]

## From Generation to Generation

Jonathan's children married and had large families: he eventually had forty-seven grandchildren. John, who had married Sarah Fiske in 1641, continued to farm and add land to his inherited holdings. Jonathan's children and grandchildren were farmers, active to varying degrees in their towns, and eager to ensure their children's prosperity through land acquisition and education. Some became or married clergymen, teachers, and doctors. Many men in the subsequent generations fought in the Indian Wars and, later, the Revolutionary War. They also began to settle in other Massachusetts towns and in Connecticut, New York, New Hampshire, Vermont, and Canada. Because our focus is on the homestead, we will follow the careers of the descendants who remained at the house.[4]

John's first and third sons, Joshua and Jonathan, died in 1661; his second son, John, had settled in Wrentham. He therefore left his Dedham properties to his two younger sons, Joseph and Benjamin, giving Joseph the first choice of houses. Joseph chose the main house. He and his wife, Dorcas, had a daughter (Dorcas, born in 1684) and a son (Joseph, born in 1687), and in 1734 the younger Joseph inherited the house. He and his wife, Abigail Deane, had six sons and two daughters. In 1752, Joseph conveyed the house and lands to his oldest son, also named Joseph. Three years later, the younger Joseph sold the property to three of his brothers—John, Israel, and

Samuel—who in turn conveyed their interest to their brother Ebenezer in 1764. Ebenezer, then thirty-two years old, had married Prudence Farrington in 1756. Lorenzo Fairbanks described him as "a highly esteemed citizen . . . a man of fine presence and dignified bearing, and associated with the best people in town. He had considerable musical ability, and was for many years a member of the church choir. He sang with the choir at the memorial funeral services, held in Dedham, on the death of General Washington, the hymn and music, written with a pen, being among the relics now preserved in the old house."[5]

Over the years, the family made alterations to the house. The original windows with diamond-shaped panes were replaced by casement windows with rectangular panes. A staircase replaced the ladder to the second floor, and the original large hearths were reconfigured for greater convenience and efficiency. Ebenezer had a large family: at various times, the household included Ebenezer and Prudence; their unmarried sons, William, Joshua, Abner, and Jason; Ebenezer's sister Abigail, who died in 1798; and their son Ebenezer Jr. and his wife, Mary, who had eight children born between 1778 and 1796. They soon outgrew the house, so Ebenezer added an east wing of one and a half stories and a west wing, both existing buildings that were moved to the site. The additions made room for the three generations and changed the appearance of the house, with the pitched roof converted to a gambrel roof and windows and doors added and altered.[6]

For five generations, throughout the seventeenth and eighteenth centuries, life at the Fairbanks homestead had been comfortable and prosperous, neither unusual nor particularly eventful. At the turn of the nineteenth century, though, dramatic events brought the family into the public eye and changed their fortunes.

FIGURE I. Fairbanks House, ca. 1890. *Courtesy of the Fairbanks House.*

## An Unsolved Mystery

Ebenezer Sr.'s first son, Ebenezer Jr., was born in 1758, and Prudence and William were born soon after, in 1760 and 1762. Joshua was born six years later, and Abner six years after him. Their last son, Jason, was born in 1780. The younger Ebenezer recalled of his youngest brother that "never was a child so caressed, so beloved, or who appeared to have so many claims upon the attachment of his surrounding family: for as he grew in stature, his prepossessing form, his intelligent mind, and his affectionate temper, made him the hope, the delight, the boast of his connections. I have seldom known a disposition so inclined to good, nor a soul more free from evil, than appeared from all the conduct, and the whole character of his first boyhood."[7]

Ebenezer recalled that when Jason was twelve years old, he was unsuccessfully vaccinated against smallpox, and "the *natural* appearance of the disease, in its most malignant state, left but little hopes of his preservation." He was treated with mercury, and "his limbs and joints became sensibly affected, and his constitution so injured, that there appeared no expectation for this darling of his family, but to remain crippled and debilitated through his remaining existence. The strength and excellence of his native stamina, in a degree counteracted the destroyer. He was restored with the loss of several bones of his right arm, by which it partly withered, and became useless from the shoulder to the wrist." Unable to do farm work, Jason was sent to school, but severe headaches, probably caused by mercury poisoning, made study impossible. He briefly held a job in the office of the register of deeds, but his health forced him to retire. In addition to headaches, he suffered from fevers and weakness. By the time he was twenty, he was often unable to dress himself.[8]

Despite his physical limitations, Jason made friends with other young people in Dedham, including Elizabeth Fales, who was always called Betsey. As he recalled, "I paid my addresses, and was received by her as a favored lover, for a whole year, living in perfect harmony with all her family, and treated with the greatest respect and affection by them." Then Betsey's family withdrew their affection. Jason believed that it was because of some slight jokes he had made at their expense, though it may have been because of his obvious inability to support their daughter. "Not long after this, *Betsey* and I agreed to part, in order to see if the tide of rage and madness would not abate; but we rather found its furious enmity to increase." A year after their separation, they met by chance, and Betsey asked Jason "*If I thought it any crime for her to acknowledge that she loved my person, and could not be happy without enjoying my conversation?"* Jason answered "that I did not conceive it any crime for two persons of different sexes to avow their affection for each other; and as to myself, I would answer, that words could not convey the ardent and passionate expression of love that filled and warmed my breast towards her." Because of the Fales family's opposition, the couple met outdoors, in one of the outbuildings on the Fales property, or at the homes of neighbors. When Jason became too ill to leave his house, Betsey met him there, frequently staying until the early hours of the morning and once spending the night. On that occasion, they talked of marriage and agreed to see each other again the next week. Jason was feeling well enough to suggest that they meet in a nearby meadow.[9]

There are two versions of what happened in the meadow on May 18, 1801, between two and three in the afternoon. According to Jason, the couple talked about the difficulties that made marriage unlikely. Betsey expressed the doubts her family had raised about his love, and Jason replied angrily that if she believed what her sisters said about him, "she might go to the devil with them, since she so well knew that I had already *possessed her person, and received the pledge of her most tender attachment!*" Betsey called him a monster, "and looking on me, as I sat whittling a small piece of wood with a pen-knife, she cried out *'give me that knife, I will put an end to my existence, you false-hearted man!—for I had rather die than live!'* " She took the knife "and began, as if in a state of distraction, to stab her breast and body—screaming out and walking violently from me . . . while I, struck with astonishment, remained without power." After stabbing herself in the chest, Betsey cut her throat. Jason "immediately seized that cruel knife which had robbed me of all my fond heart held dear! and while it yet remained wet with her blood, stabbed myself in many and repeated places; only leaving off when I had finished cutting my own throat, and when I believed all was over with me."[10]

The other version is that of the prosecuting attorney at Jason's trial on August 5, 1801: that Jason Fairbanks, "not having the fear of God before his eyes, but being moved and seduced by the instigations of the devil . . . feloniously, will-fully, and of his malice aforethought, did make an assault, and that he the said Jason Fairbanks, with a certain knife, of the value of ten cents, which he the said Jason Fairbanks, in his right hand, then and there had and held," stabbed Betsey Fales and cut her throat.[11]

There is more agreement about what happened imme-diately after the disastrous meeting. Betsey's uncle, Samuel Fales, testified that at about three that afternoon, he "saw *Jason Fairbanks* standing by my house, with his throat cut, and having a number of stabs in his body. He said, *Betsey* had killed herself . . . I went to him, took hold of his hand, and held him, till her father came to us. I told her father we had better go and look for *Betsey*." Samuel asked his son to "hold" Jason while he and Nehemiah Fairbanks went to the meadow. They found Betsey bleeding and unable to speak. "She was lying on the ground, nearly on her face, with her arms extended over her head; her head lying between them . . . Her mother came just before she died," twenty or twenty-five minutes later. Jason was put to bed in an upstairs room at the Fales house, with his brother Ebenezer attending him. A coroner's inquisition was held the next day, and Bet-sey's funeral the day after that. On May 21, Jason was carried to the Dedham jail in a litter.[12]

Jason's wounds were grave. Dr. Charles Kitteridge, who examined him in prison, sewed up "a large wound on his throat" and treated three shallow wounds in his breast, three deeper wounds in his abdomen, and seven wounds on his arms and thigh. "His wounds were very dangerous. The one in the abdomen, began to mortify, and it was with great difficulty, the mortification was stopped. It brought on the lock-jaw, that lasted seven or eight days . . . I had but little prospect of his recovering." By August, however, Jason had gained enough strength to stand trial. On August 4, a grand jury voted to indict him for murder, and on August 5 Jason pleaded not guilty. He was represented by two prominent, politically active Boston attorneys: Harrison Gray Otis and John Lowell Jr. The prosecutor was Massachusetts Attorney General James Sullivan. The case was heard on August 6 and 7 before four justices of the Supreme Judicial Court and a jury, meeting in the First Parish Meeting House. According to a local newspaper, the courthouse was too small to accommodate the "throng of anxious spectators." The high-powered legal figures involved, as well as the romantic and dramatic possibilities of the story, generated interest far beyond Dedham. One historian claims that the case "evoked greater newspaper coverage than almost any previous homicide in the region, and local printers issued more than half a dozen separate publications on the case, some of which went into multiple editions." The trial was reported in newspapers as far away as Pennsylvania and Ohio.[13]

The testimony focused on two issues: the relationship between Jason and Betsey, and the nature of Betsey's wounds. Witnesses contradicted one another on both questions. Jason's family and friends testified to the long-standing friendship between the two young people and their genuine affection for each other, while Betsey's family denied any such relationship. The defense argued that Betsey's wounds could have been self-inflicted and that Jason was not physically capable of the attack. The prosecution dismissed Jason's claims of disability and asserted that it was impossible for Betsey to have stabbed herself.[14]

The lawyers on both sides were eloquent and emotional in their pleading. The defense asked the jury to consider human nature:

> If the Jury should have been informed, that a young lady, of eighteen, with her head filled with melancholy and romantic tales, passionately in love, a passion which adverse circumstances forbade the gratification of, with every gleam of hope extinct, had in a moment of phrenzy, put a period to her own existence.
>
> If at the same moment, a witness *equally credible*, had assured them, that a young man of irreproachable character, at the unripe age of twenty years, tenderly attached to a female of his own age, with whom he had grown up in the habits of intimacy and affection, and who returned his passion with equal ardor and greater constancy, had, without provocation, without inducement, destroyed the object of his tenderest regard, and butchered the beautiful victim in so barbarous and unexampled a manner, which tale should the Jury esteem most deserving of credit?—Which of them is the most *usual* catastrophe? Which of them excites the least horror? Which does the least violence to the feelings of human nature? . . .
>
> To murder youth, innocence and beauty, defenseless, in so cool, deliberate, and brutal a manner, would require more than an ordinary portion of the most diabolical spirit.[15]

The prosecution argued against suicide: "We find the fair sex, when sick of life, generally avoiding the ghastly wounds of the knife and dagger, and seeking an avenue through the water, or by poison, or strangling. We always find it preceded by melancholy, distemper, or a disposition to solitude and retirement." Witnesses agreed that Betsey had been cheerful on the morning of her death. But the prosecution focused its arguments on the idea that Jason had been a pampered child, never taught to master his will:

> If the tender love of the parents unfortunately robs them of that firmness which they ought to use in the government of their children, one ought to be led to conclude, that this alone would incline the child to search for their wishes, and to perform them with alacrity. In a life filled with temptations to errors, fatal in their nature; in a path thro' a wilderness full of dangers and evils, one would suppose that young travellers would gladly avail themselves of the wisdom experience has given. Yet too many rush on heedlessly over the ruin of thousands, who have fallen a prey in the same ways they are pursuing . . .
>
> The parent sometimes feels a kind of animal fondness for the infant; but yet he extends his views and wishes more to the point where he shall be relieved from the trouble of guardianship and the expense of education, than to that, when he shall view the child as beloved by the world, or at least by the neighborhood, for the correctness of his morals, the benevolence of his heart, and the chastity of his manners. Hence the child observes the public opinion to be treated with contempt, and gains an unalterable habit of despising it himself. He who does not regard the opinion of the public, places no estimation upon his own character, and soon becomes an unrestrained licentious profligate, capable of the most atrocious enormities.[16]

Closing arguments ended at ten o'clock on Friday evening, and the jury delivered its verdict at eight o'clock the next morning. They found Jason guilty, and Chief Justice Francis Dana, reportedly sobbing, delivered the verdict: that the prisoner "be carried from *hence* to the gaol from whence you came, and from thence to the place of execution, and there be hanged by the neck, until you are DEAD!!! and may God Almighty have mercy on your soul." Jason's lawyer John Lowell Jr. was said to have been so shaken by the verdict that he never again practiced law.[17]

Jason's family believed in his innocence and were probably angered by the prosecution's placing blame on the gentleness with which they had raised him. Hiring the best available defense counsel had proved ineffective against public opinion. They did not attempt to appeal the verdict. Rather, on August 18, at three in the morning, Jason's brother Ebenezer, two younger family members, and three friends broke into the Dedham jail and helped Jason escape.[18]

Jason headed toward Canada. His family had provided him with excellent horses and a good deal of money. He crossed the Connecticut River on August 19 and traveled north. On August 22 he reached Lake Champlain, where he planned to cross by boat into Saint Johns, Canada. The next morning at breakfast, Moses P. Holt, one of the party pursuing the fugitive, walked into the dining room. A Hartford newspaper reported that he "seized at once on both [Jason's] arms. He then told three persons who were present, that the man he had taken was a murderer who had escaped from justice; and he desired the landlord to give him a rope—but neither the landlord nor guests afforded the least aid." Holt took Jason to Northampton, Massachusetts, and then to Boston, where he was imprisoned on August 28. Governor Caleb Strong set the date of Jason's execution: September 10.[19]

On that day, Jason was escorted from Boston to the Norfolk County border by two officers of the law and a minister, the Reverend Dr. Thomas Thacher, who had visited him in both the Dedham and Boston prisons. There the sheriff took charge of the prisoner and, accompanied by three military companies, took him to the Dedham jail. At two o'clock, Jason was taken to the gallows constructed on Dedham Common, where ten thousand spectators awaited the execution. Jason "mounted the scaffold about a quarter before three, with his usual steadiness, and soon after making a signal with his handkerchief, was swung off. After hanging about 25 minutes, his body was cut down, and buried near the gallows."[20]

Jason wrote a letter to be opened after his death. In this "declaration," he denied "that there was a previous agreement to take each others lives." He repeated his version of the events as "a true and faithful account of all those affecting circumstances which have brought my youth to its most unhappy downfall!" He hoped that by the time his relatives read his words, "a merciful GOD has, in all hope, pardoned the repented errors of my youth, and to HIM have I made the expiation of what I have committed: for HE knows the veracity of all that I have here acknowledged, and that THIS is the only cause of my CONDEMNATION."[21]

What *did* happen in the meadow? Was the verdict just? Public opinion assumed Jason's guilt; his family and friends assumed his innocence. One account expresses the ambivalence a modern reader feels: the sermon that Thomas Thacher, minister of the Third Parish in Dedham, preached on September 13, the Sunday after Jason's execution. Thacher echoed the prosecution's case, exhorting young people to restrain their passions and urging parents not to indulge their children. But when he spoke of Jason, subtle notes of doubt crept in. He reminded his congregation that more than one victim had suffered: "the *eighteenth of May* last, exhibited an event more tragical and horrid than hath been known to the most aged among us, or even recorded in the annals of this country. So extraordinary was it in itself—*so mysterious in its causes*; that notwithstanding the apparent authenticity with which it hath been reported; it will excite not merely admiration but scepticism in posterity. The train of calamities it hath introduced on two respectable families in this town, on their connections and the community, may almost tempt us to borrow the language of *Job*, when he execrated the day of his nativity . . . our sympathy and consolation shall be equally communicated to each of those distressed families implicated in that most unhappy event!" Despite his conversations with Jason, Thacher had been unable to find a motive, and he expected future generations to question the newspaper (and perhaps the official) accounts, whose authenticity was merely "apparent."[22]

Thacher then shed doubt on the prosecution's evidence by recounting his discussions with Jason before the trial: "He was very deeply affected with some impieties then propagated concerning him, which he very solemnly denied; and said he could demonstrate his innocence by unexceptionable testimony. In one of those visits, he spoke with strong feelings, but without bitterness, of some characters whom he judged to be his active personal enemies." Conversations after the trial reinforced those impressions: Thacher told him "*that if he were innocent of the death of* Elizabeth Fales—*yet there were so many probabilities of his guilt in his appearance—that the Court and Jury could not have acted otherwise.* To the justice of this remark, he fully assented; but complained of the witnesses—of two—that they had sworn falsely—of some others—that though they had related no untruths; yet they had foreborne to bring forward some facts which might have been of great advantage in his defence."[23]

Thacher denied accounts of Jason's impiety: "In every visit I paid him, one only excepted, at his own motion he desired prayers.—The like was observed by some other ministers who casually visited him. He appeared to have a strong filial piety to his parents; and desired me to visit them in their affliction—nor were their names ever mentioned, when I was present, either at prayers, or in private conversation, without extorting his tears. From which, as well as other like circumstances that might be mentioned, I have drawn this conclusion:—That though there was a want of candor which prevented such communications as were highly necessary for one in his condition—and a reserve which precluded him from exhibiting what sense he had of his past crimes, or future hopes; yet, 'that he was hostile to all religious instruction, or a hardened wretch void of all sensibility,' are charges not founded on any facts which occurred within my own observation or memory."[24]

Jason's conduct at his execution was, to Thacher, an indication of decency—even heroism: "He was not ignorant that he was an object of almost universal execration; that his wishes for the small space of life usually granted to other offenders, was denied; that the zeal and influence of individuals, was exerted to contract that narrow allowance. Yet still his mind appeared sufficient to combat death arrayed in all its terrors . . . He hath been condemned by the laws of this country, and if guilty, hath expiated them by his punishment. But this we scruple to say—that had the same measure of fortitude been possessed by a truly virtuous man, it might have made him a martyr for religion; a patriot bleeding on the scaffold for vindicating the rights of his country; or a hero crowned with glory expiring on the bed of honor." Although Thacher may not have believed firmly in Jason's innocence, the phrase "if guilty" suggests at least a reasonable doubt.[25]

Jason's niece Sukey, who was eighteen when he was executed, certainly believed in his innocence. She named her first son, born in 1806, Calvin, after a brother who had died in 1800. She named her second son, born in 1818, Jason.[26]

## The Aftermath

Without letters and diaries, we can only imagine the emotional impact of Jason's execution on the Fairbanks family. In addition to their grief and sense of injustice, they must have experienced anger, even scorn, from many neighbors. Some townspeople would have acceded to Thacher's appeal for sympathy, but not all. Fairly or not, the family of a convicted murderer is shamed. Abetting Jason's escape extended culpability to his brother and nephew.

The family also suffered financially. Ebenezer's expansion of the house had been expensive. Now he had to pay the fees of Harrison Gray Otis and John Lowell Jr., who had defended Jason. For arranging Jason's escape, Ebenezer was sentenced to four months in jail, and Nathaniel, to two. Both had to pay fines. Ebenezer's pamphlet, *Solemn Declaration of the Late Unfortunate Jason Fairbanks*, sold out three editions in a year but generated little profit. Ebenezer died in 1832, deep in debt. Nevertheless, his estate retained ownership of the homestead, which he bequeathed to his wife, Mary. At her death in 1843, the property was divided among four of their children. Joshua was given part of the land, and their unmarried daughters—Prudence, Sarah, and Nancy—were left the house for as long as they lived.[27]

## Single Ladies

Prudence, Sarah, and Nancy were middle-aged when their mother died, and they all lived into their eighties. (Prudence died only days before her ninetieth birthday.) The house was not the easiest place for older people to live. Alvin Lincoln Jones, who visited the house twenty years after the sisters' deaths, wrote that "in its primitive simplicity it brings us nearer to a true understanding of the actual appearance and characteristics of the homes of our forefathers, than any other house we have seen"—an observation that remains accurate. The most modern features were a coal cookstove and oil lamps. It was filled with "souvenirs of days gone by": cooking and sewing implements, saddles, spinning wheels, china, foot warmers, and trunks filled with clothing. The outhouse had been replaced by a two-seater privy in a small room in the lean-to, but there was still no indoor plumbing.[28]

Predictably, the sisters were the subject of neighborhood rumors. A journalist noted that gossips "asserted that they could not agree together, and that each lived in a separate part of the house, occupying individual chambers, and at times refusing to see each other for days and weeks at a time . . . We want to state, as a matter of justice, that these things are not so. It is true that the sisters occupied separate apartments during the last years of their lives; but it was not from any dislike to each other, but from the natural desire of old folks to be alone. They had their peculiarities, as might have been expected; yet as long as they lived they had their meals together, and attended to the household duties in turn, each one doing the work for a week. And although the dilapidation of the house made the task of keeping it in order rather difficult, their housekeeping was of the first order." According to another account, the sisters were said to have

FIGURE 2. Nancy and Sally Fairbanks, with some of the family heirlooms. *Courtesy of the Dedham Historical Society and Museum, Dedham, Massachusetts.*

"kept their reputation for amiability, and were great favorites with the young people, who used to visit them, to hear the stories of the olden time."[29]

When a Boston journalist visited the house in 1885, he was shown documents that told a bit more about the sisters. Nancy and Sarah had saved certificates citing their "good and amiable scholarship"; these were "treasured most carefully by the little girls who won them." He also found "a wonderful roll, which Nancy exhibited on one of the school public days, as a proof of her penmanship. It has the alphabet in various kinds of letters, in vari-colored inks; there is ornamental work of all kinds . . . there are old maxims and chronicled historical events—all these form an elaborate border for the center, which was a copy of the then celebrated poem of 'Edwin and Angelina,' written in script." The scroll includes brief essays on friendship, charity, envy, virtue, revenge, beauty, passion, sentiment, benevolence, and candor. It is an impressive display of design as well as handwriting. Nancy "would have had 'literary aspirations,' had such things been the fashion in her day. She did write verses, but the only relative to whom she confided the fact begged her to keep them to herself, else 'folks would think she was weakening.'" The poetry was never found, and the visitor thought that "the dear old lady must have destroyed it after her rebuff by the unappreciative relative."[30]

Their great niece also recalled Nancy as being "very plain, but very literary, read Scott and Shakespeare when she was very young . . . She enjoyed novels, if, at the end, the hero and heroine were married, she would look over to the end to see, if not she dropped the book." She remembered Aunt Prudence as "very witty and droll. Aunt Sally was very dainty, was quite fond of dress, and loved to use perfumery . . . She did her front locks on broom corns in the morning in order to have little curls behind her ears in the afternoon and the white hair was bound by a black velvet ribbon."[31]

The sisters were protective of the homestead. When the town built Willow Road, now Eastern Avenue, the sisters opposed it. According to Lorenzo Sayles Fairbanks, they regarded the road as merely "a 'modern convenience' . . . It made the road to the village shorter by half than the old way, but that had no weight with the inflexible women, who had inherited all the decision and firmness of a long line of Puritan ancestors. They protested against the building of the road, but when it was built, in spite of their protests, it is said that they declared they never would use it, and they kept their word. Constant attendants of the old Congregational Church in Dedham, they went persistently the longest way round, rather than, even for their own convenience, show any toleration for what they so honestly opposed." Their great niece said they "requested that their bodies, after death, should be taken the old way."[32]

Nancy outlived her two sisters, describing herself as "the greatest curiosity that the antiquated building contained." When she died, in 1879, the house passed to her niece Rebecca, Joshua's youngest daughter, who was fifty-two years old. Joshua had had six children. His two sons had predeceased him, and three of his daughters had married and were living elsewhere. Rufus Haven Mills, Rebecca's cousin by marriage—the widower of Joshua's daughter Harriet Sophia—lived at least part of the time at the homestead until his death in 1895. This was rarely (if ever) mentioned, perhaps because of the impropriety of single people of different sexes living together, even at rather advanced ages. Rebecca became the last member of the family to live in the house. She shared her aunts' pride in the homestead, as well as its inconveniences and the lack of funds. To support herself, she began selling family furniture and artifacts.[33]

One of the family's proudest possessions was a smoothbore flintlock musket, which had been in the family since at least 1745, when Lieutenant Joseph Fairbanks used it to fight the French in Nova Scotia and at the Siege of Louisbourg. The gun, for many years in family hands elsewhere, was returned to the homestead during Rebecca's tenure. In 1888, perhaps concerned about the disappearance of so many family

FIGURE 3. Rebecca Fairbanks. *Courtesy of the Dedham Historical Society and Museum, Dedham, Massachusetts.*

artifacts, the Reverend Henry Fairbanks, a clergyman and inventor from the Vermont branch of the family, bought it from her. Rebecca had refused many offers for the gun before selling it to Henry. According to one descendant, she had been "so besieged to part with the old gun that she lamented having only one to sell. So she went to market and got herself a couple. Family tradition has it that Rebecca hung each gun in its turn on the pegs in place of the genuine and, as buyers pestered her, she represented nothing—only sold them the gun which hung there." Her entrepreneurial activities were exposed around 1890, when one buyer boasted that he had purchased the Fairbanks musket. "Promptly another denied the report; said that he had it."[34]

Rebecca also sold a carved wooden chest built in the mid-seventeenth century by John Houghton that had been in the house when the first Jonathan Fairbanks lived there. It was still in the house as late as 1881, when it featured in an illustration to an article about the house in *American Architect and Building News*. The chest came up for auction at Christie's in New York in June 2003, with an expected purchase price of $6,000 to $9,000. Family members were eager to bring the chest back to the homestead. Convinced that the estimate was too low, they raised donations and pledges of considerably more. Two other serious bidders participated, but when the gavel came down, the Fairbanks Family in America Association, which owns the house, had purchased the chest for $71,700. The association is still tracing its journey from the homestead to Christie's.[35]

Rebecca appeared in the Boston newspapers in 1892, when the house was struck by lightning: "A dog under a bed occupied by Miss Rebecca Fairbanks in a sleeping room on the lower floor was instantly killed, but Miss Fairbanks escaped injury. The bolt as it came into the house resembled a large ball of blue and red fire, a form it held until it burst and tore things in pieces." Part of the building was so badly damaged that it was thought the house might have to be razed. It was soon repaired, however, and Rebecca was able to move back after a stay in Boston.[36]

Three years later, Rebecca sold the house to a Dedham real estate dealer, John Crowley, with the provision that she be allowed to live there for at least six months. She stayed in the house and, from time to time, welcomed visitors. In November 1896, for example, she entertained twenty-six members of the Adams chapter of the Daughters of the American Revolution, and in 1898 the *Boston Sunday Globe* reported that she had found four drawings in the house by an English soldier named Honeyman, illustrating the battles at Lexington and Concord. The article described the house as "a monument dedicated to the greatest thing in the world, the thing which makes great nations, 'the household.'"[37]

It was widely assumed that once Rebecca left the house, Crowley would tear it down and sell or build on the land. On April 3, 1897, the *Boston Evening Transcript* published a letter from Mrs. Nelson V. Titus, treasurer of the recently formed Fund for the Preservation of the Fairbanks House. Titled "A Last Appeal for the Fairbanks House," it set out the history and importance of the house and explained that Crowley was willing to sell it for what he had paid for it, $4,500. The letter then got down to business:

> The purpose of this appeal is to try to arouse in the members of the patriotic societies here in Massachusetts a sense of the duty which they owe to themselves and to their country to try to preserve for Massachusetts this interesting relic of the Colonial days. There are 5,000 members of the patriotic societies alone in Massachusetts. If each would contribute a little, the preservation of this famous old landmark would be assured. Miss Rebecca Fairbanks leaves the house on May 1. If the house can be preserved she will leave in it the ancient furniture and relics identified with its history. Will the "Sons" and "Daughters" of

Massachusetts allow this famous old house to be destroyed? If the preservation of the house can be assured, a chapter of the Society of the Daughters of the Revolution, which is incorporated under the laws of the Commonwealth of Massachusetts, will be responsible for the care of the house, or a board of trustees may be chosen from members of the different patriotic societies. It is hoped that this appeal will find an echo in the hearts of those to whom the history of their country is dear, and that a generous response will be made to help save to Massachusetts this famous relic of the Colonial days. All patriotic citizens of Massachusetts are asked to contribute, and the names of the donors will be preserved for future reference in the old house.[38]

Success arrived with astonishing speed. Only five days later, Mrs. Titus wrote to the *Transcript* to announce that Mrs. J. Amory Codman, heir to a Boston real estate fortune, and her daughter, Miss Martha C. Codman, had provided the funds. The change in ownership altered Rebecca's plans. She did not leave the house on May 1 but stayed on, with the understanding that she would open the house to visitors. Within days after the Codmans had purchased the house, the Fairbanks chapter of the Daughters of the American Revolution was formed, and Rebecca entertained them at the homestead.[39]

Unfortunately, Rebecca was not always hospitable. One journalist said that she felt besieged by "sketching-classes and camera clubs. A dozen at a time will plant their easels at advantageous points around the house; and once the good lady informed me that she counted twenty 'squatted down all over the yard,' as she expressed it . . . so great has been the annoyance, Miss Fairbanks has been obliged to keep the dooryard clear of these budding 'Raphaels.'" Not only strangers were turned away. John Wilder Fairbanks, the secretary

of the newly formed family association, told a Boston newspaper that Rebecca "refused admittance to Mrs. Codman's
friends and the public, and things went so far awry that
Mrs. Codman had no heart to go to see her own property."
Rebecca, he said, was hostile to "anyone who seemed desir-
ous of bringing the old place to the front . . . People were
coming there every day—singly and in numbers—only to be
turned away. No matter if they came from faraway California, as some did, the door was shut to them."[40]

The situation did not improve when the Fairbanks family
took possession. In 1902, the Fairbanks Family in America
Association was formed, to which the Codmans agreed to
sell the house, giving the association five years to raise the
funds. Rebecca said she did not want to stay in the house.
John Wilder Fairbanks said that he "told her we all wanted
her to stay, that it was the idyllic thing, that she ought to stay
there as long as she lived." In the summer of 1904, Rebecca
fell ill and told John, "I'm going right out as soon as I get up;
I know this isn't the place for me." In September, the board
members looked for a place for her to live, but John found
that "none of us could please her. Finally it was forced upon
some of the board that she didn't intend to go 'until she got
good and ready.' Winter was coming on. The home needed
fixing, and it is no place for a woman with rheumatism to
live." The board felt they had no alternative but to evict her.[41]

The action might have gone unnoticed outside the family,
except that one Fairbanks had won an important election in
November 1904: Charles W. Fairbanks had become the vice
president elect of the United States. On November 13, the
*Boston Sunday Post* filled three-quarters of a page with an
article headlined "Relative of Vice President–Elect Fairbanks
Evicted from Her Old Home in Dedham," accompanied by
several illustrations. It was pure melodrama:

A tragic occurrence took place yesterday, in Dedham, that brought tears to the eyes of the many friends who witnessed it. Pity and sympathy were mingled with indignation. It was the spectacle of a white-haired, sad-faced old lady, a relative of the Vice-President elect of the United States, within but two milestones of her 80th year mark, being taken away in her wheel chair from the old, weather-beaten home, where all the sweetest and dearest memories of her life had been gathered.

Evicted at the age of 78, the last one of that branch of her family that had occupied the homestead for 268 years continuously, with the associations of a lifetime clustered about the celebrated old place in her mind, the old lady sat bravely in her invalid's chair and outside the tumbling old fence that inclosed the dearest spot in the world to her looked in tearful farewell for the last time upon her home. It was the first time that she had been outside the house for three years—the first time in 30 years that she had gone away from it to remain even overnight, this time she was going for good, because the members of her own family—not strangers—were compelling her to leave. . . .

At the last moment she trembled a little and the tears came to her eyes and she begged for a few moments longer in which to remain and take her farewells. If it were for some other reason, she thought, if it were not the members of the Fairbanks family itself who were turning me out from the dear old place, I could endure it better.[42]

The newspaper did allow John Wilder Fairbanks to tell the family's side of the story in the article. He described Rebecca's refusals to admit visitors and then added further details: "From the very first Miss Rebecca has evinced no love for the place . . . I have known Miss Rebecca for the past eight years . . . Many and many a time during these years has she told me that she hated thoroughly the place; she had no love for it whatever. She has showed to us all these past few years she has sold off at exorbitant prices almost everything of intrinsic value and has even replaced other things to sell again. She was not born in the house, as the papers stated; it came to her by inheritance from her three maiden aunts. She has had a lonely life, yet she has many nephews and nieces, none of them scarcely ever coming there; for, as they say out at Dedham, she has turned everyone against her."

Rebecca died in 1909. Two years later, her personal effects were auctioned off, including a medal, dated May 1854, "awarded to Becky Fairbanks for superior appetite, industry and good looks."[43]

## The House Becomes a Museum

As John Wilder Fairbanks had said, the house needed a lot of work. The women who had been living in it for more than half a century could afford only the most urgent repairs. The association formed in 1902 needed to finance the building's maintenance, repairs, and possible restoration. It was fortunate that the family did *not* have a great deal of capital, because they were at first advised to undertake work that would have diminished the historical value of the homestead.

In 1910, when William Sumner Appleton founded the Society for the Preservation of New England Antiquities (SPNEA, now Historic New England), some preservationists favored restoring houses to their appearance when the first owners moved in. An extreme advocate of this approach was Wallace Nutting, whose interest focused on the interiors and furnishings of colonial houses. His ideal was "a worthy house of the Seventeenth Century restored and furnished as the second Pilgrim generation would have had it . . . a house of harmonious style throughout . . . with interior decorations also in keeping with its time." He acquired and refurbished five houses between 1914 and 1915, creating what he called his "Colonial Chain."[44] Appleton suggested that the family association lease the house to Nutting for fifteen to twenty-five years, "on condition that Mr. Nutting restore and repair the house perfectly and keep it in repair during the period of lease." A few months later, he wrote that "there is no doubt in my mind but that much should be done to the Fairbanks House[,] the house resilled, girts made true, the missing portions of the wall filling replaced, and most important of all, the old windows should be put back in their original location and style." Some of these actions were needed, but others would have seriously diminished the value of the house for architectural historians, social historians, and visitors. Fortunately, the association did not turn the house over to Nutting and undertook only necessary repairs.[45]

In the meantime, Appleton and his colleagues were rethinking their principles. By the 1920s, the emphasis was generally on *preservation* rather than restoration. "Turning away from heavy restoration," Appleton "argued that buildings should display the visible record of change over time," because "what is left today can be changed tomorrow, whereas what is removed today can perhaps never be put back." His advice to the Jackson family in the 1920s applied to the Fairbanks family as well: "Generations of your forebears have lived there and made this a part of their lives too. It seems to me that we can't willingly erase aspects of history." He also insisted that changes to buildings should be documented and photographed. The family's care of the house adhered to Appleton's later approach.[46]

New England winters, aging trees, and other natural dangers constantly threaten old houses. The roofs, clapboards, windows, plaster, and structural elements of the house have all been restored according to the rigorous—and expensive— standards of modern preservation practice. Throughout the first half of the twentieth century, repairs were made to the foundations, footings, sills, floors, and chimney. In 1964, the house suffered serious damage when a seventeen-year-old driver lost control of his car on East Street and crashed into it. The association built a fence, and later a stone wall, to protect the house from further collisions. Three years later, someone tried to set the house on fire, but passing motorists extinguished the flames before much damage was done. Floodlights, and later an alarm system, were installed, resulting in the 1980 capture of two would-be burglars hiding under the canopy bed.[47]

The Fairbanks House was initially preserved through the efforts of the family, with support from privately funded groups, such as SPNEA. Beginning in the 1960s, however, historic preservation became an official concern of federal and state governments. The National Historic Preservation Act, the National Register of Historic Places, the Historic American Buildings Survey, and other public and private efforts brought both interest and funding to historic sites. When the first national historic landmarks were recognized in 1960, the house was one of seventeen honored in Massachusetts. The Fairbanks Family in America Association was quick to tap into newly available resources, and it received grants from the Department of the Interior and the Massachusetts Historical Commission. The family developed a conservation plan with help from SPNEA. Nevertheless, most of the costs have been met through dues, donations, bequests, and the sale of souvenirs.[48]

All repairs to the house are documented and photographed, and they offer opportunities to study the construction techniques and materials of past centuries. For example, in November and December 2006, the oldest part of the roof was reshingled. As the curator reported, "We cleaned and photographed exposed portions of the roof, including the join between the lean-to and the original house, and the oak sheathing boards on the south side of the roof that have been dated by dendrochronolgy to circa 1652–55. The sheathing boards were found to be riven rather than sawn. The 1650s date of these boards suggests that the family replaced their original roof very early in the house's history. One intriguing possibility is that the Fairbanks House's original roof may have been thatch, quickly replaced because it was such a fire hazard."[49]

The family association has also undertaken archaeological research to locate and identify outbuildings and artifacts, as well as genealogical research to extend the 1897 volume into the present and publish it as a CD.[50] And once a year—every year since 1902—the family has held a reunion at the homestead.

## Homecoming

On August 13, 2016, Fairbanks descendants from the Midwest, vacationing in New England, visited the homestead. The site was unexpectedly busy, with about a hundred people chatting and wandering around the house and grounds. Much to their surprise, they were greeted as cousins. They had come, by accident, on the day of the 114th Fairbanks family reunion.

The descendants of Jonas and Lydia had held a reunion in 1901, and the larger group decided to follow their example. They issued three thousand invitations, and more than seven hundred descendants attended the reunion on August 27, 1902, when the Fairbanks Family in America Association was formed. By 1906 the association had identified fifteen thousand descendants. In the early years, family members traveled to the homestead from Boston by train and returned to the city for a banquet. Many dressed in period costumes, and in 1907 the *Boston Post* headlined its coverage of the event, "Beauty of the Fairbanks Family Admired for Artistic Posing." It included a photograph of Miss Coralu Schutz of Pittsfield, Illinois, seated at a spinning wheel in the kitchen in "an old-fashioned dress patterned after those of a century ago."[51]

Many guests at the 2016 reunion had been attending all their lives. Some could recite all their Fairbanks ancestors going back to Jonathan, while others knew only that they were descendants. Those visiting the house for the first time ducked their heads as they went through the low doorways and up the steep stairs. The docents held even the small children spellbound: this was the house where their family had lived fourteen or fifteen generations earlier. The attendees enjoyed seeing old friends, meeting new "cousins," and learning more about the house and family. The house is the magnet that draws them each year and holds them together with a common purpose.

Arthur W. Fairbanks, who created the certificate sent to each descendant upon joining the association, urged parents to give their children the certificate, with its picture of the house, to hang on the wall of their rooms, "that each morning, during childhood, when they awake, and each evening when they go to rest, their eyes may look on the picture of this old place and they will think of how many little children that old bent roof has sheltered; how many little ones have played about those quaint old doors and windows; and how many nights, through the long years, those little children have dropped to sleep safe in the protecting arms of its old oaken beams. And when, in the later years, life's troubles begin to crowd upon the dreams of childhood, these older children shall go from their rooms with courage strengthened in the thought of how many of their forefathers have, in the mornings of the past, gone forth to meet successfully the duties of *their* day. And when tired and worn at evening they return, seeking rest, their spirits may find a measure of hope and comfort in this evidence of their heroic past." Family members in 2016 chose different words to express the same thoughts: visiting the house gave them a sense of connection to the past, the knowledge of having roots, a conviction that they had come home. Their commitment to the house reaffirms the sentiments of Marshall P. Wilder, a descendant who had attended the 1903 reunion: "To know nothing of our ancestry, or whence we came, to have no reverence for the precious memories of the past or interest in those who are to succeed us, is to ignore the elements and influences that have made us what we are."[52]

## To Visit

The Fairbanks House offers an experience very different from those in fully restored houses. Because no changes beyond essential repairs have been made for over a hundred years, visitors get an immediate sense of life in the house from the earliest days through the nineteenth century. Architectural historians and those interested in building techniques and materials will have a field day. In 1912, the association erected a Sears Roebuck Craftsman-style bungalow near the house as a caretaker's home. The bungalow is now itself a historic house—one of the few Sears kit houses in its original condition.

The house is open for tours Tuesday through Sunday from May through October (www.fairbankshouse.org). If you arrive on Tuesday through Friday, you can add a visit to the Dedham Historical Society and Museum (www.dedham-historical.org), which publishes a booklet leading you on a self-guided walking tour of the town, including interesting houses, churches, and public buildings, such as the Norfolk County Courthouse, where Nicola Sacco and Bartolomeo Vanzetti were tried. Much farther afield, you can visit the house that John Boylston and Sarah Van Wagoner Fairbanks built between 1856 and 1862. In 1981, this adobe house was moved from Payson, Utah, to This Is the Place Heritage Park in Salt Lake City (www.thisistheplace.org). It is open daily, year-round.

## To Learn More

In 1897, Lorenzo Sayles Fairbanks compiled *Genealogy of the Fairbanks Family in America, 1633–1897*, available in print or as a CD from the house website and online through Google Books. For detailed information and photographs about the construction and preservation of the house, see Abbott Lowell Cummings, *The Fairbanks House: A History of the Oldest Timber-Frame Building in New England*, 2nd ed. For more information about the construction and materials used in the colonial era, see Cummings's *The Framed Houses of Massachusetts Bay, 1625–1725*. The documents related to the case of Jason Fairbanks in 1801 are collected in *A Massachusetts*

*Mystery: The 1801 Tragedy of Jason Fairbanks and Elizabeth Fales*, compiled by the Fairbanks House and the Dedham Historical Society. It includes an introduction by Dale H. Freeman, the *Report* of the trial, Jason's *Declaration*, Ebenezer's *Life and Character*, and the Reverend Thomas Thacher's *Discourse*, each separately paginated. Freeman provides an excellent narrative in "'Melancholy Catastrophe!': The Story of Jason Fairbanks and Elizabeth Fales (1801)," *Historical Journal of Massachusetts* 26, no. 1 (January 1998): 1–26. An earlier version is available on the house website. The Boston *Post*, *Transcript*, and *Globe*, accessible through several digital newspaper collections, reported on the house, on reunions, and extensively on the eviction of Miss Rebecca Fairbanks. The association's archives, in the caretaker's cottage, contain the association newsletter, copies of newspaper and magazine articles, documents, and artifacts from the house. There is a useful finding aid.

# 2

## First Families

*Adams National Historical Park, Quincy*

ONE small saltbox house in North Braintree, now called Quincy, was the birthplace of John Adams, second president of the United States, and his two brothers. A few yards away, a nearly identical house was the birthplace of John Quincy Adams, sixth president, and the childhood home of his sister and two brothers. About a mile away sits Peace Field, or the Old House, where John and his wife, Abigail, were living when John became president. Other family members, too, lived in these houses. Fortunately, John, John Quincy, John Quincy's wife, Louisa, and their son Charles Francis all kept journals. Husbands, wives, brothers, sisters, and children—frequently separated by service to the country—wrote thousands of letters. Nearly four centuries later, we can discover from their words what those three houses meant to each of them at different times in their lives.

### "Still, Calm, Happy Braintree"

In 1720 Deacon John Adams, a twenty-nine-year-old farmer and shoemaker, bought a farm and very small house in rural Braintree, southeast of Boston on Boston Bay. The house had only two rooms, plus a lean-to. In 1734 he married Susanna Boylston, a socially prominent Bostonian seventeen years his junior. Their three sons—John, Peter, and Elihu—were all born there. He later bought the house next door, and the farm and houses became known as Penn's Hill. In 1750 he added rooms to the original house that made it the saltbox we now visit. Even with the addition, it was small for five family members plus servants.[1]

His son John left home to attend Harvard in 1751, and after graduating he taught school in Worcester and studied law. In his autobiography, John wrote that in 1758, when he was admitted to the bar, "My Father and Mother invited me to live with them, and as there never had been a Lawyer in any Country Part of the then County of Suffolk, I was determined at least to look into it and see if there was any chance for me." After a socially active life in college and among his fellow law students, he returned to his remote boyhood home. Writing to a friend, he said, "I am removed from Worcester to Braintree where I live secluded from all the Cares and Fatigues of busy life in a Chamber where no mortal Visits but myself except once in a day to make my Bed." From his solitary chamber, he began to develop his law practice and renew friendships.[2]

When Deacon John died in 1761, he left the original house to his son Peter and the second house to John, but the living arrangements remained unchanged until 1764, when John married Abigail Smith and they moved into the house he had inherited. Just as Susanna Boylston had moved a step down the social ladder when she married Deacon John, Abigail was marrying beneath her. Her father, a Harvard graduate and the minister of the First Church of Weymouth, owned a house far grander than either of the Adamses' saltboxes. Abigail, her sisters, and her brother had grown up in a two-story house with a gambrel roof and decorative trim. Her mother was a Quincy, a family of wealthy landowners whose name would later be given to the part of Braintree where the

Adamses lived. Her sister Mary married Richard Cranch, a friend of John's, and lived in Braintree; Elizabeth married the Reverend John Shaw and moved to Haverhill. Hundreds of letters among the sisters survive.[3]

As John's law practice grew, he and Abigail moved back and forth between Braintree and Boston. He needed to be in the city to expand his practice, but he was happiest in the country, in what he called in his diary "still, calm, happy Braintree": "From Saturday to Wednesday Morning I staid at Braintree, and rode, walked, rambled and roamed. Enjoyed a Serenity and Satisfaction to which I have been 3 Years a Stranger." Much of his work was in circuit courts, which required him to travel far afield, and he dreamed in his diary of being a commuter: "My Heart is at Home. It would be more for my Health to ride to Boston every fair Morning, and to Braintree every fair Afternoon. This would be riding enough and I could there have one Eye to my office, and another to my farm." He did not long for a Boston townhouse or a country mansion, writing in his autobiography that his "house humble as it was, with a few repairs and a very trifling Addition served for a comfortable habitation for me and my family, when We lived out of Boston . . . The Uncertainty of Life as well as of Property, which then appeared to me, in the prospect of futurity, suppressed all thought of a more commodious Establishment." Three of their children were born in Braintree: Abigail, known as Nabby, in 1765; John Quincy in 1767; and Thomas Boylston in 1772. Charles was born in Boston in 1770. Between 1772 and 1774, when they were living in Boston, John leased the Braintree house to his mother and her second husband, Lieutenant John Hall.[4]

In 1774 the family decided to make Braintree their only home. John bought fifty-three acres of land and the neighboring house from his brother Peter, consolidating his

FIGURE 4. The John Adams Birthplace and the John Quincy Adams Birthplace. G. N. Frankenstein, oil painting, 1849. *Courtesy of the National Park Service.*

ownership of the Penn's Hill farm.[5] They returned to Braintree just in time for John to become involved in revolutionary politics. That fall, he was off to Philadelphia as a delegate to the first Continental Congress, and Abigail would spend most of the next ten years raising their children and running the farm on her own. John's "still, calm, happy Braintree" soon became something quite different to his family.

## Revolution

From Braintree, Abigail and the children could see and hear the fighting in Boston. Abigail wrote that "the constant roar of the cannon is so [distre]ssing that we can not Eat, Drink or Sleep. May we be supported and sustain in the dreadful conflict. I shall tarry here till tis thought unsafe by my Friends, and then I have secured myself a retreat at your Brothers who has kindly offerd me part of his house. I cannot compose myself to write any further at present." Abigail did not accept Elihu's offer of shelter in Randolph, but it took courage to stay. In old age John Quincy recalled: "The year 1775 was the eighth year of my age . . . For the space of twelve months my mother with her infant children dwelt, liable every hour of the day and of the night to be butchered in cold blood, or taken and carried into Boston as hostages, by any foraging or marauding detachment of men . . . My father was separated from his family, on his way to attend the same continental Congress, and there my mother, with her children lived in unintermitted danger of being consumed with them all in a conflagration kindled by a torch in the same hands which on the 17th. of June lighted the fires in Charlestown. I saw with my own eyes those fires, and heard Britannia's thunders in the Battle of Bunker's hill and witnessed the tears of my mother and mingled with them my own."[6] Abigail told John that "our House has been upon this alarm in the same Scene of confusion that it was upon the first—Soldiers comeing in for lodging, for Breakfast, for Supper, for Drink &c. &c. Sometimes refugees from Boston tierd and fatigued, seek an assilum for a Day or Night, a week—you can hardly imagine how we live."[7]

In addition to war, she had to deal with illness. In September 1775, an epidemic of often fatal dysentery spread through the town. Three of Abigail's servants and farmworkers fell ill, and soon she, too, was sick. She wrote to John: "Since you left me I have passed thro great distress both of Body and mind . . . Our House is an hospital in every part, and what with my own weakness and distress of mind for my family I have been unhappy enough . . . And such is the distress of the neighbourhood that I can scarcly find a well person to assist me in looking after the sick." She resorted to the only remedy thought to prevent spread of the disease: "A general putrefaction seems to have taken place, and we can not bear the House only as we are constantly clensing it with hot vinegar."[8]

Abigail feared another epidemic disease: smallpox. Inoculation was available, but it was risky. All patients being inoculated had to be isolated, and some became seriously ill. Boston had been free of British troops since March 17, 1776, and in July Abigail took the children to the city for treatment. Her uncle and aunt, Isaac and Elizabeth Smith, invited the family to stay with them. All were inoculated, and although Abigail suffered few ill effects, the children did not do as well. Charles and Nabby were frighteningly ill, and the family had to stay quarantined in Boston for nearly two months.[9]

While recovering from her inoculation, Abigail heard the product of John's work in Philadelphia and wrote to him about it:

> Last Thursday after hearing a very Good Sermon I went with the Multitude into Kings Street to hear the proclamation for independance read and proclamed. Some Field peices with the Train were brought there, the troops appeard under Arms and all the inhabitants assembled there (the small pox prevented many thousand from the Country). When Col. Crafts read from the Belcona [balcony] of the State House the Proclamation, great attention was given to every word. As soon as he ended, the cry from the Belcona, was God Save our American States and then 3 cheers which rended the air, the Bells rang, the privateers fired, the forts and Batteries, the cannon were discharged, the platoons followed and every face

appeard joyfull. Mr. Bowdoin then gave a Sentiment, Stability and perpetuity to American independance. After dinner the kings arms were taken down from the State House and every vestage of him from every place in which it appeard and burnt in King Street. Thus ends royall Authority in this State, and all the people shall say Amen.[10]

Finally back in Braintree, Abigail wrote to John: "Last monday I left the Town of Boston . . . then came Home, which seem'd greatly endeard to me by my long absence." Toward the end of her stay in Boston, though, she had been dreaming of greater comfort: "I have possession of my Aunts chamber in which you know is a very conveniant pretty closet with a window which looks into her flower Garden. In this closet are a number of Book Shelves, which are but poorly furnished, however I have a pretty little desk or cabinet here where I write all my Letters and keep my papers unmollested by any one. I do not covet my Neighbours Goods, but I should like to be the owner of such conveniances. I always had a fancy for a closet with a window which I could more peculiarly call my own."[11]

Abigail was also managing the house that the Adamses still owned in Boston. Soon after the British had left the city she wrote to John that "our House . . . has been occupied by one of the Doctors of a Regiment, very dirty, but no other damage has been done to it. The few things that were left in it are all gone." She was "determined to get it cleand as soon as possible and shut it up." A few months later, the house was "going to ruin. When I was there I hired a Girl to clean it, it had a cart load of Dirt in it. I speak within Bounds. One of the chambers was used to keep poultry in, an other sea coal, and an other salt. You may conceive How it look'd. The House is so exceeding damp being shut up, that the floors are mildewd, the sealing falling down, and the paper mouldy and falling from the walls." She repeatedly expressed concern about the state of their finances, but she did not lose sight of the purpose of John's absence: "I trust we shall yet tread down our Enemies."[12]

John's duties sent him to Philadelphia, Yorktown, Baltimore—wherever the revolutionary government met. Writing from Philadelphia, he told Abigail: "The green Grass, which begins to shew itself, here, and there, revives in my longing Imagination my little Farm, and its dear Inhabitants. What Pleasure has not this vile War deprived me of? I want to wander, in my Meadows, to ramble over my Mountains, and to sit in Solitude, or with her who has all my Heart, by the side of the Brooks." He returned to Braintree for a short visit in 1777—long enough for Abigail to become pregnant. She was alone in July when she gave birth to a stillborn daughter.[13]

For a few weeks, it looked as though John might come home to stay, but in November he was sent to France. Except for a brief visit home in 1779, he would spend the next ten years in Europe, Abigail not joining him until 1784. Their frequent letters are full of information about the war, domestic and international politics, financial transactions and worries, and family news. Both of them wrote often and movingly about the pain of separation, concerns for each other and the children, and their love. But the hazards of navigation during wartime meant that months passed before letters were received—if they arrived at all. In 1781 Abigail wrote: "O that I could realize the agreable reverie of the last Night when my dear Friend presented himself and two Son[s] safely returnd to the Arms of the affectionate wife and Mother. Cruel that I should wake only to experience a renual of my daily solicitude. The next month will compleat a whole year since a single Line from your Hand has reachd the longing Eyes of Portia."[14]

John was often nostalgic about the farm and the landscape. He told Abigail, "I know not the reason but there is some Strange Attraction between the North Parish in Braintree and my Heart." In Paris, he was impressed by the grandeur of the Palais Bourbon but wrote in his diary that "I had rather live in this Room at Passy than in that Palace, and in my Cottage at Braintree than in this Hotel at Passy." When he became discouraged and frustrated with diplomatic negotiations, he told Abigail that he "had rather chop Wood, dig Ditches, and make fence upon my poor little farm."[15]

Abigail was not romantic about the farm: she was too busy running it. Her letters tell of the difficulties of hiring workers, the high cost and scarcity of supplies, and the severity of New England weather. In 1780, returning from a visit with a friend, her thank-you note was grim: "From your Hospitable Mansion of Benevolence and Friendship, I reachd my own Habitation . . . the Scenes around me wore a dismal aspect—the dyeing Corn, the Barren pastures and the desolated Gardens threaten us with distress, and Hunger." Any romanticism about Penn's Hill was linked to John's return: "What do you think will become of us. If you will come Home and turn Farmer, I will be dairy woman. You will make more than is allowd you, and we shall grow wealthy. Our Boys shall go into the Feild and work with you, and my Girl shall stay in the House and assist me."[16]

Abigail was better at farming than predicting the future. A friend wrote to John: "I don't know but Mrs. Adams Native Genius will Excel us all in Husbandry. She was much Engaged when I came along, and the Farm at Braintree Appeared to be Under Excellent Management."[17] In fact, Abigail not only kept the farm going, she increased the

Figure 5. Abigail Adams. Jane Stuart after Gilbert Stuart, oil painting, ca. 1800. *Courtesy of the National Park Service.*

family's assets significantly. She bought land, found tenants for their properties, managed their investments, and sold cloth and luxury goods not yet made in America that John shipped from Europe. But by 1782, patience on both sides of the Atlantic was running out.

## Peace

There were many reasons why Abigail had not joined John in Europe. It was never clear how long he would be there, and he moved from country to country as his assignments changed. Both parents were concerned about their children's education and feared that living in Europe would corrupt them. Abigail told John that they agreed on that point: "A European life would, you say, be the ruin of our Children. If so, I should be as loth as you, to hazard their embibeing sentiments and opinions which might make them unhappy in a sphere of Life which tis probable they must fill, not by indulging in luxuries for which tis more than possible they might contract a taste and inclination, but in studious and labourious persuits." Yet John Quincy and Charles had both sailed with their father and attended Dutch schools. John Quincy had even accompanied Francis Dana to St. Petersburg as his secretary and traveled back to western Europe on his own.[18]

Abigail's main reason for staying at home seems to have been her fear of sailing across the ocean. With the end of hostilities, the danger from Great Britain was much reduced, and by October her loneliness overcame her fears. She wrote to John: "I cannot be reconcild to living as I have done for 3 years past. I am searious. I could be importunate with you. May I? Will you let me try to soften, if I cannot wholy releave you, from your Burden of Cares and perplexities? . . . I Hardly think of Enemies of terrors and storms. But I resolve with myself, to do as you wish. If I can add to your Happiness, is it not my duty? If I can soften your Cares, is it not my duty? If I can by a tender attention and assiduity prolong your most valuable Life, is it not my duty? And shall

I from Female apprehensions of storms of winds, forego all these Calls? Sacrifice them to my personal ease?"[19]

John had been in Paris since April, working with John Jay and Benjamin Franklin to negotiate the peace treaty with Great Britain. He was unhappy with the way Congress had treated him, and his letters home were resentful and discontented. He had little confidence that the negotiations would succeed, and he was unsure about his future. From The Hague, he wrote in October 1782: "Your proposal of coming to me would make me the happiest of Men, if it were probable that I should live here where I am well settled." He feared, though, that he would have to go to Paris or Vienna. "If Peace should be made this Winter," he added, "I intend to go home in the Spring."[20]

From October 1782 to July 1784, John and Abigail wrote back and forth, neither of them certain which should cross the ocean. Abigail sometimes seemed determined to join John in Paris, but at other times she encouraged him to return, citing his love of Penn's Hill: "I do not wish you to accept an Embassy to England, should you be appointed. This little Cottage has more Heart felt Satisfaction for you than the most Brilliant Court can afford." John tendered his resignation to Congress in December 1782 but received no response. In September 1783 he suggested that Abigail and Nabby come to London in the fall and that they all return home the following spring. The long delays between the time a letter was written and the time it was received added to the confusion.[21]

Finally, in the first days of 1784, Abigail made up her mind: she and Nabby would sail. She arranged for her uncle Cotton Tufts to oversee the business of the farm and gave him a power of attorney and detailed instructions. Charles and Thomas would board with her sister Elizabeth Shaw and be taught by her husband, John, in preparation for entering Harvard. Their house would be cared for by William and Phoebe Abdee. (Phoebe had been a slave in Abigail's father's house, freed and given an income under his will.) On May 25, she booked passage for herself and Nabby, and they boarded the *Active* on June 20, 1784.[22]

Communication was so poor, and John so indecisive, that while Abigail was being seasick on the *Active*, he wrote: "My own Opinion is, you had better Stay. I will come home . . . and leave Politicks to those who understand them better and delight in them more, Breed my Boys, to the Bar and to Business, and My Girls too, and live and die in primaeval simplicity and Innocence." As late as July 19, he did not know whether Abigail and Nabby were coming: "They must let me know it by the French & English Packet and by every opportunity that I may not sail west while they are sailing East." Four days later, Abigail and Nabby arrived in London, and Abigail wrote to him at The Hague. He said that her letter "has made me the happiest Man upon Earth. I am twenty Years younger than I was Yesterday." John Quincy joined his mother and sister on July 30, and John arrived a week later. The family soon settled in Auteuil, four miles from Paris.[23]

## "Depraved beyond Conception"

A few weeks in Europe convinced Abigail that the United States and its citizens were morally superior to the French and the English. She told her sister that "the Morals of Europe are depraved beyond conception, Love of Country and publick virtue, mere visions."[24] Although John disliked the formality and artificiality of life at court, he had learned to move effectively in those circles. Abigail never achieved that level of comfort. She was not made for city life or for socializing with strangers. Yet during their four years in Paris and London the family enjoyed comfortable quarters and intellectual stimulation. Both she and John began to view their "homely house," their "little Cottage," through different eyes.

Abigail told her sister that the family's temporary home at Auteuil was "large, commodious, and agreeably situated." It was, however, "much larger than we have need of," dirty, and inadequately furnished. She also feared that "it must be very cold in Winter." Despite its elegance and beautiful gardens, it was "not so dear to me as my own little Cottage connected with the Society I used there to enjoy, for out of my own family I have no attachments in Europe, nor do I think I ever shall have." Nabby, too, was homesick. She was having difficulty learning French, and although she was impressed with the grandeur of Parisian architecture and the elegance of Parisian fashions, she found the people dirty and dishonest. "I do not see an American that does not ardently wish to return to their Country . . . At the end of twelve months I shall be quite satisfied with Europe, and impatient to return home."[25]

Abigail's opinions gradually softened: "I have found my taste reconciling itself to habits customs and fashions, which at first disgusted me." She grew to love the theater and dance and to enjoy the company of French women, even those with titles, and especially the Marquise de Lafayette. As the garden at Auteuil came to life in March, she felt free to "brag" about it. Nabby, too, admired the garden and loved the opera.[26]

Early in December it became clear that the family would not be returning home soon. John had been chosen as minister to the Court of St. James's, an appointment that would be confirmed in February. Abigail reported that John Quincy, miraculously uncorrupted by living in Europe for seven years, would return to America in the spring to study at Harvard, "that he may become acquainted with the Youth of his own Standing and form connextions in early life amongst those with whom he is to pass his days." John, Abigail, Nabby, and their servants arrived in London on May 27 and quickly began to enjoy the city's musical and dramatic productions. In their first month in the city, Abigail attended a performance of Handel's *Messiah* at Westminster Abbey, and her daughter saw two plays. They found a comfortable house to rent in Grosvenor Square.[27]

Representing the United States in London so soon after the end of the war was bound to be politically difficult for John and socially awkward for Abigail, who described being presented at court: "The Queen was evidently embarrased when I was presented to her. I had dissagreeable feelings too. She however said Mrs. Adams have you got into your house, pray how do you like the Situation of it? Whilst the princess Royal looked compasionate, and asked me if I was not much fatigued, and observed that it was a very full drawing room." The newspapers were full of anti-American writings, and the news from home focused on Shays's Rebellion and the need for a new constitution, in which John would not have a voice. Nevertheless, Abigail told her friend Mercy Otis Warren, "I have made some few acquaintance whom I esteem and shall leave with regret." Perhaps she suspected her criticisms of England were exaggerated. She asked her sister, "Do you know that European Birds have not half the melody of ours, nor is their fruit half so sweet, or their flowers half so Fragrant, or their Manners half so pure, or their people half So virtuous. But keep this to yourself, or I shall be thought more than half deficient in understanding and taste."[28]

Although the Adamses were still writing fondly about their house at Penn's Hill, they were in fact having thoughts about that "more commodious Establishment" that John had long suppressed. Early in 1787, about a year before they planned to return, John wrote to friends that he feared his land would be in poor condition and asked them to order a vast quantity of manure. He added, "I shall hardly find my homely house a Scene of tranquility or of Pleasure." Abigail was thinking of redecorating. She asked her sister Mary to send her the measurements of two rooms so that she could buy new floor cloths: "I am thinking Seriously of returning to you & trimming my little cottage once more." She added, "Should I ever have a better I will rejoice if I cannot I will be content." Mary advised her not to bother: "You can never live in that house when you return it is not large enough. you cannot crowd your Sons into a little bed by the side of yours now, & you will never inlarg it you had better buy mr Bowlands or Build one. He has offer'd to sell it I hear."[29]

The Borland house was in John and Abigail's sights. It was a "fine country seat," built around 1731 as a summer residence for Leonard Vassall, a sugar planter from the West Indies, and left to his daughter Anna and her husband, John Borland, when he died in 1737. John Borland died at the beginning of the Revolution, and Anna, a loyalist, fled to England. Early in the war it was used to house refugees from Boston and was then leased to various tenants. After the war, Anna Borland reclaimed the property and conveyed it to her son, Leonard Vassall Borland, and in 1783 they sold it to Royall Tyler, a young lawyer and aspiring writer.[30]

Tyler also aspired to marry Nabby, and he courted her and sought Abigail's support. Abigail at first seemed to approve of Tyler, but John responded to the news forcefully: "I confess I dont like the Subject at all. My Child is too young for such Thoughts, and I dont like your Word 'Dissipation' at all. I dont know what it means—it may mean every Thing.

There is not Modesty and Diffidence enough in the Traits you Send me. My Child is a Model, as you represent her and as I knew her, and is not to be the Prize, I hope of any, even reformed Rake." The courtship continued for two years, and by 1784, John and Abigail hoped that they would not marry, but they were also unwilling to forbid it. Taking Nabby to Europe was in part an effort to bring the matter to a head. On August 11, 1785, Nabby wrote to Tyler from London—a single sentence, returning his letters and ending the connection. Less than a year later, she married William Stephens Smith, secretary to the American Legation.[31]

His marital hopes dashed, Tyler defaulted on his payments, and once he had settled with the Borlands, the house was back on the market. Cotton Tufts had purchased various farm properties for the Adamses, and in June 1787 he told John that the Borland house "will be very soon open for any Purchaser." John asked him to make an offer, and the Adamses became the owners on September 26. The news spread quickly. Even before the sale was final, Mary Smith Cranch told Abigail: "I am rejoic'd that you will have a house big enough to hold your self & Friends when they visit you . . . It will take one large room to hold Mr Adams Books If you make it with Alcoves like the college Library it will make a beautiful appearence—We are amuseing ourselves with the alterations which it is probable you will make."[32]

Abigail had been contemplating repairs and decorating since the prospect of buying the house came up. In July she wrote to Cotton Tufts: "I should like to know the heights of the rooms & the paper they will take to paper them as well as the bigness of them, painting will be a necessary buisness both without and within." In his letter describing the negotiations and conclusion of the sale, he promised to send her the dimensions but reminded her that "all paper Hangings are prohibited from Importation If I remember right—and the best & neatest are made here at a very reasonable Price." Richard Cranch sent a plan of the house, measurements, and descriptions.[33]

Abigail was planning in great detail and for years to come:

> with regard to the repairs painting both without & within I should be glad to have compleated as soon as possible in the Spring, as the Smell is always pernicious to me. the east lower room to be painted what is calld a French Grey and as the furniture is red, a paper conformable, will look best. the Chamber over it will have Green furniture, and may be in the same manner, made uniform by a paper Green & white. the mahogany room, I know not what to say about it, making the two windows into the Garden will dispell much of the Gloom, & if it is not much abused & injured, had it not better remain as it is? can there be a Closset contrived in the Room when the windows are made, I could wish to have one, to make a uniform appearence, must there not be windows in the Chamber above, in the east Room. I think there are two clossets by the side of the Chimney. what would be the expence of taking them away & making arches in the Room of them? Iron Backs to the Chimneys & Brass Locks upon the Doors of the two best rooms & Chambers are all the particular directions I think of at present with regard to the other part of the House I shall leave it wholy to your judgment to make such repairs as you deem necessary and consistant with economy. as to any aditional building we cannot at present afford any. in some future day perhaps we may think of making the House Square by adding a Library, which mr A will really want, but at present, some chamber must be a substitute.[34]

After the Adamses did some last-minute sightseeing and John said good-bye to his friends in Holland, they left London. The *Lucretia* sailed later than planned, but by the end of April they were on their way home—not to the saltbox in Penn's Hill which had been the subject of so much nostalgia but to the much larger house of their future hopes. In Boston they were greeted by an official salute, church bells, and cheering crowds. After spending the night at the home of Governor John Hancock, they rode to Braintree, where they would stay with the Cranches until their furniture arrived. Soon they were in the midst of family and friends—John's mother, whom he had not expected to see again; a grown-up John Quincy; sons Charles and Thomas, now Harvard students, whom John had not seen since they were small boys; and Shaws, Cranches, Quincys, and many others.[35]

The Borland house, though, was a disappointment. The repairs were far from complete, Abigail told her daughter: "Ever since I came, we have had such a swarm of carpenters, masons, farmers, as have almost distracted me—everything all at once, with miserable assistance." The furniture they had brought with them had not survived the voyage very well. Abigail had remembered how large and elegant the house was compared to their cottage, but now she was comparing it with the grand homes in Auteuil and London: "I own myself most sadly disappointed. In height and breadth, it feels like a wren's house . . . Be sure you wear no feathers, and let Col. Smith come without heels to his shoes, or he will not be able to walk upright." By August, she told Nabby: "I have get more reconciled to the spot than I was at first, but we must build in the Spring an other kitchen a dairy room & a Libriary of the two last we are quite destitute, and distresst for want of."[36]

Abigail paid special attention to the garden. She planted flowers, shrubs, and trees in the front garden, including roses that she had brought from England. She planted lilacs and rose of Sharon along the walkway and created rectangular beds for fruit trees—apple, plum, peach, pear, apricot, quince, and cherry. She also planted a kitchen garden with potatoes, peas, beans, cabbages, squash, pumpkins, turnips, onions, asparagus, and lettuce.[37]

Eventually the repairs were completed, and John and Abigail settled in for their planned peaceful country life. In the midst of the house negotiations, John had told Cotton Tufts: "My View is to lay fast hold of the Town of Braintree and embrace it, with both my Arms and all my might. there to live—there to die—there to lay my Bones—and there to plant one of my Sons, in the Profession of the Law & the Practice of Agriculture, like his Father.—To this End I wish to purchase as much Land there, as my Utmost forces will allow, that I may have Farm enough to amuse me and employ me, as long as I live. that I may not rust, alive."[38] John was not going to rust, but neither was he going to farm.

In less than a year, he had been elected the first vice president of the United States; four years later, he was reelected; and four years after that, he was elected president. He spent those years in New York, Philadelphia, and Washington, returning to Braintree—his section now renamed Quincy—for the summers. In 1796, he began calling the house Peace Field, to honor his contribution to the Treaty of Paris. When he arrived home in the summer of 1798, he found the house dramatically changed. With the help of Cotton Tufts, Abigail had secretly made the additions she wanted. A wing had been added, with higher ceilings, providing an elegant parlor on the first floor and a library for John on the second. Servants' quarters were expanded, and a woodshed was converted into a kitchen. In 1800, a new east wing added several rooms and a second front door. The house was then twice its original size. And in 1801, after being defeated for a second term as president, John returned at last to his farm, where he would spend the last twenty-five years of his life.[39]

## The Next Generation

John Quincy Adams took little interest in domestic arrangements until he was married. He had lived in Braintree only as a child, and he had spent much of his life in rented lodgings—in Europe during his teens, in Cambridge while a student, and in Boston while practicing law and writing pseudonymous essays. He resumed his rootless existence in 1795, when George Washington appointed him resident minister to The Hague. In his diary, John Quincy wrote that "neither my years, my experience, my reputation nor my talent, could entitle me to an office of such respectability." In fact, there were few if any young men with his experience at European courts, his mastery of languages, and his political knowledge. In September he sailed, with his brother Tom as his secretary.[40]

Diplomatic affairs often took John Quincy to London, where he visited the elegant home of Joshua Johnson, the American consul. Joshua had seven marriageable (or soon-to-be-marriageable) daughters, and the young diplomat fell in love with the second, Louisa Catherine. The courtship ended in a long engagement, with John Quincy at The Hague, uncertain about his political and financial future. Abigail was uneasy about the marriage, which recalled her concerns about the effects of living in Europe. Mr. Johnson was American, the brother of a Maryland governor, but Mrs.

FIGURE 6. John Quincy Adams. Unknown artist after John Singleton Copley, oil painting, 1796. *Courtesy of the National Park Service.*

Johnson was English, and in Abigail's eyes Louisa was "*half-blood.*" She was also used to a style of living far beyond John Quincy's means. Finally, both sets of parents decided that the marriage should take place quickly. John Quincy sailed to London, and he and Louisa were married in July 1797.[41]

John Adams, now president, appointed his son minister to Prussia. The couple traveled to Berlin, arriving in early

November. The Adamses could not afford the lavish quarters enjoyed by diplomats with private means and more generous allowances. They lived in rented apartments and, occasionally, country homes offered by friends. It was not a happy time. John Quincy was uncomfortable outside his official role, and although Louisa enjoyed the gossip and female companionship of the court, she was unwell. She suffered several miscarriages, and both she and her husband feared they would never have children. Finally, in April 1801, their first child, George Washington Adams, was born. One of President Adams's last acts before leaving office was to recall his son. John Quincy, Louisa, and George sailed for America in July and arrived in September.[42]

They first visited Louisa's family in Washington, where they had been living since leaving London in 1797, and in November went on to Peace Field. John Quincy's account of this momentous occasion is brief: "I had the pleasure of introducing my wife and child to my parents." Louisa's emotions were far more complex. She feared that she did not live up to Abigail's expectations, and she was taken aback by the company and customs of Quincy: "What shall I say of my impressions of Quincy! Had I steped into Noah's Ark I do-not think I could have been more utterly astonished . . . It was luck for me that I was so much depressed, and so ill, or I should certainly have given mortal Offence." Social life was unlike anything she had experienced: "The dressing and the dinner hour, were all novelties to me: and the ceremonious partys, the manners, and the hours of meeting ½ past four were equally astounding to me." She was uncomfortable in church. Louisa had attended a Catholic school in Nantes during the Revolution and Anglican churches in London. She loved ritual and well-performed music, neither of which was to be found in Congregational Quincy: "Even the Church,

its forms, The snuffling through the nose, the Singers."[43] Fortunately, John Quincy had bought a house in Boston.

For the next seven years, John Quincy and Louisa divided
their time between Washington and New England. Until
1803, it was a happy arrangement. He was elected to the state
senate and then to the U.S. Senate, and a second son, named
after John, was born. Louisa enjoyed their time in Washington, where they lived with one of her sisters in a large,
comfortable house, and she made friends in Boston. But in
1803, financial disaster struck. On John Quincy's recommen-
dation, John and Abigail had invested funds with Bird, Sav-
age & Bird, a reputable London banking house. When the
bank failed, John Quincy felt honor bound to reimburse his
parents for their loss. That meant selling the house in Boston
and purchasing his birthplace from his father as a place to
spend the summers.[44]

In April 1805, John Quincy, Louisa, their sons, and her
sister Eliza stayed at Peace Field until their house was ready.
A carpenter and a mason made necessary repairs, and they
brought the furniture they had used in Boston. John Quincy
saw the move as an undesirable necessity: "Early in the Evening came *home* to the house in which I was born; but in
which I have not before pass'd the night for upwards of
twenty-five years . . . On coming into my own house I am
entering upon a new mode of life, as it regards my family and
myself. It is attended with many circumstances upon which
I am not anxious to dwell, but as it was dictated by necessity
so I hope it will eventually prove highly advantageous to us
all. That it will enure us to some of its inconveniences, and
enable us to remove others—That it will reduce our desires
to a level with our circumstances, and compensate to us in
safety, whatever it may take from us in elegance or ease."[45]

Louisa saw her husband's actions as "highly honourable and meritorious," and she took up the unaccustomed chores of country life with good spirits: "not being able to procure any Servant or more properly *help* I had to cook and perform all the duties of the house with the assistance of my Sister who was more successful in milking the Cows as I confess with all my labor for want of *knack* I could not get a drop of milk." At the end of the summer, much to Louisa's dismay, John Quincy decided that George and John should not accompany them to Washington. Decisions about where the boys should live and be educated became a continuing source of disagreement.[46]

When John Quincy returned to Braintree in April for the next summer, he stayed with his parents at Peace Field. Louisa was pregnant and remained in Washington. In June, "under circumstances of the most imminnent danger," she "gave birth to a dead Child with Thermometer at a hundred and neither Father or Children near me to console me for my sufferings." John Quincy responded to the news: "If the tears of affliction are unbecoming a Man; Heaven will at least accept those of gratitude from me, for having preserved you to me." A month later, Louisa and her sister Caroline arrived. It was not a happy reunion: "We went out to Quincy and were kindly greeted but my Children recieved me as a stranger and I was almost forgotten . . . John would go back to his Grandmothers and it was with great difficulty that I could keep him at home."[47]

The house was also the scene of great embarrassment for Louisa when family friends from Maryland—"the elite of Baltimore"—came calling: "I was making and baking Cake, and was obliged to *dress* before I could appear—The rooms of my house were literally too small to hold my company . . . There was something truly ridiculous in my position—The shaking off of the kitchen drapery for the parlour finery; and the assumption of the fashionable manners of my Station: was such a transition: as robes Cinderella as a Princess . . . Mrs. Harper had lived with my family in England and knew full well what I was used to." When the summer was over, they moved to a rented house in Boston. Except for summer visits, they would never live in Quincy again.[48]

Despite the inconvenience and even humiliation, John Quincy wrote in his diary of his love for the place: "This afternoon I took George with me over part of the farm; with the view to familiarize him at this season of his life with the scenes upon which my own earliest recollection dwells. I feel an attachment to these places more powerful than to any other Spot upon Earth. Precisely because they are associated with the first impressions of which the traces remain upon my mind—These attachments are connected with Some of the Sentiments and opinions which I most cherish, and which I should wish my children to possess." Louisa's attitude toward the farm was not at all sentimental. In 1821, she and her father-in-law rode to Penn's Hill "to see the Farm which has been new painted it is the old Gentlemans hobby and as he has made it over to my husband he fancy's it must be mine also—The situation is beautiful and as a property in good hands it would no doubt be valuable."[49]

John and Abigail had three other children. Nabby lived in New York after her marriage and, except for visits, returned to Quincy only when she was terminally ill. In 1811 she came to be cared for by her mother when she had a mastectomy, performed without anesthesia. She died there two years later. Charles, charming but irresponsible, practiced law in New York and in 1795 married Sally Smith, the sister of Nabby's husband, William. Their two daughters were born in 1796 and 1798. While at The Hague, John Quincy had asked

Charles to manage his investments, and he lost $4,000 in speculation. By then he had become an alcoholic, and he died of cirrhosis in 1800. His widow and daughters were frequent visitors to Peace Field.[50]

The youngest son, Thomas Boylston, did live in the family homes. He had practiced law in Philadelphia but in 1805 married Ann Harrod and settled in Quincy. He was active in town affairs and in 1811 was appointed chief justice of the Circuit Court of Common Pleas for the southern circuit of Massachusetts, a job that led family members often to refer to him as "the judge." But, like Charles, he was an alcoholic, and he was never financially independent. He lived in the saltbox known as the "John Adams birthplace" from 1810 to 1820. After Abigail died, he and his family moved into Peace Field with his father. When John died in 1826, the house was left to John Quincy, who asked his brother to leave. John Quincy reported that Tom did not take the news well: "He is quite unprepared for the change which must take place." He left the house in 1829 and died three years later.[51]

## Grandsons

John Quincy and Louisa outlived all but one of their children. Their only daughter died in infancy. Their oldest son, George, practiced law in Boston but became an alcoholic. On his way to join his parents in Washington in 1829, he fell or jumped from the ship and drowned. John married one of Louisa's nieces, Mary Catherine Hellen, in the White House in 1828. The two families lived together in Washington during the winters and in Quincy in the summers. John, too, was an alcoholic, and his father thought that a move to Quincy might improve his health and reduce his drinking.

In July 1834 he wrote a long letter that demonstrated his love of his son and of Peace Field: "Here so long as I live and have a house over my head, it shall be yours and your children's and when I depart it may with prudence, industry, and frugality secure to you and them an independent existence. Here my father began his career upon nothing, he lived a long life of vicissitudes, but always a life of honour, always with a modest competency . . . Here he found a refuge from the Hurricane of Political conflict. I have done the same . . . My preservation from ruin hitherto has been my retirement here, and here is a last resort for my children to maintain their independence when they meet with nothing but disappointment elsewhere." John died of alcoholism three months later. John Quincy became the guardian of his two granddaughters, and the families continued to live together.[52] The youngest son, Charles Francis, had the closest ties to Peace Field and Penn's Hill.

When Charles Francis was at Harvard, he enjoyed spending time with his grandfather at Peace Field, but his Uncle Tom's drunkenness made the visits difficult. In his diary, he described Tom as "one of the most unpleasant characters in this world, in his present degradation, being a brute in his manners and a bully in his family." Nor did he have a kind word for Anne Harrod Adams, Tom's wife: "Extravagant without the means and knowing that she plunges her husband deeper in his wretchedness, at every step she takes, she does not mind it, cunning and deceitful, hypocritical to a degree beyond belief and malicious as a serpent." John Adams had confided to his grandson that he was concerned about Tom and Anne: "My Uncle and Aunt have so little prospect before them after his death, he spoke feelingly, the children also, if he could have done anything for them but it

was entirely impossible . . . he has done much for that family, but I am afraid all the assistance he can give will avail
little."[53]

Charles was never convinced that his aunt and uncle
would leave Peace Field, despite John Quincy's ultimatum.
He arrived in April 1829 and "found the family quiet and
apparently not yet started to move at all. They were evidently
in distress about it." But leave they did: "My Uncle this day
vacated the house, an event I have long looked for but which
when it came surprised me. The mansion looks melancholy
and old and ill used and gave me many ideas which I would
have preferred not to have had." A month later, though, his
parents arrived: "The house looked poorly but the presence
of it's owner made it seem more cheerful."[54]

Charles assumed that John Quincy would retire to Peace
Field after losing the 1828 presidential election, but he misunderstood his father badly. In 1830, John did the unthinkable:
he ran for Congress and spent the rest of his life representing
Quincy in the House of Representatives. He and Louisa continued to spend the summers at the Old House, and Charles
became his father's agent, managing the land and houses he
owned in Quincy and Boston. At the Old House, he had the
assistance of a cousin, Louisa Catherine Smith, a niece of
Abigail's. She had lived there since she was a child and had
cared for John Adams in his old age. When John Quincy was
there without Louisa, she took over the housekeeping.[55]

Charles always found the empty house depressing. He
wrote: "There is a sort of cheerlessness about the lonely
appearance of an uninhabited Country house before vegeta-
tion bursts forth that discourages. And this old house without the large family which I have always seen in it, strikes me
as peculiarly dismal." The farm at Penn's Hill also needed

FIGURE 7. Charles Francis Adams. Charles Bird King, oil painting, 1827. *Courtesy of the National Park Service.*

much attention: "The houses are old and the barns decayed. The difficulty is to know how and where to begin."[56] Gradually, though, Charles's attitude toward Quincy mellowed.

Part of the reason was his personal situation. In 1829, he married Abigail Brooks, the daughter of Peter Chardon Brooks, one of the wealthiest men in Massachusetts. Brooks built a house in Boston for his daughter, and Charles spent a lot of time with his in-laws. It was a large, close family, very different from his own. And in 1831, their first child, Louisa Catherine, was born, followed in 1834 by a son, John Quincy. Charles was also becoming better established professionally. In short, he was growing up. After many difficulties restoring order to the house after Tom and Anne's tenure, by 1832 he had the old place under control. That spring he was surprised to find the house in good order, and when Louisa arrived she wrote to thank him "for the improvements which you have made in the house which looks altogether different from what it was last year."[57]

That summer was a turning point. He and his family spent six months at the Old House: "I have enjoyed the time very much. The Society of my father and mother has been agreeable to us, and our's, we are assured, has not been unpleasant to them. We have lived quietly, without the parade of public life and without its anxieties. Nothing has happened to annoy us with disagreeable or painful feelings, or harass us with care. Perhaps in the history of a life it may be difficult to say this for any period of six months time." As he was getting the house ready in 1833, he "had far less than usual of the cheerless feeling which seems to spread itself round the old Mansion in Quincy." In 1835, he again enjoyed being at Peace Field: "though the want of comfort there is very great, yet the kindness of the family and the agreement in which we have lived has more than compensated for it all." The next year he decided to build his own house in Quincy. By then another son had been born: "My children require very much the Country air and their number is now rather large for my father's house." John Quincy was delighted.[58]

The presence of her son, daughter-in-law, and grandchildren softened Louisa's attitude toward Peace Field. She had never been happy there. As she anticipated John Quincy's defeat in 1828, she had planned to live in Washington. She

wrote to Charles that she had "neither affections nor community" at Quincy and would not "expose myself to a repetition of insults which beggar as I am . . . I am too proud to
submit to." Her son hoped that she would change her mind,
"that she will find some things to recommend this part of the
Country to her, and that finding herself now more independent than she ever was before, she will relish having a house
of her own." Louisa did accompany John Quincy to the
Old House in the summers, but when he died in 1848, she
remained in Washington, where she died four years later.[59]

Charles Francis and Abigail inherited the Old House
from his father and a great deal of money from hers. Charles
achieved public recognition when he was appointed to the
important and prestigious post of minister to the United
Kingdom during and after the Civil War. They made a major
addition to the house in 1869, built the Stone Library in 1870,
and added a carriage house in 1873. By the 1860s, Charles
Francis owned 885 acres in Quincy. He died in 1886, and
Abigail remained there until her death three years later. Their
youngest son, Brooks, spent summers there, preserving it as
much as possible in its original state. After his death, the
Adams Memorial Society managed the property and opened
it for public tours, and in 1946 the society transferred it to the
National Park Service.[60]

## Different Lenses

Knowing how family members viewed these houses at different times makes visiting them an often confusing experience.
One house at Penn's Hill was the place where John Adams
began his life and career, but it was also the place where

his youngest son's life and career began to disintegrate. The house where John Quincy was born was his father's idyllic farm, his mother's place of wartime struggle, his own happy (if war-torn) childhood home, and the place where he and Louisa came to live at a time of financial embarrassment. The Old House was the first generation's peaceful retirement home, the retreat of Thomas as he sank into the disrepute of alcoholism, a place for John Quincy to escape increasingly unpleasant national politics, the site of Louisa's discomfort, a nuisance to Charles Francis, and the place where he finally came to feel at home. The houses echo with all of these lives.

## To Visit

The presidential birthplaces and Peace Field (the Old House) are part of the Adams National Historical Park in Quincy (www.nps.gov/adam/index.htm). They are open from mid-April through mid-November. The two-hour tours begin at the Visitors Center. The Abigail Adams birthplace (www.abigailadamsbirthplace.com) is open on some Sunday afternoons between April and November. Private tours can be arranged as well. The crypt of the United First Parish Church, 1306 Hancock Street, contains the tombs of John, Abigail, John Quincy, and Louisa Catherine.

Nearby is Quincy House (www.historicnewengland.org), built in 1770 and home to a distinguished family of Revolutionary statesmen, Boston mayors, and intellectually prominent women. It is open on the first and third Saturdays of each month from June 1 to October 15.

## To Learn More

The best source for information about the Adams family is the Massachusetts Historical Society, where the Adams Family Papers Project is publishing the diaries, family correspondence, and official papers. The material is available in three forms: print editions, which can be found in most research libraries; microfilm, also available in research libraries; and digital editions (at www.masshist.org). The online resources include digital editions of the print volumes, which you can easily search or browse; the diaries of John Quincy Adams, available as images that can be searched by date but not by word, and (for some entries) searchable transcriptions; and useful research aids, including brief biographies, a family tree, and a detailed timeline. The Online Adams Catalog (OAC, www.masshist.org/adams/catalog/catalog.php) lists every known Adams document, including those held by other institutions.

# 3

## Decline and Rise

*The Otis House, Boston*

THE Otis House is a nearly perfect presentation of the house as it looked when Harrison Gray and Sally Foster Otis lived there from 1797 to 1801. It creates the illusion of uninterrupted elegance. But this *is* an illusion—something like reading the first and last chapters of a novel with a happy ending. You have no idea of the perils the heroine has survived over the past two centuries or the ordeals of those who rescued her. As the West End of Boston was developed and redeveloped and the city's population embraced new residents from the countryside and from Europe, the house was divided, partitioned, defaced, and—with the threat of destruction looming—picked up and moved. Only in the twentieth century, when the movement to preserve historic houses took hold, did it begin the long process that restored its initial elegance. The house's journey tells the story of a city, its population, and the way it values its past.

### Developing Neighborhoods

Samuel Eliot Morison, Otis's biographer, wrote in 1913: "Of pure English stock, strengthened by five generations on New England soil, and refined by three generations of public service and social position, he could have asked nothing more of heredity." A childhood friend claimed that Harry Otis "was always the handsomest, brightest, and most charming boy of all our companions. Everything he did was better done than any of the rest of us could do it." With family wealth and influence, intelligence, and charm, he became a respected lawyer, orator, and politician, but his personal wealth came from his success as a real estate developer. At the age of twenty-five, he married Sally Foster, the daughter of a wealthy Boston merchant, who was as hospitable and charming as her husband and extremely beautiful. In welcoming her to the family, Otis's father quoted Homer, comparing Sally to Helen of Troy, "whose 'bland accents' and 'female attractions steal the heart of the wise.'"[1]

The couple at first lived in a rented house, but in 1795 they hired the architect Charles Bulfinch to design a three-story mansion at the corner of Cambridge and Lynde Streets, on land purchased from Sally's father. The area, which came to be known as the West End, was connected to Cambridge by a bridge constructed in 1793, only a few blocks from their new house. By the time they moved into the house in 1797, the Otises had five children. The house was elegant and much admired, but the family lived there for a little less than five years before moving to the second house that Bulfinch designed for them, at 85 Mount Vernon Street. The move was due to Otis's participation in the Mount Vernon Proprietors, a real estate syndicate formed to purchase land on Beacon Hill and develop it as a fashionable residential neighborhood. The property was near the new state house and faced the Common and Back Bay—which at that time was still a bay. The Otises and other investors built houses in the area to establish it as *the* place to live. Five years later, Otis commissioned Bulfinch to design his third and final house, at 45 Beacon Street, on a lot large enough for gardens and courtyards. With eleven bedrooms, it could comfortably

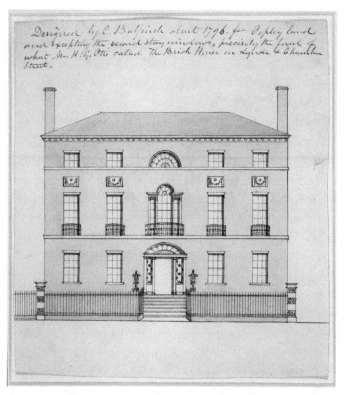

FIGURE 8. Front elevation of the first Harrison Gray Otis House, Boston. Charles Bulfinch, ink, wash, and watercolor on paper. Annotation thought to be in the hand of Sally Foster Otis. *Collection of the Massachusetts Historical Society.*

accommodate the eight surviving children born to him and Sally. The house faced the Boston Common and enjoyed a view of the Blue Hills.[2]

The Otis homes were more than investments. The couple were known for their devotion to family and their hospitality. Otis served two terms in the U.S. House of Representatives and one in the Senate but turned down other political opportunities that would have kept him away from Boston, choosing instead to serve in the state legislature and as mayor of Boston. Early in their marriage, he wrote to Sally, "I always knew that my habits were naturally domestic and that my happiness was to be found only in the bosom of my family," and he made his children "feel that home was the best place on earth." At their first house, guests were welcomed into a hall with high ceilings, an elaborately carved staircase, and carefully chosen artwork. They dined in a room with wall-to-wall carpeting imported at great expense (and protected during meals by a crumb cloth), a highly ornamented fireplace, and elegant furnishings. The parlor and drawing room were similarly decorated—colorful and tastefully furnished. Invitations to the large parties that the couple gave were much sought after, and they frequently entertained smaller groups.[3]

Otis and his father had had several political disagreements with both John Adams and John Quincy Adams, and it was Otis who extended the olive branch, by inviting the older Adamses to a small dinner in their third house. The reluctant guests were charmed: Abigail wrote, "I know not when I have past a pleasanter day, and I could not but regret the hour of separation." John told his son, "I never before knew Mrs. Otis. She has good Understanding. I have seldom if ever passed a more sociable day." Despite his political differences with Otis, John Quincy responded: "It has not fallen to my lot to meet a man more skilled in the useful art of entertaining his friends than Otis; and among the many admirable talents that he possesses, there is none that I should have been more frequently and more strongly prompted to Envy . . . his warm domestic Affections, his active Friendship, and his Generosity, always commanded my esteem . . . Mrs. Otis is and always has been a charming woman and I am very glad you have seen them both in the place where of all others they appear to the greatest advantage—their own house."[4] Today the house on Cambridge Street once again reflects the elegance, grace, and hospitality of its first owners. But what happened to the house and neighborhood after the Otises moved on?

## Growth and Change

At the turn of the nineteenth century, Boston prospered and grew. The population more than tripled between 1780 and 1810, from 10,000 to 34,000, and the small peninsula was growing crowded. The city and developers solved the problem by filling in wetlands and annexing neighboring areas. Otis invested in many land-making projects, including India Wharf and the nearby commercial streets, the land near the Cambridge Street bridge, and the Mill Pond. He was also involved in the annexation of Dorchester Neck (now South Boston) and related bridge building and land reclamation. Half of what is now Boston was built on newly created land, as was half of the West End.[5]

In addition to the fashionable residential area on the south slope of Beacon Hill, the West End had a lively African American community on the north slope, but neither slope remained purely residential for long. In 1811, another Bulfinch building, the Massachusetts General Hospital, hastened development. Cambridge Street filled with row houses and commercial buildings. Nearby industrial development encouraged the construction of housing for workers. Gradually, the economic status and ethnic origins of the area's residents changed. People arriving from rural areas and from Europe needed places to live. In addition to single-family houses, demand rose for tenements and boardinghouses. The new residents also required places to worship, and synagogues

and Catholic churches joined the older Protestant congrega-
tions. And shops sprang up to provide goods and services.[6]

The Otis House reflected these changes. Otis had sold
the house to John Osborn in 1801, and the Osborn family
remained in possession for most of the next twenty years.
In 1822, though, the house was divided into two unequal
parts, to accommodate two sets of residents. The division
required a number of structural changes, including parti-
tions, supporting beams, and an additional entrance, staircase, and kitchen. In the 1820s, stores were built on a strip
of land between the house and Cambridge Street. The new
neighbors were a shoemaker, barber, plumber, and laundry.
And in 1833 the larger, western part of the house acquired
new tenants: Dr. Richard Dixon Mott and his wife, Elizabeth, "the celebrated female physician," author of *The Ladies'
Medical Oracle, or Mrs. Mott's Advice to Young Females, Wives
and Mothers.*[7]

The establishment of the Massachusetts General Hospital and the Harvard Medical School attracted a variety of
medical practitioners to the West End. The term *doctor* was
used loosely in this period, covering graduates of reputable
medical schools, self-taught practitioners of traditional medicine, bone setters, and advocates of alternative medicine who
used homeopathy, water cures, herbal medicine, and other
approaches to disease. Although the range of practice was
wide, there was probably little difference in efficacy between
traditional and nontraditional treatments. Graduates of Harvard Medical School were still purging and bleeding patients,
applying leeches, and using drugs—like mercury—that had
serious long-term side effects. Herbal treatments probably
did less harm.[8]

Shortly before the Motts moved into the house, they
had been consulted by two sisters, Sarah and Harriot Kezia

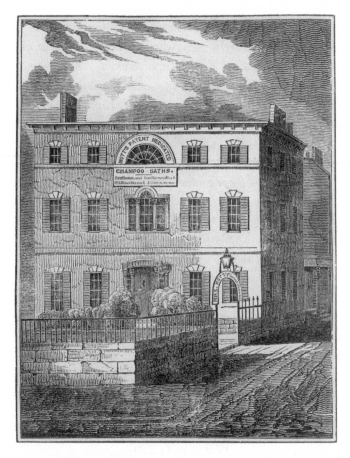

FIGURE 9. Woodcut of Harrison Gray Otis House, Boston, Mass., copied from *The Ladies Medical Oracle, or Mrs. Mott's Advice to Young Females, Wives, and Mothers*, Boston, 1834. *Courtesy of Historic New England.*

Hunt. A number of "regular" physicians had failed to cure Sarah of a serious illness, and Harriot thought that the Motts might be able to help her. They diagnosed her disease as tuberculosis, and whether or not this diagnosis was correct, their herbal treatments cured her. Baths were given to patients in a rubber tent filled with herb-scented steam to "cover the surface of the body, when the pores are in a proper state to receive them," the Motts explained. This "champoo vapour bath" was followed by massage. In 1834, the Motts hired Harriot Hunt to help manage the business side of their practice, and the two sisters and their mother moved into the third floor of the house. Harriot and Sarah also became apprentices to the Hunts, and after Mrs. Mott returned to Europe in 1835, they moved out of the house but continued to practice there, alongside Richard Mott. Mott treated male patients, and the Hunts treated the women. After Mott died, Harriot practiced independently at the corner of Spring and Leverett Streets and later at 32 Green Street.[9]

Harriot was eager to learn more about medicine, and in 1847 she applied to Harvard Medical School. She was not optimistic about her chances, because she "well knew that the conservatism of Harvard would blind the trustees, professors, etc. to the importance of recognizing woman as a physician." It took the president of the university only three weeks to declare her admission "inexpedient." She continued to practice and reapplied two years later, this time successfully in that she was permitted to attend lectures, though she would not be granted a degree. Her admission was rescinded when the students protested the admission of African American applicants and Hunt, claiming that their inclusion would harm "the dignity of the school" and their own self-respect. Hunt was finally able to append "M.D." to her name in 1853, when the Female Medical College of Philadelphia awarded her an honorary degree.[10]

Hunt continued to fight for women's rights to education and to the vote, and for many years she contested her tax bill on the grounds that it was equivalent to taxation without representation. Year after year, she protested "against the injustice and inequality of levying taxes upon women, and at the same time refusing them any voice or vote in the imposition and expenditure of the same." She was particularly incensed about the city's failure to provide public education for girls beyond grammar school. In addition to treating individual patients, she gave lectures to women on health care, believing that "if women could be induced to meet together for the purpose of obtaining a knowledge of physical laws, it would enable them to dispense in great measure with physicians, put them on their own responsibilities, and be a blessing to themselves and their children."[11]

As the nineteenth century advanced, the West End—like the North End—saw its population gradually change from wealthy to middle-class to poor immigrants: Irish, Italian, and Jewish. "Along the slope of Beacon Hill," one contemporary noted, "the 'struggling people' and the 'prosperous and responsible Boston citizens' were physically only blocks apart." It also lost its African American community, whose residents moved to other neighborhoods. By the turn of the century, three African American churches in the West End had become synagogues.[12]

The Otis House bowed to the changing needs of the neighborhood, and in 1854—no longer divided in two—it became a "first class" boardinghouse operated by the four Williams sisters, home to middle-class people who had come to the city from outlying areas. Young men studying law or medicine, for example, could live in homelike surroundings with which both they and their families were comfortable. Among the Otis House boarders were John A. Andrew, a future governor of Massachusetts; Admiral Henry Thatcher, executive officer of the Boston Navy Yard, and his family; the Reverend George Punchard, who later became secretary of the New England branch of the American Tract Society, and his wife; and Samuel Emerson, author of arithmetic text-books. They were served three meals a day in the basement dining room and socialized in the parlor. The neighborhood became more convenient—and more crowded—in 1856, when the city introduced horse-drawn streetcars, which were replaced by electric trolleys in 1887. The once gracious street became "a narrow, cobbled, crooked thoroughfare with streetcars running up and down the center. Here were shops, bakery, ice cream parlors, Chinese laundries, drugstores and bar rooms with swinging doors and 'Ladies Entrance' signs on the side."[13]

After the Williams sisters, the boardinghouse was managed by Alfred Carr (1868–83) and then Lydia A. Smith (1883–97). Most of their boarders were white, middle-class New Englanders. By the turn of the century, though, the boarders began to reflect the socioeconomic changes in the neighborhood. Among the twenty-one boarders in 1900 were first- and second-generation immigrants, generally skilled manual workers. By the early twentieth century, when a Mrs. King kept the boardinghouse, its residents were "poorer and more transient," and in 1910 it became a lodging house, where no meals were served. In 1916 the once elegant mansion carried a sign, "Furnished Rooms to Let." Inside, a visitor reported, a divided third-floor room "was occupied for many years by one man, who lived a sort of hermit life and finally died in this space which he rented at the rate of $1 a week. The room when we found it was dirty and shabby and it was sad to think it was all the space on earth that this poor man was able to call his own."[14]

In March 1916 the Benoth Israel Sheltering Home, which since 1891 had provided housing and services for new immigrants, bought the Otis House but never moved in. At the request of William Sumner Appleton, corresponding

FIGURE 10. The Otis House, ca. 1916. *Courtesy of Historic New England.*

secretary of the Society for the Preservation of New England Antiquities (SPNEA), Lee M. Friedman, a founder of the American Jewish Historical Society and member of SPNEA, intervened. Benoth Israel sold the house to SPNEA on August 1, and its decades-long restoration began. It was a daunting and expensive physical task, and serious thought and research were needed to determine how best to re-create and present its lost elegance. It was initially to be a historic house, a museum, and the offices of SPNEA. Because it became the headquarters of the leading historic preservation organization in New England, decisions about its preservation and restoration affected the fate of historic houses throughout the region.[15]

## Restoration Begins

When William Sumner Appleton founded SPNEA in 1910, he was worried about the loss of seventeenth- and eighteenth-century buildings to neglect and demolition. Preservationists' dedication to these ancient buildings came from a variety of motivations. Some were attached to a house because of family connections or love of its setting. They were concerned less with architecture than with commemorating the past as they wished to remember it. Although some historians attribute these attitudes to female preservationists, they were also prevalent among male proponents of the Colonial Revival movement.[16]

For others, preservation was a matter of patriotism—often with a strong component of nativism. Some found the influx of immigrants a physical and existential threat. The Paul Revere house, the object of a 1905 restoration effort, was the leading example. A historian of preservation noted that "on all counts, the situation was dire for tradition-minded Bostonians. The Revere house, along with other cherished symbols of the Puritan-Yankee past . . . was located in the city's North End. With a population density rivaling Calcutta's, the North End held tightly packed, multi-storied lodging houses that adjoined Boston's historic treasures." One antiquarian complained of "the vile odors of garlic and onions" and the conversion of "Father Taylor's old brick Bethel" into a Catholic church: "Has it come to this, that a mass-house should stand within the very pale of the thrice consecrated old Puritan sanctuary?" The Revere House had been the home of "model" immigrants who had anglicized their name and become true, patriotic New Englanders. Once restored, its advocates claimed, it would "serve as a daily lesson to the youth of that district in Massachusetts' ideals of loyalty, simplicity and civic pride," "a reminder to new citizens of the service due from them and their children to the Commonwealth."[17]

Appleton shared commonly held nationalistic sentiments, but he also contributed his knowledge of architecture and art to the movement. Equally important, he brought economic and political realism, seeking to involve a new generation of politicians and business leaders who were not all Boston Brahmins. When a building could not be preserved in its entirety, he advocated what is now called "adaptive reuse," in which the facades of historic buildings are retained, while their interiors are modernized and used for commercial purposes. In its first decade, the organization acquired seven buildings, mostly simple rural houses. The Otis House—an opulent city dwelling—was an exception. Several elite members of the group, including the young Harvard historian (and Otis biographer) Samuel Eliot Morison, provided the funds to buy it. It was also an exception because the goal was restoration rather than preservation.[18]

As important as Appleton's role in acquiring houses was what he did with them once SPNEA owned them. The sentimentalists wanted to present houses in an ideal state. They were more concerned with the appearance of the house than with its structure, integrity, and historical accuracy. Appleton wanted to base both preservation—stabilizing a house in its present state—and restoration on the principles of historical archaeology. He explained the idea underlying his work: "What is the object of a restoration? There can be but one answer. It is to restore a given object to the appearance it had at the beginning or some other selected time or times of its existence." All work on the houses was documented and was based on knowledge of the construction techniques and materials of the time at which it was built. His approach took hold, not only at SPNEA but in the National Park Service, the American Institute of Architects, and throughout the nation. William J. Murtagh, the first keeper of the National Register of Historic Places, "credited SPNEA with 'almost single-handedly' reorienting the field from a preoccupation with romanticized history to one stressing architectural aesthetics, scientific method, and historical scholarship." What SPNEA did at the Otis House exerted influence far beyond Cambridge Street.[19]

The first task was to make the building safe and to remove what Appleton called "later accretions to the house, changes and additions made to update the building's appearance in keeping with mid-nineteenth century taste, and to accommodate boarders." Safety required replacing badly damaged floors, removing gas fixtures and installing electric lighting, and updating the plumbing. (Because part of the house was to be used as offices, modern heating, plumbing, and electricity were essential.) Undoing alterations was more complex. For example, modern four-pane windows had replaced the originals, which had twelve small panes. Appleton explained that restoring each to its original appearance required constructing a "new window frame of the original design and mouldings like the only one still remaining in place, repairing the chopped out shutter box, repairing the large shutter leaf which has been shortened and narrowed and nailed into the box, supplying new interior shutter leaves to replace those long since discarded, and replacing the missing iron shutter bars." Radiators and heat risers were moved. Wallpaper was stripped (some rooms had more than a dozen layers), and samples were kept. Missing or anachronistic hardware was replaced with replicas of the originals; decorative plaster and woodwork were repaired. All changes were photographed and documented, and the restorers developed ingenious ways of differentiating new materials from old, for the benefit of future scholars and restorers.[20]

The front entrance of the house had been altered during its boardinghouse years, and Appleton resisted suggestions that the replacement be made more elegant than the original, noting that although "it would have been very easy to have designed a larger and more imposing porch which would have given the house more distinction," historical accuracy was the goal. "To ignore the evidence and make what may be more beautiful in the eyes of those having the work in charge is not to restore but to build anew, falsifying the old and telling an archaeological falsehood."[21]

The house was still cut off from Cambridge Street by the row of shops constructed in the 1820s. In 1919, SPNEA bought the buildings with the intention of tearing them down, though they did not yet have the funds for demolition. Six years later the shops were finally demolished, but not according to the original plan.[22]

## Moving Day

Cambridge Street was an early nineteenth-century thoroughfare, unsuited to the needs of 1920s Boston. In 1925, the city decided to widen it, which would require demolishing the Otis House. Now the house's white knight, SPNEA devised a way to save it. In 1924, the organization had bought the neighboring houses at 10, 12, 14, and 16 Lynde Street, tearing down the first two and remodeling the others for use as offices and a museum. On the land where the houses had

been demolished, they built a new foundation and cellar for
the Otis House. And on June 27, 1925, the *Boston Evening
Transcript* reported: "Sometime this afternoon the Harrison
Gray Otis house will arrive at its destination. An eventful
journey it has been . . . the historic building was speeding
ahead at the rate of one foot per hour when the road was
clear." Using a system of trestles, beams, rollers, and hand-
turned screw jacks, a crew took a week to move the three-
story brick house, weighing approximately nine hundred
tons, more than forty feet back from its original location.
The furniture and artifacts remained in place during the
move, and "all the service paraphernalia was moved with the
house, except the furnace . . . by the use of rubber hose to
connect the pipes in the house with the pipes in the street,
the telephone and electric light service being maintained,
of course, with extra lengths of wire."[23] Newly settled, the
house was ready for the next round of work.

Soon the slate roof and underlying wooden shingles were
removed and the slate relaid. The dormers that had been
added to the third floor were eliminated. The space acquired
with the purchase of the Lynde Street houses made it possible to use the entire house as a museum, with a mixture of
period rooms and exhibits. The combination did not please
all visitors. In 1930 Eleanor Early, a New England travel
writer, found it "depressing and rather horrid. There are radiators and ugly modern lights, and dusty things in glass cases.
It has been completely denuded of its ancient splendour, and
the work of restoration scarcely begun. It belongs now to
the Society for the Preservation of New England Antiquities,
and I wish they would tear out those dreadful radiators and
open the fireplaces. And hang damask in the windows, and
cover the bare floors. Then, if they could furnish it in proper

FIGURE 11. Exterior view of Otis House during removal, as seen from the other side of Cambridge Street, near Joy Street, Boston, Mass., ca. 1925. *Courtesy of Historic New England.*

fashion, and make it look like a home instead of a musty museum—it would be perfectly beautiful."[24]

The work did proceed slowly. The radiators were removed and the fireplaces opened: today the house is heated only by the warmth that comes through from the offices next door. Bare floors were carpeted, draperies hung, and furniture and ornaments placed—but not overnight. Progress was hampered by a lack of funds during war and depression. And Appleton was determined to do the job right, which was always more time consuming. Great care was taken to ensure historical accuracy, with painstaking research and at great expense. The preservation of the wallpaper that had been removed early on made it possible to identify most of the patterns used during the Otises' residence, and reproductions were commissioned and hung.[25]

Art historians contributed information by studying paintings by Henry Sargent, which their research proved to represent accurately the decoration of similar Boston homes during the period. Diaries, letters, wills, accountings, and inventories helped identify furniture, china, artwork, and other artifacts that then had to be located. The Otises chose their furnishings with great care. Letters between them when Harry was in Washington often discuss furniture to be purchased. In 1821, when the French ambassador Jean-Guillaume, Baron Hyde de Neuville, sold the contents of his Washington home, Harry bought silver that is on display in the house.[26]

Paint was more complicated. The research of the art historians provided information, as did the work of chemists. Initial paint analysis proved inaccurate, because it did not account for the effects of light and interactions with the chemicals of later applications. Only in the 1960s was the staff confident that they had discovered the original color scheme. Richard C. Nylander, the curator in charge of the restoration, was "not prepared for the discoveries we made and the revolutionary impact they had on the interpretation of other Federal interiors. Most striking of all were the paint colors, which were reproduced far more accurately than had formerly been possible thanks to sophisticated new analytic techniques. The combination of brilliant woodwork colors and vibrant wallpapers . . . brought the rooms to their appearance during Otis's residence. The effect was dramatically different from the harmonious pastel tones that curators and decorators had previously considered appropriate for Federal rooms. The opulence of the walls was, if anything, exceeded by the luxurious wall-to-wall carpeting."[27]

Today's visitors share their astonishment. The colors are bright and in unexpected combinations. The dining room has patterned carpeting with muted pinks and greens. Above the chair rail, the walls are deep yellow with bright wallpaper borders; festoons in blue, orange, and gold hang below the cornice; below the chair rail, the walls are bright blue. The mantel is the same blue, with ornamentation painted in white, reminiscent of Wedgwood Jasperware. Red draperies with gold fringe adorn the windows. The doors are painted with faux mahogany grain. In the parlor, green replaces the blue, and the wallpaper borders illustrate scenes of Pompeii. The upstairs drawing room, with a more pastel color scheme, sparkles with mirrors on walls and doors and the house's only chandelier. Other rooms are more restrained, but all feature wallpaper, decorative borders, and colorful carpets.[28]

According to Nylander, by 1970 the house "was interpreted as a whole rather than as a series of period rooms," with the interiors re-created "as they may have been during the Federal era." It would be impossible to be sure that everything was exactly as it was during the Otises' time, but work continues to approximate it more closely. On the second floor, one room is dedicated to the era of the Mott clinic, and another is furnished as it would have been during the "genteel" boardinghouse era.[29]

## Another Close Call

After World War II, the federal government offered funds to cities for programs variously called "urban renewal" and "slum clearance." The West End was now the home of immigrants from Italy, Greece, Poland, Russia, Albania, and Ukraine—poor people with little political power. With its crowded tenements and narrow streets (which some said were a hazard because fire trucks could not navigate them), the neighborhood was a promising target. Many residents saw the West End as "beautiful and unique," reminiscent of European cities. A newspaper reporter said that the area had "taken on an aura of romance." But the sense of community was real. Decades after the demolition, dozens of former West Enders met weekly to talk about their old lives. They recorded seventy hours of oral histories and raised funds to create a museum.[30]

The Boston Planning Board, however, saw a dangerous slum, crowded with poor people. In 1953 a project was announced to clear the West End of substandard housing, displacing more than two thousand families. Initially, residents were told that new construction would include low-rent housing units for which they would be given preference. As the plan developed, the involvement of private investors increased, and costs rose higher than expected. The promise that residents could return vanished. As one historian noted, "By the time tenants finally received their official eviction notices in the spring of 1958, there was no mention at all of low-rent public housing," and the rents "placed the project firmly in the luxury-housing category."[31]

An architectural historian described the project as "a carpet-bomb act of urban renewal," and the Otis House stood at ground zero in the way of progress. Fortunately, the West End plan made an exception for religious and historic buildings. A dramatic photograph exhibited in the Otis House shows the fifty-two-acre West End after demolition. It looked like a rubble-strewn war zone, with only Massachusetts General Hospital, St. Joseph's Church, the Charles Street Jail, and the Otis House with its neighbor, the Old West Church, still standing. As another historian wrote, the project "symbolized all that was wrong with city planning in the 1950s, because it bulldozed the homes of poor people and replaced them with an enclave for the wealthy." The handling of the clearance, and its results, were so reviled that plans to treat the North and South Ends similarly were abandoned.[32]

The Otis House is now a short walk from the Charles-MGH T station. The high-rise buildings, heavy vehicle and pedestrian traffic, and noise make it impossible to imagine what the street looked like when the Otises lived there—until you walk through the door. Then the house works its magic, and you are back in 1800, surrounded by elegance and luxury. Even the sirens vanish, and you can imagine yourself as a dinner guest—graciously welcomed, well fed, and surrounded by good conversation. A happy ending.

## To Visit

The Otis House (www.historicnewengland.org), at 141 Cambridge Street, is open Thursday through Sunday from April to November with tours on the hour and half hour. The Paul Revere House and the adjacent museum in the Pierce/Hichborn House (www.paulreverehouse.org), at 19 North Square, are less than a mile away. Three other historic houses are open within a mile of the Otis House. The Nichols House (www.nicholshousemuseum.org), built in 1804 and attributed to Bulfinch, is at 55 Mount Vernon Street. The 1808 Prescott House (www.nscda.org), at 55 Beacon Street, includes an excellent collection of clothing. The Gibson House (www.thegibsonhouse.org), a Victorian townhouse built in 1859, at 137 Beacon Street, is just a little farther along. The West End Museum (TheWestEndMuseum.org), dedicated to the community destroyed in the 1950s, is also nearby, at 150 Staniford Street. Admission to the West End Museum is free.

## To Learn More

The Harrison Gray Otis Papers are in the collections of the Massachusetts Historical Society. In 1913, Samuel Eliot Morison published a collection of Otis's letters and some biographical material in *The Life and Letters of Harrison Gray Otis, Federalist, 1765–1848*. His 1969 biography, *Harrison Gray Otis, 1765–1848: The Urbane Federalist*, is the only book-length study. Harriot Hunt's autobiography, *Glances and Glimpses, or Fifty Years Social, including Twenty Years Professional Life* is available online. Myra Glenn has just completed a biography of Hunt: *Dr. Harriot Kezia Hunt: Nineteenth-Century Physician and Woman's Rights Advocate* (Amherst: University of Massachusetts Press, 2018).

*Gaining Ground: A History of Landmaking in Boston*, by Nancy S. Seasholes, is a thorough and well-illustrated study of how the landmass of the city has been doubled. For photographs of the West End from the Otis era on, see Anthony Mitchell Sammarco, *Boston's West End* (Charleston, S.C.: Arcadia, 1998).

# 4

## Cousins

*County Street, New Bedford*

THE city of New Bedford began at the harbor, where the boats that harvested fish and whales from the world's oceans docked with their catch. At first, the men who made fortunes from the sea built houses near the docks, but as their wealth grew they moved up the hill to County Street. From their new mansions, they could see the harbor but not hear or smell it. Three families—the Rotches, Rodmans, and Morgans— combined to dominate the city's business, industry, and landscape from the late eighteenth to the late nineteenth century. They enhanced their power with intermarriage. Ralph Waldo Emerson once compared William Rotch Sr. to "Father Abraham himself," for every Quaker that Emerson met was related to him.[1] A Rotch could scarcely set foot on County Street without running into a relative.

### Generations

William Rotch (1734–1828) and Elizabeth Barney (1735–1824) were married in 1754 and had five children. William had been born in Nantucket, where he bought and sold whale oil. His three sons—William Jr., Benjamin, and Thomas—joined him in his business. His daughters were Elizabeth and Mary. Thomas Rodman (1724–66) was a merchant and ship's captain in Newport. He and his wife, Mary Borden (1729–98), had five children who lived to maturity: Samuel, Eliza, Anna, Hannah, and Charity. Thomas died at sea in 1766, leaving Mary to manage his real estate, store, the brig *Dove*, and other commercial interests. The Rotches and Rodmans were Quakers.[2]

The Revolutionary War disrupted both families. According to one historian writing about Nantucket, "three wealthy oil merchants, William Rotch, Timothy Folger, and Samuel Starbuck . . . formed in fact a super-government, a tight little whaling oligarchy which, superseding the town meeting, dominated the dealings with both British and American authorities." Rotch always described his stance as neutrality. Certainly, as a Quaker, he played no military role. A Quaker historian reported that he threw bayonets into the harbor to prevent their use by American soldiers. But the merchants interpreted neutrality to mean that they could sell to either side. Their ships carried two sets of papers, so the captain could present the set that would gain the most favorable treatment from British or American officials or privateers. After the war, Rotch claimed, the punitive taxes imposed by the British on American oil made it impossible for him to earn the profit he expected. He and other Nantucket merchants also faced possible charges of treason in Massachusetts. Some left Nantucket for Nova Scotia, New York, or Connecticut. William Rotch Sr. and his son Benjamin went to France and established their business at Dunkirk. William Jr. moved to New Bedford, on the south coast of Massachusetts midway between Cape Cod and Providence. His father and most of the family joined him there in 1795, when the coming war between France and England threatened the safety of their ships. Benjamin went to England to conduct the family's business there.[3]

The Rodmans had their own problems during the war. Mary Rodman's four daughters were all beautiful and accomplished. A visiting Englishman was said to remark that "Newport was the garden of America, and her three daughters the choicest flowers therein." (Charity, by far the youngest, may have escaped his notice.) Newport was swarming with British soldiers and sailors. Fearing that the girls might fall in love with British officers, Mary moved the family to the inland safety of Leicester, Massachusetts. Samuel Rodman returned from Nantucket, where he had been apprenticed to a whaling firm after his father's death, and joined the family in Leicester, acting as tutor to his sisters. After the war, the Rodmans returned to Newport.[4]

Samuel Rodman's apprenticeship had taught him how the whaling business worked and how to keep the books of a complicated enterprise. Even before the war ended, he was eager to get his career started. He would naturally gravitate toward New Bedford, which was rapidly displacing Nantucket as the center of the whaling industry. The Rotches were a valuable business connection for an ambitious young Quaker, and they embraced Samuel as a member of the firm and the family. In 1780, he married William and Elizabeth's daughter Elizabeth. Two years later, his sister Elizabeth Rodman married William Rotch Jr. Two years after that, the Rotch family traveled to Newport for a gathering of Friends, and they stayed with Mary Rodman. Thomas Rotch and Charity Rodman met, and they married in 1790. In a letter to Charity's mother, William Sr. said their union created "a triple alliance . . . which meets our full approbation." Having run out of sons, he endorsed Hannah's marriage to Samuel Rowland Fisher.[5]

The next generation of Rotches and Rodmans were too interwoven to marry one another, but there was room in the business and the clan for another family. In Philadelphia, a Quaker couple, Thomas and Ann Waln Morgan, had had six children. Thomas died in 1804, and Ann, ten years later. Their son Charles, then twenty-two, became the head of the family. Their daughter Rebecca married Samuel Rodman's son William Rotch Rodman; sister Susan married Samuel's son Benjamin; and Anne married Francis Rotch, son of Benjamin and Elizabeth Barker Rotch (the English branch of the family). Charles Waln Morgan married Samuel Rodman's daughter Sarah in 1819 and joined the family firm.[6]

There remains only one relative to complete the County Street scene. William Rotch Jr. and Elizabeth Rodman Rotch had a daughter, Sarah (1786–1860), who in 1807 married James Arnold (1781–1868), the descendant of two wealthy Providence families, the Arnolds and the Browns. He had come to New Bedford to work for Rotch, and with his marriage came a partnership in the firm. The Arnolds had one daughter, Elizabeth.[7]

The history of one marriage gives some insight into how these alliances were engineered, for they surely did not happen by accident. Benjamin Rotch, who had stayed in England while the rest of the family settled in New Bedford, conducted the firm's business very profitably in Milford Haven, in South Wales. He purchased an elegant home on more than a hundred acres, with extensive gardens, orchards, greenhouses, woodlands, and fishponds. He and Elizabeth Barker had five children who survived infancy—Francis, Eliza, Benjamin, Maria, and Thomas Dickason. Francis and Thomas worked in their father's business, and Benjamin became a barrister who represented his father in a successful lawsuit and later became a member of Parliament. Quakers generally did not approve of the legal profession, and the Rotches shared that opinion. Benjamin Sr. defended his son in a letter to his father: "Now my dear Father don't let this dear grandson of thine sink in thy estimation from

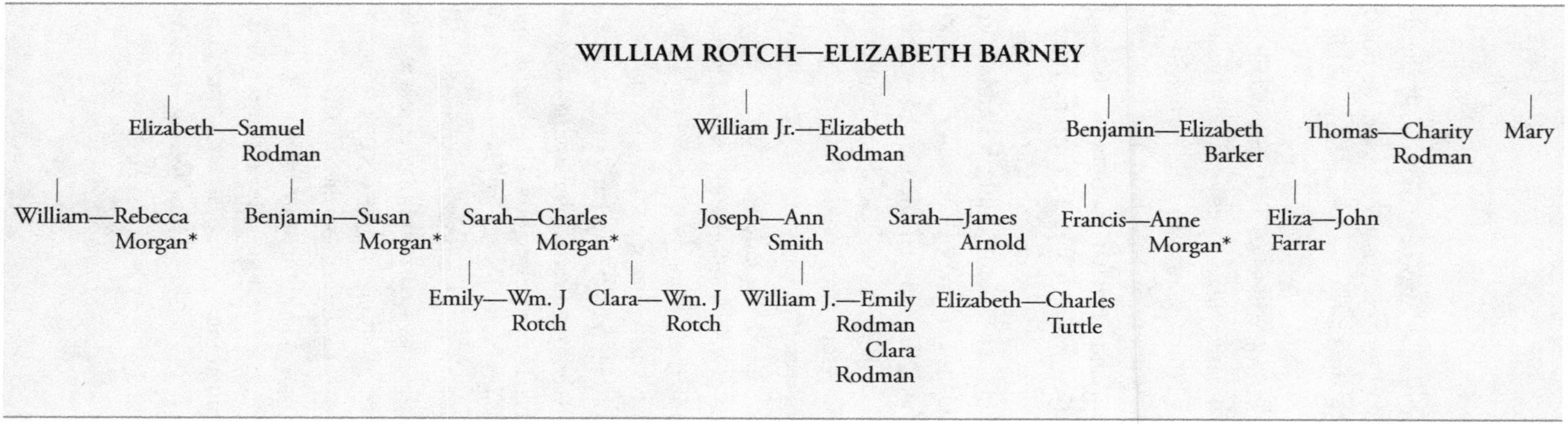

## WILLIAM ROTCH—ELIZABETH BARNEY

| | | | | |
|---|---|---|---|---|
| Elizabeth—Samuel Rodman | William Jr.—Elizabeth Rodman | Benjamin—Elizabeth Barker | Thomas—Charity Rodman | |
| | | | | Mary |

Benjamin—Susan Morgan*

William—Rebecca Morgan*

Sarah—Charles Morgan*

Joseph—Ann Smith

Sarah—James Arnold

Francis—Anne Morgan*

Eliza—John Farrar

Elizabeth—Charles Tuttle

William J.—Emily Rodman

Clara Rodman

Emily—Wm. J Rotch

Clara—Wm. J Rotch

FIGURE 12. The Rotch, Rodman, and Morgan families.

*Children of Thomas and Anne Waln Morgan

supposing him a Lawyer or Attorney, who do all the dirty work in the law—No—he possesses an honourable mind, is qualifying himself for the highest and most honourable part of the profession."[8]

In 1814, the market for whale oil in London collapsed, and Benjamin Sr. was bankrupted. Creditors took his house, and according to his father, Benjamin had been selling his furniture to survive. William Sr. sold land and other property "to assist him, as now he has nothing of any consequence." Thomas stayed with his father's firm, and the two of them eventually rescued it from bankruptcy, paid their creditors, and were able to live comfortably in London. Francis, however, decided to emigrate. Benjamin Rotch's close friend, Morris Birkbeck, had visited the United States and had purchased land in Illinois for a settlement he named "English Prairie." He wrote two books about the wonders of the American Midwest to recruit settlers. According to Eliza Rotch, "This induced my eldest brother to emigrate also, and it was deemed expedient for William to accompany him." Francis's grandfather wrote that "poor Fran's lost the chief of his property by his father say £2000 Stg. and comes away with only £500 Stg., passages to pay out of that, but I intend helping him out of my Estate, I believe he is a deserving young man, and feels a great weight, by having his young brother under his care."[9]

The brothers sailed from Liverpool in April 1818. They spent some time on the East Coast, in Philadelphia and New Bedford, and during that time Francis became engaged to Anne Waln Morgan. His future brother-in-law, Charles, was not altogether pleased. Although he believed Francis to have "a sincere and ardent attachment for my sister," his letters were lacking something. "What is this something—it has elegance of composition, warmth of feeling—beauty of description—and elevated morality to recommend it but he seems anything but a Quaker and seems ready to become even less than he is." In June, Francis's father, Benjamin, wrote to his father, William Sr., to say that William's approval of Anne "is highly gratifying & secures to him mine and my dear wife's approbation.—altho a fortnight's Acquaintance is too short a time to decide on so important a choice for life." The brothers then continued their journey to English Prairie.[10]

The plan was for Francis to establish a home where the couple could live following their marriage. In less than a year, though, Francis grew disillusioned with the settlement and with Birkbeck. His land, he told his uncle, Thomas Rotch, was excellent, but his fellow pioneers were not the sort of people he was used to living among, governance of the settlement was chaotic, and "the rifle is our only law." (As a Quaker, Francis noted, he refused to own any weapon.) He was confident in the strength of his own character, but— given the doubts he now had about Birkbeck—"for my younger brother William I have many very anxious fears . . . I tremble for the influence of such a creed from the lips of a man, who he has been taught to value and respect; whom he sees me in habits of intimacy with; and under whose roof he is sheltered." He asked for Thomas's counsel: "I am cheerfully inclined to follow the advice of my friends; and if it be judged best by them that I do not again return to this settlement till things are settled, and Society a little more under the influence of religious and Social government I shall believe it is best for me."[11]

Two days later, he wrote to Anne's brother, Charles W. Morgan. He had stopped working his land and, indeed, was beginning to sell it. At English Prairie, he wrote, "such society is not at present here to be found for ladies . . . I have naturally turned my thoughts to the peaceful home of my grandparents and the generous offer of my grandfather to interest me in a whaling outfit . . . I feel all its advantages, all its attractions as a residence for a married man." What, then, was stopping him? Charles Morgan, Francis noted, was beginning his career "under the auspices and by the advice of those whose support will ensure success." Not so Francis: his uncles had mostly been silent about his situation. The exception was William Jr., who had advised him "to wander yet further in search of a spot to pitch my tents!" He "could not venture a removal to N. Bedford with a view to any mercantile pursuits unless under the approbation and expressed wish of my uncles." He also sought the support of Aunt Mary and his sisters, though they had not been answering his letters either. He ended the letter on an ominous note: "Give my love to the several individuals of your family and offer to Anna those sentiments from her absent friend most congenial to her own feelings but I w' suggest the propriety of not raising in her affectionate heart a hope that may be the taunt of disappointment."[12]

Francis's tactics were successful: he and Anne were married in December 1819. Whatever his uncles' objections may have been—his cosmopolitan Englishness? his facile charm? the weakness of his Quaker principles?—he was able to settle in New Bedford under generous terms. His wife brought a settlement of $15,000; his grandfather gave him a similar amount; and James Arnold built a candleworks factory for him. William returned with him and lived with his grandfather.[13] The negotiations among Rotches, Morgans, and Arnold must have been complex. Other marriages were probably less difficult to arrange, but we can assume that they were not all simple boy-meets-girl stories.

## "Patrician-like Houses"

Marriages require houses, and as the families' businesses grew more varied and profitable, their houses grew bigger and grander—despite the Quaker commitment to simplicity. Many wealthy families were building houses up the hill from the harbor—the Russells, Howlands, Grinnells, and others. House after house rose along County and intersecting streets. Charles Francis Adams, visiting New Bedford with his father John Quincy Adams in 1835, wrote in his diary: "The fortunes suddenly made at this place have poured themselves out upon the surface in the shape of Houses and grounds. We were taken to see the street which has lately risen like Magic and which presents more noble-looking mansions than any other in this Country."[14] Some of these houses have been razed; some have become institutions or offices; some are looking a bit seedy. Only three are now open to the public: the first and last houses that William Rotch Jr. built and the house built by James Arnold and later expanded by another William Rotch (1819–93, the son of Joseph Rotch and grandson of William Sr.). Nevertheless, we can imagine what County Street looked like in its heyday, as the carriages and sleighs of the Rotches, Rodmans, Morgans, and Arnolds took them visiting.

Herman Melville's Ishmael left the Spouter Inn and wandered up the hill: "Nowhere in all America will you find more patrician-like houses; parks and gardens more opulent than in New Bedford."[15] He was in Rotch country. He might have started near the docks at the corner of Water and William Streets, where William Rotch Jr. had built his first house, in 1791. Three stories tall, of brick with clapboard on the front, it was large enough to accommodate his family. Sarah, William, Joseph, Thomas, and Mary all grew up there. It

FIGURE 13. County Street, New Bedford. *Courtesy of the New Bedford Whaling Museum.*

was later moved to Johnny Cake Hill and is now open as a museum. Quakers generally frowned on brick houses, which were considered ostentatious. Covering the front with clapboard hid the ostentation and evaded the New Bedford tax on brick dwellings.[16]

William was living only a block or two from his father's house at Union and Second Streets, where his sister Mary lived until their father's death in 1828. A few short blocks west, on the north side of William Street just before County, was the brick mansion that William Jr. built for his son Joseph in 1823. A long flight of stairs led to the entrance of this simple, elegant house that was distinguished by columns extending to the roof, with a porch on the ground floor and a balcony above.[17] William Street ends at County Street, and at its head loomed Charles W. Morgan's Greek Revival mansion, built in 1821, with an uninterrupted view of the waterfront district. Six two-story pillars supported the roof, with its square cupola. It was built of stone covered with concrete painted a light beige.

Turning left, one block south on County is the James Arnold mansion, one of the houses that can be visited. When completed in 1821, it was a three-story Federal house, red brick with white Ionic columns supporting a second-story balcony. The symmetrical front had a central door with a fanlight, with two windows on either side. A central hallway led to double parlors on one side and smaller rooms on the other. Marble mantels, ornate plasterwork, and polished woodwork decorated the interior. John Quincy Adams described its appearance in 1835 as "graceful and comfortable, and furnished with elegance and at great cost." When he visited again in 1843, he found it "embellished with many articles of exquisite luxury from Italy." Sarah Rotch Arnold was especially pleased with her bathroom, with stoves to warm the room and heat water.[18]

When James Arnold died in 1868, predeceased by both his wife and daughter, he left the house to Sarah's nephew, William J. Rotch, son of Joseph and Ann Smith Rotch. Arnold stated one condition and one wish. The condition was that William add $20,000 to Arnold's residuary estate, in payment for the house. His "earnest wish and desire" was that William "will immediately after my decease move into and take possession of my said Mansion House and the described appurtenances, keeping them during his life as nearly as possible in the same order as has been done by his late lamented Aunt and myself.—This wish and desire is not intended as a positive condition of the bequest, but only as a wish with which I presume he would prefer to comply unless in his opinion circumstances may forbid."[19]

William's circumstances did forbid. He had seven children from his first marriage, to Emily, and a daughter from his second marriage, to Clara. (His wives were the oldest and youngest daughters of Charles W. Morgan.) The Rotches enlarged the house to accommodate their large family, adding wings, towers, and a cupola. In 1924, the Wamsutta Club purchased the house and expanded it further.

As notable as the house were the gardens, which were open to the public but have not survived. The eleven acres included a greenhouse, a walled garden with trellised fruit trees and grape vines, a great variety of trees and shrubs, and a maze. Charles Francis Adams wrote that when he and his father visited in 1835, Arnold "took us over his garden which has been laid out with much taste. The presence of a female of taste is perceptible in it." Indeed, Sarah shared her husband's interest in horticulture and participated in the development of the garden. Charles Francis also enjoyed the products of the garden in "a beautiful fruit collation"—a frequent feature of the Arnolds' entertaining that his father also commented on after his 1843 visit. In 1852, Herman Melville visited "Mr Arnolds beautiful garden" with his father-in-law, Lemuel Shaw, chief justice of the Massachusetts Supreme Judicial Court. Arnold's interest in horticulture survives near Boston in Jamaica Plain, at Harvard's Arnold Arboretum, which he endowed through a trust dedicated to the advancement of agriculture and horticulture.[20]

Across the street from the Arnold mansion is the home of Samuel Rodman Jr., at 92 Spring Street, built in 1827–28. A three-story house, nearly square, it is constructed of granite covered with concrete painted a light brown. It more than meets the Quaker expectation of simplicity and plainness. Its one adornment is a cupola, where Samuel used a telescope and other instruments to make meteorological observations. Nearby on Spring Street was the Quaker Meeting House. Next to the Rodman House on County Street is the gothic Grace Episcopal Church, built on land donated by Samuel's son Thomas Rotch Rodman and with money donated by Samuel's daughters. The next block includes the stone gothic-style home of Samuel's son Samuel W. Rodman, built between 1841 and 1845. Originally it occupied the entire block.

None of the families lived in the next block, but at the southeast corner of County and Madison sits the other house that is open to visitors. Known as the Rotch-Jones-Duff House and Garden Museum, it preserves the era beautifully. The house was built for William Rotch Jr. in 1834, when he was seventy-five years old, and he lived there until his death in 1850. It was sold in 1851 to Edward Coffin Jones. The Greek Revival house, with its gardens and outbuildings, occupies one acre—a full city block. It is brick covered with clapboard, painted a cheerful yellow with white trim. Pairs of Doric columns support a second-story portico, and porches extend the house into the gardens. A central hall leads to parlors, the dining room, and rooms whose uses have varied over time. With its large rooms, high ceilings, generous windows, and simple woodwork and mantels, it is the epitome of Quaker elegance. The main staircase exemplifies the aesthetics of the house: it curves gracefully to the right, with tapered wood balusters that evoke Shaker furniture. Like his son-in-law James Arnold, William was a founding member of the New Bedford Horticultural Society, and he created elaborate gardens. At Arnold's suggestion he included a knot garden, which survives, although most of the current garden design belongs to the period when the Jones family owned the house. After William Rotch Sr. died in 1828, his unmarried daughter Mary had a house built just behind, at 47 South Sixth Street, for herself and her companion, Mary Gifford.

South of the Rotch-Jones-Duff House is the William Rotch Rodman mansion, built for a son of Samuel Rodman and Elizabeth Rotch in 1833–36. It is a massive three-story structure of granite, with six Corinthian columns, reminiscent of an oversized mausoleum. The interior is less forbidding, with a central hall and a graceful divided staircase that curves to the right and the left from a landing brightened by a large window. It remained a private residence into the 1850s but is now converted into offices. The house mirrors the Joseph Grinnell mansion diagonally opposite, built in 1830. Although born in New Bedford, Grinnell had spent the years between 1810 and 1825 in New York, where he and his cousin, Captain Preserved Fish, founded a successful trading company. He returned to New Bedford in 1825. Both houses were designed by Providence architect Russell Warren, and they are nearly identical. The Grinnell House, however, has only four Corinthian columns, and the granite is rougher. Its large third floor was added later.

By the 1840s, then, most members of these families were living in great comfort along a seven-block stretch of County Street. What was happening in those houses? How were the family members—three or more generations of them— getting along? As complex as the genealogical table and arrangement of houses might seem, these relationships are even harder to discover.

## Close Quarters

It is impossible to separate business from family in this story. All three families built their wealth on whaling—a risky business in which trust was paramount. The greatest risk, of course, was to the men at sea, who in these generations were rarely members of shipowners' families. The captains of the ships were entrusted not only with crew, cargo, and ship but sometimes with important business decisions. A captain might be empowered to alter his route and destinations or to decide where, when, and whether to sell a cargo. He was expected to know about the commodity markets in the ports where he was headed and the state of the currency markets. Fortunes depended in good part on access to skilled, smart, honest captains.

The risk of losing a ship was real, and owners dealt with this in two ways: they insured their ships, and they shared the risk. It was far more prudent to own one-tenth each of ten different vessels than to own a single vessel. Owners needed partners they could trust. Family members headed the list, followed by men whose prosperity demonstrated their ability and who went to the same church, joined the same organizations, and had reputations for honesty. The men who married into these families were made partners in the business, as were their sons. The first Rodman-Rotch marriage—Samuel Rodman to Elizabeth Rotch—was ideal in this sense. Samuel had learned the whaling business in Nantucket, and the men to whom he had been apprenticed were known and trustworthy. He was a Quaker. He was good at bookkeeping, and making him a partner and family member would give him a double incentive to do that job carefully and honestly.

Another way to reduce financial risk was to diversify investments. Whaling required ships, but also rope, casks, lumber, wharves, icehouses, and storage buildings. The Rotches, Rodmans, and Morgans invested in all of these. They rented out wharfage and storage space, and they sold ship supplies, oil, bone, and spermaceti candles made in their own factory.[21]

The family also invested in banks. Whaling involved huge sums of money at a time when the banking industry was in its infancy. It was an international business when there were no institutions to handle international credit or currency exchanges. Whaling companies relied on agents in foreign ports. For example, William Rotch Sr. used Thomas Dickason as one of his English agents before and after the Revolution. Dickason was engaged in whaling himself, but he was also a principal, or "Name," in Lloyd's of London and insured Rotch's ships operating out of England and France. William Rotch used him as a banker, leaving money with him for his captains and creditors to draw on. The relationship was extremely close. In 1807 William's son Benjamin named his youngest son Thomas Dickason, and when Dickason died in 1827, Benjamin was one of the people for whom a mourning ring was made. Thomas Dickason Rotch stayed in England, acting as one of the family's agents, until his death in 1855. As their fortunes grew, the families invested in western lands and railroads. When the textile industry came to New England, family members invested in the mills. Joseph Rotch owned a silk mill, and other members of the family held shares in the large cotton and woolen mills being built in New Bedford and Fall River.[22]

Because they shared ownership of vessels and other business ventures, the family's fortunes to a large extent rose and fell together. When the English Rotches were bankrupted, they recovered in part by acting as agents for the American

Rotches and Rodmans. Even family members no longer active in whaling benefited from a prosperous voyage. From her upstate New York farm, Anne Morgan Rotch wrote to her brother: "O Charles how grandly the *Hector* has done— one such arrival to us *small owners* is a great affair. how amazingly this sperm oil does mount up . . . Francis . . . is well pleased in this instance as you may believe . . . I felt *rich* at once—for my views you know are comparatively humble." Feeling rich, she decided to send some of the profits to the children of Tom and Charity Rotch, who were Quaker missionaries in Ohio.[23]

Most of the men in the family worked together, the women socialized and participated in charitable organizations, and the families all attended the Quaker Meeting—at least until 1824. About ten years earlier, a movement called New Light had begun to gather strength among the Friends. In one sense, it was simply another manifestation of the liberal ideas that were spreading throughout New England churches. But among Quakers, it was a divide between conservative church members and those who believed that by departing from tradition they were returning to "the Inner Light as the early Friends had known it," as a historian explains. Prosperity and greater contact with "worldly" people outside the church were thought to motivate the New Lights. Certainly the Rotch-Rodman-Morgan family fit that description. An anonymous writer, describing the phenomenon in New Bedford, saw a younger, affluent generation that "suddenly threw aside their broad-brims and poke bonnets, and came forth . . . from the bondage of their youth." But even older family members who still dressed in the plain style of Friends and addressed one another as "thee" and "thou" were drawn to New Light.[24]

Some family members were very much in touch with "worldly" people and their writings. Aunt Mary Rotch,

William Sr.'s unmarried daughter, belonged to a reading and discussion group whose studies ranged far beyond Quaker literature. In 1803 she reported reading John Locke's *Essay concerning Human Understanding*, Johann Kasper Lavater's *Essays on Physiognomy*, a biography of the Catholic theologian François Fénelon, Robert Southey's *Letters from England* and the *Memoirs* of the English dramatist Richard Cumberland. She attended lectures on chemistry, took French lessons, sewed clothes for the poor, and kept up a lively correspondence with her nieces and nephews. She and a group of friends wrote and exchanged papers that were read aloud at their monthly meetings. She was well informed about Transcendental thought, and in the 1830s she and Ralph Waldo Emerson became correspondents and friends. Margaret Fuller visited her in New Bedford, staying in her home, and they corresponded extensively.[25]

Her intellectual circle had been broadened when her niece Eliza (Benjamin's daughter) arrived from England. She lived with Mary from 1820 to 1828 and helped to take care of her aging grandparents as well as visiting nieces and nephews. She apparently had had no domestic experience. She wrote to a cousin in Boston: "As I am for the first time in my life occupied with housekeeping affairs you must not wonder if they show their common place heads in every few lines of my letter. If I was writing of the war with the Turks I should be sure to think of *Russian Towelling*." Her English parents seem to have been more intellectually inclined than most of their American relatives. In 1828, Eliza married John Farrar, a professor of mathematics and astronomy at Harvard. She wrote that "if I had sought the world over, for a husband who would be acceptable to my parents, as a son-in-law, I could not have pleased them better than I did in giving them John Farrar. His refined appearance, good manners, and gentle nature endeared him to my mother, whilst my father delighted in adding to his own knowledge of Natural Philosophy, the more accurate information and late discoveries, which the Professor could give him."[26]

Having been raised among the upper classes of English society, Eliza was more cosmopolitan in her views than her New Bedford relatives. She became active in intellectual circles in Cambridge and Boston and introduced Aunt Mary to people she thought she would enjoy meeting. One of these was Margaret Fuller, whom Eliza took under her wing. As the author and social reformer Thomas Wentworth Higginson reported: "She readily saw the remarkable intellect of Margaret Fuller, and also perceived the defects of her training. She undertook to mould her externally, to make her less abrupt, less self asserting, more comme il faut in ideas, manners and even costume. She had her constantly at her own house, reformed her hairdresser, and instructed her dressmaker."[27]

Eliza extended her views on the behavior, appearance, and education of women more broadly by writing children's books (Higginson called her "one of our first and best writers for children") and *A Young Lady's Friend: A Manual of Practical Advice and Instruction to Young Females on Their Entering upon the Duties of Life, after Quitting School*. She was the Miss Manners of her day, and her advice extended far beyond using the right fork: "The great business of early education is to form habits of industry, to train the mind to find pleasure in intellectual effort, and to inspire a love of knowledge for its own sake."[28]

Aunt Mary and the others of her generation had little interest in changing their plain Quaker dress, but they did become thoughtful and questioning about religious matters. For her, and for her nieces and nephews, new ideas about the beliefs and practices of Quakerism were worth exploring. The New Light movement had already appeared north of Boston in Lynn, where in 1816 Mary Newhall and a few other women had preached New Light beliefs. The elders of the church asked Newhall to stop preaching, but she refused, so the elders disowned her and her followers. Tempers on both sides rose so high that—throwing pacifism to the wind—violent altercations broke out in the meetinghouse, one involving a sword. The sheriff came to the meetinghouse and literally read the riot act. In the ensuing trial, several of Newhall's supporters were found guilty of rioting and disturbing public worship. Similar disruptions occurred in Salem.[29]

One of the people attending worship during the disturbances at Lynn was Benjamin Rodman, who sided with the rebels. His growing discomfort with the Society of Friends was shared by James Arnold, who requested dismission in 1822 and eventually joined the Congregational Church. Elizabeth Rodman, writing to a relative in Pennsylvania in 1820, said that New Bedford Quakers were wondering why "the Rotch family in its various branches were so tinctur'd with the 'New System!'"[30]

In January 1823, Mary Newhall came to New Bedford to preach in the Spring Street meetinghouse. When she knelt to pray, most stood to show their support, including Elizabeth Rodman and Mary Rotch. The Old Light elders remained seated. Soon the meetings became so contentious that Elizabeth wrote that she felt "at liberty to omit attending." In January the Select Meeting responded to the apostasy by threatening to depose Elizabeth and Mary from the eldership, thinking that would solve the problem. "But," as one historian noted, "the Old Lights reckoned without the familial loyalty of the Rotch-Rodman clan." Elizabeth Rodman reported that William Rotch Rodman had made his advanced thinking known more blatantly by holding New Bedford's first dance in his home that same month. Elizabeth Rodman Rotch seems to have been the only member of the family who sided with the Old Lights.[31]

For a full year the conflict was aired at nearly every business meeting of the Friends, and even worship meetings were disrupted. An elder visiting from England commented that he "had never before . . . discovered so much activity on the part of those related by blood and affinity to the persons under notice . . . The Rotches and Rodmans hotly riposted that their fundamental concern was not for their relatives but for the principles of their religious society." Finally, on March 5, 1824, the Old Lights voted to remove Mary Rotch and Elizabeth Rodman as elders. Samuel Rodman wrote in his journal that their action "involves such a restriction of the right of conscience, such an arrogant spirit of Self Righteousness, and such want of Christian Charity . . . that the proceedings on that complaint were opposed on the ground of principle with much animation and energy." Nevertheless, the censure passed, and the clerk entered the action as unanimous.[32]

At the end of the meeting, Benjamin Rodman announced that disowned members would gather that afternoon. At another worship meeting, Samuel reported, "Benjamin kept his seat during a prayer by D. Otis . . . which was not meant to condemn either the prayer or those who conformed to the usage, but . . . he could not from form apparently unite in a prayer which he did not feel." After refusing to meet with a church committee, he too was disowned, but "it gave him no pain to disconnect from the society." Soon nearly all the New Lights had been disowned or had resigned, shifting their allegiance to the Unitarian Church, though a few Rodmans became Episcopalians. Aunt Mary began attending

FIGURE 14. Benjamin Rodman. *Courtesy of the New Bedford Whaling Museum.*

Unitarian services, but she always left quietly before communion (then part of the Sunday service) because she disliked ritual. Family unity survived better than did the New Bedford Society of Friends, which was much diminished in numbers.[33]

Benjamin Rodman's principles created some embarrassment for the family. He was strongly opposed to the Massachusetts law that allowed creditors to imprison delinquent debtors, a practice abolished under federal law in 1833. In 1840, when his protests fell on deaf ears, he decided not to pay back about $1,500 that he owed to the Duxbury Bank. The bank had him imprisoned, depositing $100 for his upkeep. His brother Samuel visited him frequently, sometimes bringing Benjamin's children. His journal reports that he always found Benjamin cheerful, busy, welcoming to visitors, but stubbornly unwilling to discuss "the reasons of his own course in remaining there." Benjamin spent his time in prison writing newspaper articles that he combined, along with other documents, into a pamphlet, and he vowed not to seek release until the pamphlet was published. On September 16, he noted that he had been in prison for three months, and he was still there twelve days later. His hundred-day incarceration strengthened his commitment to prison reform, to improving the lot of sailors (who often ended up in jail after drinking sprees), and to temperance.[34]

Benjamin also noted the need for a home for sailors, a goal accomplished in 1850 when James and Sarah Arnold donated her father's home at Water and William Streets for that purpose and it was moved to its present site on Johnny Cake Hill. Benjamin did not forget his fellow inmates after his release, and he raised money to buy a hundred turkeys to be delivered to the prison for Thanksgiving.[35]

Benjamin's sister-in-law Anne Rotch expressed her conflicting feelings about his actions in a letter to her brother, Charles W. Morgan, feelings that were probably shared by other family members: "Dear Ben remains status quo—well everything has been said by his friends that could be—every expedient presented—he has chosen to stand alone—to place himself separate from the help of any one . . . I feel so much for Susan [Anne's sister, Benjamin's wife]—that I am provoked at him . . . it is a hard case—and were Bens being

in prison a mere matter of opinion I should wage uncondi-
tional war against it—but as it is in the ground of duty—no
one has a right to controvert it—may he continue to find it a
recompense for the privation and suffering which he necessarily inflicts on others—that to a feeling mind must be a
cause of regret."[36]

Generational differences, too, became evident. When
Francis and Anne Morgan Rotch visited his parents in England in 1828, Anne's letters to her sisters, copied in her journals, talked much more about fashions, furniture, and decor
than her parents' generation would have thought proper.
Judging by her purchases, she certainly was not dressing as a
traditional Quaker. Her initial enjoyment of Francis's sister
Maria faded in the face of Maria's extreme piety and commitment to good works. And sisterly love could give way to
cattiness. Her sister-in-law Isabella (Benjamin Rotch's wife),
she wrote, "is tall with a small waist but I do not call hers a
good figure—She has no bust, which is uncommon for an
Englishwoman."[37]

All three generations were eager to amass fortunes, but
William Sr.'s grandchildren grew up in a wider world than
had their grandparents. They were less concerned with
modesty and discretion, as their houses demonstrated, and
they were less willing to be confined by Quaker principles.
The generation gap between Samuel Rodman and his son
William Rotch Rodman became an abyss. William, his
father complained, had "never been satisfied with reasonable
and moderate things . . . In his determination to be rich he
has embraced schemes that common judgement and fore-
sight would have turned from with disgust." William had
invested, largely on credit, in nonwhaling businesses. In 1819,
those businesses failed spectacularly, and he appealed to his
father for help. Samuel told a correspondent that William

had ignored his teachings and had been seduced by "an imprudent, insatiable, appetite for some phantom," but he guaranteed $25,000 of his son's debt. Then he learned that William owed $60,000 more, due immediately, and the same amount again in longer-term debt. He refused further aid and regretted that he had "lifted a finger to help him."[38]

William suffered little from the experience. He negotiated successfully with his creditors, and by 1851 a listing of the wealthiest men in Massachusetts claimed he was worth more than half a million dollars: "A son of old Samuel, and a go-ahead, gain-or-lose sort of man. He owns in everything . . . he is affable when he pleases, pays his bills when he pleases, and does as he pleases generally."[39]

## Trust Betrayed

None of these problems approached the severity of what became known far beyond the family as "The New Bedford Scandal." In November 1830, James and Sarah Rotch Arnold were looking forward to the marriage of their only daughter, Elizabeth, to a young man from Boston. Shortly before her wedding, she came to them and said she could not go through with the ceremony. For several years, she told them, she had been molested by an older, married man. When she had tried to end the abuse, he threatened her with exposure and, according to some, violence. She disclosed his actions to her parents anyway. Her molester was Francis Rotch, her mother's cousin, the husband of Anne Waln Morgan Rotch, a man her father had helped to become established in New Bedford. He was forty-two, and she was twenty-one. The molestation had begun at least two years earlier; according to some accounts, it had begun when Elizabeth was fourteen.[40]

Francis was confident that the matter would be hushed up to spare Elizabeth's reputation. But James Arnold saw clearly that the shame was not hers. He made sure that the family and the prominent merchants and bankers of New Bedford were fully informed of Francis's character. Francis fled the city on the packet to Naushon Island (just east of the New Bedford harbor). According to a contemporary letter written by someone outside the family, the affair was "a common topic of conversation with everyone—such was the excitement in Bedford that a mob collected on the Wharf as . . . they meant to tar and feather him." Francis's wife was the last to know. She "went in to Mr. Rodman's Monday afternoon and seeing several members of her family assembled and looking gloomy she made the remark and wished to know what was the reason . . . they did not wish to name the thing to her but were obliged as she expected some company in the evening, she would not however believe it until she went to the Island and found it was really too true." According to Samuel Rodman, Anne's "unsuspicious confiding and ardent affection made [the disclosures] fall with lacerating power on her gentle and innocent mind."[41]

Everyone was outraged by Francis's behavior. Samuel Rodman, who was among those James first spoke with, wrote in his diary that he had learned of "a depravity surpassing any possible previous conception . . . exciting on the one hand in the assembled friends the strongest abhorrence and on the other hand the deepest commiseration for its victims." But some members of the family neither understood nor sympathized with James Arnold's decision to make the events public. One wrote that he was surprised, "seeing there was not likely to be exposure from any thing happening to her; That this dreadful intercourse was not in some way hid from the public ear—if money could have shut up this foul stain, on account of his wife or widow, and fatherless children

FIGURE 15. Portrait of Elizabeth Arnold, Narcisse Othon, 1837. Graphite on cream wove card. *Harvard Art Museums/Fogg Museum, Gift of Misses Aimée and Rosamond Lamb, 1965.536. Photo by Imaging Department © President and Fellows of Harvard College.*

—would it not have been better." (There was no indication that Francis was about to kill himself; perhaps the writer thought that would be the honorable course.) A few—very few—called for mercy and forgiveness.[42]

The story spread quickly to Boston. Elizabeth Peabody, a prominent member of Transcendental circles and the proprietor of a school, learned of the events because Francis's son

Frank, then seven or eight, was one of her students. Despite friends' warnings not to interfere, Peabody made several trips to New Bedford to comfort Anne, offering her "deepest religious sympathy" and suggestions for "reform of the criminal." Anne was not receptive and accused her of indiscretion. Soon nearly all her students' parents withdrew them from her school because of her connection to the scandal. Louisa Catherine Adams, wife of John Quincy, wrote that "Boston has been in a state of consternation owing to a little scandalous peccadillo which has occurred and crushed all the interest of the European News and almost of internal politics. It is as high in its grade as the Knap murder and conducted with all the deliberation, which rendered that incident so awful . . . It is a New Bedford affair. The Mother gone distracted." When Louisa's son Charles Francis visited the Arnolds in 1835, the story was still very much on his mind. He wrote in his diary: "The melancholy story which has saddened this family for life made me feel surprised to see Miss Arnold. But I conversed with her for some time and found her a woman whose mind will always prevent her from being despicable in any body's eyes."[43]

Samuel Rodman wrote in his journal entry for November 7 that Francis Rotch "left the Island of Nashaun as is supposed on the 5th Inst.—possibly never more to be seen in this place where he has proved himself so base a villain." He moved to Morris, in Upstate New York, and established himself as a farmer and stock breeder. His wife and their young children joined him six months later. Anne continued to correspond with her sisters and brother but missed being physically close to the family. When Benjamin Rodman was in prison, she wrote to her brother, Charles W. Morgan, of her feelings toward Benjamin's wife, her sister Susan: "It would have been a great comfort to me to have been near her at this time of trial—it is so painful to think of her loneliness —and to know one has no power to alleviate her feelings." It is tempting to read that as a reflection of her own loneliness. Charles never forgave James Arnold for separating him from his sister Anne because of Francis's crime.[44]

Elizabeth Arnold lived with her parents until she married in 1859, when she was forty-nine. She and her mother both died the following year. James Arnold lived alone in their house on County Street until his death in 1868. At his funeral, the minister spoke of the mansion, of "the deadly pain at the heart of all that beauty; of the tragic agonies those walls enclosed." He reminded the mourners that "this was the end of a household, the funeral of a family; that a home, the most conspicuous among all our homes, for culture, for hospitality, for charity, is utterly emptied, and exists no more."[45]

## To Visit

The Rotch House, now the Mariners' Home, is a collaboration between the New Bedford Whaling Museum and the Port Society. Exhibits are open daily to those with tickets to the Whaling Museum across the street (www.whalingmuseum.org). It is next door to the Seamen's Bethel, built in 1832, which is open free of charge seven days a week, from 9:00 A.M. to 5:00 P.M. (seamensbethel.org). The Arnold Mansion, now the Wamsutta Club and the nonprofit Arnold House, is being developed as a museum. The original parts of the house give a sense of what it looked like in Arnold's day, although none of the furniture or other artifacts remain. The Rotch-Jones-Duff House (www. rjdmuseum.org), beautifully restored, tells the story of the two families that owned the house in later years, as well as that of William Rotch Jr. The handout for the self-guided tours and the lists in each room explain which period the furniture and fittings belong to. The permanent exhibits include clothing, toys, china, and silver; other items are shown in changing programs. The garden is also open to visitors.

The Rotches and other Quaker families were abolitionists, and the New Bedford Historical Society (nbhistoricalsociety. org) offers resources to learn about the movement in the city, including a map of the New Bedford Black History Trail and an Underground Railroad Walking Tour. They are restoring the Nathan and Polly Johnson House, where Frederick Douglass lived, and collaborating with the New Bedford Whaling Museum in the creation of Captain Paul Cuffe Park, adjacent to the museum. Cuffe (1759–1817) was a Quaker businessman, sea captain, patriot, and abolitionist of Wampanoag and Ashanti descent who helped colonize Sierra Leone.

## To Learn More

The New Bedford Whaling Museum Research Library holds papers of the Rotch, Rodman, and Morgan families. The G. W. Blunt White Library at Mystic Seaport, Connecticut, holds business papers and some personal correspondence of Charles W. Morgan, as well as ship's papers for the whaling ship *Charles W. Morgan*, which was launched in 1841. The ship itself is open to visitors to Mystic Seaport. Published sources include John M. Bullard's *The Rotches*, available in print and online, and Joseph L. McDevitt Jr., "The House of Rotch: Whaling Merchants of Massachusetts, 1734–1828." The *New-Bedford Mercury* is included in America's Historical Newspapers. The New Bedford Whaling Museum (www.whalingmuseum.org) has photographs of several of the houses that are no longer standing. Search its photo collection for "County Street."

# 5

# Home and Family

*The Alcott Houses,
Concord and Harvard*

WE come to Orchard House in Concord in search of the March family, knowing that Meg, Jo, Beth, Amy, Marmee, and Father can be found only in the pages of *Little Women* and our imaginations. To find the Alcott family—Anna, Louisa, Elizabeth, May, Abigail, and Bronson—we need to visit two other houses as well. The March home was modest, but solid and permanent, the place where the family took root and grew. The Alcotts, though, moved thirty times before coming to rest in Orchard House. They lived in the house now called The Wayside during the girls' adolescence, the period of their lives in which the novel's story occurs, though Louisa wrote the first half while living at Orchard House and set the story there. Fruitlands, a day's carriage ride to the west in Harvard, was the scene of a family crisis—omitted from the March story—that changed the Alcott family forever. For the Alcotts, home was less a place than what Bronson called "the dear family."

## Beginnings

Bronson Alcott came to Boston to start a new kind of school. He was self-educated and well read, and he had progressive ideas about educating young children. When he had tried these ideas in Cheshire, Connecticut, parents became dissatisfied and started a competing school. Bronson thought a big city would be more accepting. Abigail May had grown up in Boston, a descendant of distinguished Massachusetts families, including the Sewalls and the Quincys. Her father, Joseph May, had lost his fortune, but with help from relatives his family was comfortable though far from wealthy. She had been living in Brooklyn, Connecticut, with her brother, Samuel, when Bronson came to consult him about starting a school. Abigail, a spinster at twenty-six, fell in love with the idealistic caller. After a three-year courtship, they were married on May 23, 1830.[1]

Bronson taught briefly in Boston before being invited to open a school in Germantown, near Philadelphia. He welcomed the invitation, in part because Abigail was expecting their first child, and he believed that children fared better in the country. Anna was born in March 1831, and when she was two months old they moved to a rent-free cottage that Abigail described as a "little paradise." The baby gave Bronson an opportunity to study child development and test his educational theories. Unlike most fathers of his time, he interacted constantly with Anna. He also recorded her activities, moods, and physical development in minute detail. Only he and Abigail took care of Anna, the happy object of constant attention.[2]

The idyll came to an abrupt close when Louisa was born on November 29, 1832. Abigail's attention turned to the new baby, and Anna (not quite two years old) was jealous. She began hitting and scratching both her mother and the baby. Nothing in Bronson's image of innocent children or his philosophy of kind treatment could deal with her anger. To make matters worse, Bronson's sponsor had died, and he had to close the school in Germantown. He tried his luck in Philadelphia, but that school failed as well. Finally, in July

1834 the family returned to Boston, where Bronson hoped to try again. They lived first in boardinghouses, then with Joseph May, and later in a large rented house on Front Street, with a study for Bronson, a large yard and garden, and two servants. The Alcotts did not live there alone: guests, Elizabeth Peabody (who taught in Bronson's school), and several boarding students were needed to pay the rent.[3]

The move did not resolve the struggle between Anna and Louisa. As Louisa grew bigger and stronger, she became a worthy rival for her older sister. Anna had become more passive and Louisa more aggressive, hitting and pinching her father as well. Bronson blamed the problems on Abigail's faulty mothering and Louisa's "deep-seated obstinacy of temper." In June 1835, a third daughter, Elizabeth, was born. Elizabeth was a mercifully easy baby, but Louisa—like Anna before her—was jealous of the newcomer. One day she horrified Abigail by crying, "I don't love little sister, I wish she was dead, I will throw her out of the window." Bronson and Louisa then had a conversation about contrition and forgiveness that he felt resolved the issue. Throughout their lives, Bronson believed that Anna shared his temperament, while Louisa was like her mother. When Louisa was a teenager, Bronson wrote in his journal: "Two devils, as yet, I am not quite divine enough to vanquish—the mother fiend and her daughter."[4]

With the financial and intellectual support of several influential Bostonians, Bronson created what he considered a nearly ideal learning environment at the Tremont Masonic Temple. He made a large investment, noting in his journal: "I have spared no expense to surround the senses with appropriate emblems of intellectual and spiritual life. Paintings, busts, books, and not inelegant furniture have been deemed important." When the school opened in September 1834, the schoolroom was arranged with custom-made children's desks in a semicircle facing the teacher. A large library gave students access to classic and religious literature, as well as fairy tales, and busts of Plato, Jesus, Shakespeare, and Socrates provided beauty and inspiration. Rather than the rote drills common in schools at the time, Bronson engaged the students in Socratic dialogue to elicit their understanding and develop their power to reason. He was joined in teaching, at various times, by Elizabeth Peabody and Margaret Fuller, both well known and respected among Boston intellectuals. By all accounts, Bronson was a gifted teacher and spellbinding speaker, and his school attracted the children of distinguished Bostonians. He also held successful "conversations" with adults on a wide range of topics. For nearly three years, the experiment thrived. One of his students later said, "I never knew I had a mind till I came to this school." Yet this experiment failed too.[5]

Bronson Alcott's failure was not due to the quality of his thought or his teaching. He was, however, tone-deaf to the sensibilities of mid-nineteenth-century Boston. To pro-mote the school and to inspire other educators to follow his example, in 1835 he published *Record of a School*. With Elizabeth Peabody's help, he created a clear, well-written account of what he was accomplishing. The favorable atten-tion it attracted inspired him to publish a two-volume sequel, *Conversations with Children on the Gospels*, recording his students' responses to questions about religion and human development. Against Peabody's advice, he included passages that might cause offense and used the children's first names. Readers bridled at excerpts like the one in which "Augustine" said there were "a great many" idolaters in Boston: "They worship money." And, when asked whether there were any holy ghosts in Boston, "Frank" replied, "No *very* holy ghosts here." The conversation that caused the most controversy was one in which "Josiah" explained being born: "The spirit comes from heaven, and takes up the naughtiness out of other people . . . And these naughtinesses, put together, make a body for the child." It did not help that "Josiah" was the grandson of Josiah Quincy, president of Harvard and former mayor of Boston. Newspapers attacked the book as blasphemous and obscene, calling Bronson a charlatan and a madman. Bronson regretted that "subjects treated of with reverance by the children, have been profaned by impure readers." Parents withdrew their children, and Bronson could no longer pay the rent. He moved to smaller and smaller quarters as enrollment declined. In 1837 he was forced to sell his library and, a year later, to move his family to a small house on Cottage Place and then to a shared house on Beach Street. The last straw was his admission of an African American student. The parents of all but one white child withdrew them.[6]

Bronson once told his mother that he was "still at my old trade, *hoping*," but relying on baseless optimism was financially disastrous. Even before the school failed, he confessed to his journal: "My income is small, inadequate to meet the necessary claims of my family and also carry on the school. I am involved in debt, arising from the unsuccessful issue of previous experiments in human culture. What I earn is all pledged by obligations to others, and I have already anticipated the earnings of the next two or three years, even should I be successful . . . Yet a day of deliverance shall come . . . great results are to spring from the little seed that I shall sow." With the closing of the school, he was $6,000 in debt and had no prospect of earning a living as a teacher. Abigail wrote to her brother, "We are as poor as rats."[7]

Bronson's lectures and conversations for adults had been enthusiastically received. According to Ralph Waldo Emerson, "He will willingly talk the whole of a day, and most part of the night, and then again to-morrow, for days successively." But, Emerson added, "when the conversation is ended, all is over." In a sermon preached at Bronson's death, Cyrus A. Barton recalled that "Mr. Alcott wanted to be heard. He coveted every ear . . . Conversation was his passion, but it became monologue: he soliloquized in company." Bronson hoped to reach a wider audience by publishing the ideas he offered in these sessions. Unfortunately, his oral skills did not transfer to paper. Robert Lowell described the problem:

> While he talks he is great, but goes out like a taper,
> If you shut him up closely with pen, ink, and paper;
> Yet his fingers itch for 'em from morning till night,
> And he thinks he does wrong if he don't always write;
> In this, as in all things, a lamb among men,
> He goes to sure death when he goes to the pen.[8]

Emerson read several of Bronson's efforts and almost always advised against publication. When, with his reluctant encouragement, Bronson's "Orphic Sayings" were published in *The Dial*, the critics were devastating. One suggested calling them "Gastric Sayings," while another thought that "Alcott's unintelligibles" would be more appropriate. Yet another described the work as "a train of fifteen railroad cars with one passenger." But Emerson admired Alcott as a thinker and did his best to advance his work. He encouraged him to move to Concord, northwest of Boston, where he might make a fresh start, and Abigail's father and brother provided enough money for the family to rent Dove Cottage in 1840. Anna, then seven, wrote in her journal, "Father told us how people had treated him, and why we came to live at Concord, and how we must give up a good many things that we like. I know it will be hard, but I mean to do it. I fear I shall complain sometimes about it." Bronson told Samuel

May, "I have again planted myself, and am seeking to strike my roots into the soil, if it shall prove productive of even the scantiest sustenance for our common wants." In July a fourth daughter, May, was born.[9]

Sustenance from Bronson's efforts was indeed scanty. Abigail wrote to her brother in August: "Must we too embrace some device to *get money* that we may live? . . . We *must* or starve, freeze, go thirsty and naked." She took in sewing, and Anna and Louisa helped her. She did not object to hard work: "I have labored, hand and brain, for the support of my family. The conditions of our life have been complicated, and difficult to understand; but we have submitted to no mean subterfuge, no ignoble surrender." Abigail was supportive emotionally as well. She believed in Bronson and his ideals, defended him against her father's criticisms, and shared his hopes. But she was more practical than he: "Mr. Alcott cannot bring himself to work for gain; but we have not yet learned to live without money or means." As their finances grew more and more strained, she began to doubt his principles. Her brother, Sam, who had repeatedly come to the family's rescue, pointed out that Bronson's friends were growing tired of supporting him. She questioned: "They have to labor. Why should not he?—It is a difficult question to answer . . . His unwillingness to be employed in the usual way produces great doubt in the minds of his friends as to the righteousness of his life, because he partakes of the wages of others occupied in this same way. It is certainly not right to incur debt and be indifferent or inactive in the payment of the same."[10] Abigail was willing to work, in defiance of the norms of the time. But when Bronson's principles threatened the unity of the family, she rebelled.

## Fruitlands

Although Bronson's schools had failed in the United States, a group of English reformers had taken his first book as a model for their own school near London, named Alcott House in his honor, and suggested that he visit. Emerson, seeing how low Bronson's spirits had fallen, gave him money for the trip. In May 1842 Bronson sailed to England, leaving his brother Junius to help Abigail at Dove Cottage. Abigail, at first unhappy with the idea, began to bloom in his absence. Her father died, and a small sum from his estate enabled her to pay off some of their creditors. Despite her sewing, she had time to read. "I am enjoying this separation from my husband," she wrote.[11]

Bronson spent six months with congenial thinkers— Henry Gardiner Wright, William Oldham, and Charles Lane. On July 6, they decided to try an experiment, a "consociate family" living in a self-sufficient community somewhere in New England, whose members could escape the confines of the nuclear household. On October 20, 1842, Bronson arrived in Concord with Wright, Lane, and Lane's son, William. They all crowded into Dove Cottage while they searched for a suitable farm and recruits for their community. Abigail wrote, "Circumstances most cruelly drive me from the enjoyment of my domestic life. I am almost suffocated in this atmosphere of restriction and gloom . . . perhaps I feel it more after five months of liberty." They eventually chose a run-down farm in Harvard, Massachusetts, paid for with Lane's money and a note from Samuel May. They moved in that spring and named it Fruitlands in honor of its few scraggly apple trees and their commitment to a strict vegan diet that also excluded coffee, tea, and molasses. Root vegetables were prohibited, either because eating the

FIGURE 16. Fruitlands. *Image courtesy of the Trustees of Reservations, Archives & Research Center.*

root kills the plant or because growing downward suggests a base nature. Only unleavened bread was allowed, possibly because yeast is a living thing.[12]

The Alcotts and the Englishmen were joined by a few recruits who did not stay very long. They wore only linen (wool belonged to sheep, silk to silkworms, and cotton was harvested by slaves), which worked well in summer but provided little warmth in cold weather. Bronson believed that "even the canker-worms that infested the apple trees were not to be molested. They had as much right to the apples as man had." The most important addition to the community was Joseph Palmer, who owned a nearby farm and had a practical knowledge of agriculture. Alcott and Lane refused to use animals to plow or manure to fertilize, but Palmer convinced them that the use of his "team" (an ox and a cow) would be a wise temporary measure. Except for Palmer, the men were not used to hard work, and they spent too little time at it.

As Samuel Hecker, who lived there only two weeks, noted, "Alcott and Lane were interested in literature and writing at the expense of the success & immediate prosperity of their object." He added that "Mr. Alcott looked benign and talked philosophy, while Mrs. Alcott and the children did the work." The house was in poor repair and, in any case, too small for the number of people living in it. The three older girls slept in a windowless attic with ceilings so low that they could barely stand. For at least part of the time, Bronson and Abigail slept apart.[13]

The practical difficulties of life at Fruitlands paled in comparison to the war of principles and personalities between Abigail and Charles Lane. Lane believed that attachments to one's own family were destructive of community, and he advocated celibacy and breaking familial bonds. When Bronson balked, Lane wrote that "constancy to his wife and inconstancy to the Spirit have blurred over his life forever." Abigail expressed the same idea differently: "Mr. Alcott's conjugal and paternal instincts were too strong for him." The conflict was obvious to the children. Louisa wrote in her journal, "In the evening father and mother and Anna and I had a long talk. I was very unhappy, and we all cried. Anna and I cried in bed, and I prayed God to keep us all together."[14]

Abigail took immediate action. First, she convinced her brother Sam not to pay the November installment of the note he had signed, putting the loan into arrears. Abigail thanked him: "Your letter was already received and pleased me better than it did the other proprietors of the Estate." Two weeks later Lane wrote to William Oldham: "Mrs. Alcott gives notice that she concedes to the wishes of her friends and shall withdraw to a house which they will provide for herself and her four children. As she will take all the furniture with her, this proceeding necessarily leaves me alone and naked in a new world. Of course, Mr. A. and I could not remain together without her."[15]

The experiment had lasted less than a year, and its failure broke Bronson's spirit. Abigail and the girls rarely referred to Fruitlands, but eventually Louisa wrote a satiric but light-hearted account, "Transcendental Wild Oats." According to Franklin B. Sanborn, Bronson's acolyte and biographer, "the final expulsion from this Paradise nearly cost Mr. Alcott his life. He returned to his chamber, refused food, and was on the point of dying from grief and abstinence, when his wife prevailed on him to continue longer in this ungrateful world." The family moved into three rooms in a nearby farmhouse. That winter Abigail wrote in her journal: "The end I desire [is] to obtain by some concert of means and action a home for me and my family . . . a house and [a] few acres of land for us to occupy . . . I ask but little—but that little I must have or perish."[16]

## Hillside

The family moved from place to place until the spring of 1845, when the estate of Abigail's father was finally settled, four years after his death. After the claims against Bronson remaining from the Tremont Temple school were settled, about $2,000 remained in the trust established for Abigail. The trust acquired a house in Concord for $850, and Emerson donated $500 to acquire eight acres of nearby land that Bronson could farm. The house, built in 1714, needed work, but it had large rooms and possibilities. Bronson named it Hillside. He used outbuildings to add wings to the main house, built a large kitchen, and put in a new staircase. Bronson took special care with the garden, planting to feed his family.[17] Hillside was a place of great happiness for the Alcotts. It provided something that Abigail sensed was lacking in all their previous homes: space and privacy.

For most of their lives, the Alcotts had lived with others: boarding students, teachers, the English visitors, or frequently the owners of homes who welcomed them in times of need. Even when living on their own, they were often crowded. Privacy was almost nonexistent because Bronson considered it undesirable: children should have no secrets. The girls all kept journals, but their parents read them, commented on them, and insisted on changes. Abigail censored Bronson's journals with scissors; he altered hers and tore pages out of Anna's.[18] At some point, the togetherness wore thin—perhaps when Abigail noticed how much she enjoyed being on her own while Bronson was in England.

In 1842, before the move to Fruitlands, Abigail had visited Emerson's home and wrote in her journal: "I left this scene of enchantment for once dissatisfied with my home. I have ever felt that with Mr. Alcott's ideas of beauty we have suffered for want of room. We have always been too crowded up. We have no room to enjoy that celestial privacy which gives a charm to connubial and domestic intimacy." The months in Fruitlands must have enhanced her wish for physical and emotional breathing space. Before they moved in, Louisa had told her mother, "I have been thinking about my little room which I suppose I never shall have. I should want to be there about all the time and I should go there and sing and think." At Hillside in March 1846, she wrote happily: "I have at last got the little room I have wanted so long, and am very happy about it. It does me good to be alone, and Mother has made it very pretty and neat for me. My work-basket and desk are by the window, and my closet is full of dried herbs that smell very nice. The door that opens into the garden will be very pretty in summer, and I can run off to the woods when I like." Anna, too, had her own room.[19]

Bronson had not lost his desire for communal living. He wrote to his brother Junius: "The house is a convenient structure, and with some additions and repairs would serve two families . . . I will not abide in a house set apart for myself and family alone. The law of Love opens arms and doors to our spiritual kindreds nor selfishly appropriates the gifts offered to those related by ties of blood only." After the disaster at Fruitlands, though, the power in the family had shifted to Abigail. Except for a brief period in which a young woman lived with them to teach the girls, Hillside was home only to the Alcotts. Another change in their lives was the abandonment of strict vegetarianism by all except Bronson.[20]

Anna and Louisa were now teenagers, experiencing more independence than they had ever known. The girls explored the countryside, made friends, presented home theatricals, and, according to one biographer, "were actively inventing nooks, both physical and mental, where no overly inquisitive parent or teacher could enter." Emerson invited Louisa to use his library, and she began reading intensely and writing—not just theatricals but also poems and stories. Bronson reshaped the landscape with trees, terraces, stone walls, arbors, and a summer house, enjoyed the company of Emerson and Thoreau, and conducted conversations, for which he sold tickets. Abigail rejoiced in the house and her family's happiness, but soon financial worries returned. Bronson's income from conversations was small, and they needed cash for wood, clothing, and food that they could not raise themselves. It had become clear to her that Bronson could not be left in charge of the family's fate. She wrote to her brother: "I have taken the ship into my own command, but whether I shall

FIGURE 17. A. Bronson Alcott seated on the bench he constructed around one of the "Revolutionary Elms" in the front yard of Orchard House. *Used by permission of Louisa May Alcott's Orchard House.*

do better as Captain than I have as mate, the revenue and record of the year must decide. At least I think I shall keep better soundings, and ascertain oftener and more correctly whether I am sailing in deep waters or in shallows. We have been nearly wrecked twice."[21]

In 1848, they rented out Hillside and moved to Boston, where Abigail could find work. The next four years were, according to one biographer, "the bleakest era in the Alcotts' lives . . . a succession of dreary, cramped abodes in struggling, graceless neighborhoods." Louisa wrote in her journal that they were "poor as rats & apparently quite forgotten by every one but the Lord." Bronson claimed that for him, poverty was a small matter, "but to the thinker's family, if he have one, it is no small matter, but a serious; and for the wrongs it suffers there is, nor can be, no recompense." Abigail worked among those even poorer than they; Anna lived elsewhere as a governess. Louisa spent two unhappy years teaching, continuing to write. They were saved by selling Hillside to Nathaniel Hawthorne for $1,500 in 1852, and for the next five years they lived in a rented four-story house in Boston and in a house in Walpole, New Hampshire, loaned by a relative. Abigail continued to work among the poor; Bronson traveled, earning some money from his conversations; Anna moved to Syracuse, where she taught school; and Louisa lived in Boston, where she took in sewing and wrote stories which began to earn some income. Her first book, *Flower Fables*, was published for Christmas 1854. But living and working among the poor took a toll: in 1850 the entire family had smallpox, and in 1856 Lizzie and May contracted scarlet fever. Both diseases probably originated with families that Abigail was helping.[22]

In 1857 Bronson, his confidence restored by the reception of his conversations, decided the family should return to

Concord. He found a seventeenth-century house on twelve acres, desperately in need of repair. He told his daughters: "All this I can have for $950 . . . leaving your mother's investments untouched." He promised to "take the reins a little more firmly in hand . . . You may rely upon me for supports of labour and money . . . [I] shall command the respects of your mother's connexions." Keenly aware of his position in the family, he pleaded: "Let me be the central figure of the Group, and try our family fortunes so, for a little time . . . Please give me my last chance of redeeming my goodsense and discretion." He did prevail, one last time, and the family moved to a rented house while Bronson made their new house livable. He named it Orchard House; Louisa called it Apple Slump.[23]

## Orchard House

By the time the Alcotts moved into Orchard House in the summer of 1858, the family was much changed. Louisa wrote, "All seem to be glad that the wandering family is anchored at last. We won't move again for twenty years if I can help it. The old people need an abiding place; and now that death and love have taken two of us away, I can, I hope, soon manage to care for the remaining four." "The old people": Bronson was fifty-nine and in good health; Abigail was a year younger but worn down by years of work and want. Death: Elizabeth had died in March of heart disease—probably a result of scarlet fever. Love: Anna had become engaged to John Pratt, and the couple would marry in the Orchard House parlor in 1860. And Louisa would manage to care for the remaining family with income from her writing. In fact, Abigail and Bronson were living alone there. As one biographer wrote, they "had

FIGURE 18. Orchard House (ca. 1865) with Alcott family members in the foreground (*from left to right*—Louisa May Alcott seated on ground; Abigail May Alcott; Frederick Alcott Pratt in baby carriage; Anna Alcott Pratt; A. Bronson Alcott). *Used by permission of Louisa May Alcott's Orchard House.*

finally found a permanent family home, just in time to watch that family disperse." Anna was staying with the Pratts, and May lived in Boston briefly before moving to Syracuse. Louisa was in Boston, among a circle of literary friends that included Henry Wadsworth Longfellow, Harriet Beecher Stowe, the actress Fanny Kemble, Oliver Wendell Holmes Sr., and the publisher James Fields. Bronson was thriving in the company of Transcendentalists and abolitionists, and in 1859 he was appointed superintendent of the Concord schools. He was paid only $100 a year, but recognition as an educator was important to him. He described Orchard House as "this loved spot, so largely now of my own creation . . . where I have had . . . the most profitable and agreeable occupation since our married life opened."[24]

The house was indeed of his own creation (with some help from May). The writer and reformer Lydia Maria Child described its transformation: "When they bought the place the house was so very old that it was thrown into the bargain, with the supposition that it was fit for nothing but firewood. But Mr. Alcott has an architectural taste more intelligible than his Orphic Sayings. He let every odd rafter and beam stay in its place, changed old ovens and ash-holes into Saxon arched alcoves, and added a washerwoman's old shanty to the rear. The result is a house full of queer nooks and corners, with all manner of juttings in and out . . . The capable Alcott daughters painted and papered the interior themselves. And gradually the artist-daughter filled up all the nooks and corners with panels on which she had painted birds and flowers; and over the open fireplaces she painted mottoes in ancient English characters. Owls blink at you, and faces peep from the most unexpected places."[25]

Bronson supervised the work carefully. He hired a bricklayer to build a fireplace "after my design, the bricks projecting from the jambs and forming an arch." He moved a one-room house from up the hill, thoughtfully placed it over the well, and made it into a kitchen. He designed and constructed a fence with "grotesque designs, the effect both from house and grounds being picturesque and appropriate." He prided himself on rescuing the house "from deformity and disgrace by these touches of grace and plainkeeping which I have contrived to give it." As the furniture was placed and May attended to the wallpaper ("chaste and of the right tints"), he wrote to Abigail: "Every piece is now in its place. We all think it suitable and tasteful. Your (and my) room

Our room,—I mean dutifully to say—now prides itself in the added ornaments of the bureau and mirrors, worktable, pictures &c. and awaits your arrival to take pride in it and praise it also . . . our house only waits for its matron to be completely furnished." For Bronson, Orchard House was "a home, in a sense, that neither 'Hillside' nor the Cottage at Germantown or at Hosmer's could be said to have been"; Louisa, he noted, was "less attached."[26]

The house now is almost exactly as it looked when the Alcotts lived there. Most of the furniture is theirs, May's paintings adorn the walls, and the small semicircular desk that Bronson built for Louisa remains in her study, with pen and inkwell. May's bedroom, with the arched ceiling that Bronson added to make it roomier, has the drawings she made directly onto the walls, as well as some of her paintings. Louisa's room also is decorated with some of May's paintings. The bust of Bronson in his study was created by Daniel Chester French, who had studied with May and became one of America's leading monumental sculptors.[27]

Louisa, in fact, avoided "Apple Slump" as much as possible, living there only when she was ill or her parents needed her care. Her first extended stay there was in 1862. *Little Women* begins during the Civil War, with Mr. March away at war. Bronson was too old to fight, and it was Louisa who served her country, as an army nurse. She was in camp only a few weeks before she became seriously ill with typhoid pneumonia. The experience gave her the subject matter for the stories that were brought together in 1863 in a volume called *Hospital Sketches*. It also destroyed her health. Throughout the early and mid-1860s she earned her living from writing: a novel, *Moods* (1864), and short fiction, including many sensational stories published under the pseudonym A. M. Barnard. Bronson, too, was writing, and he hoped

FIGURE 19. Louisa May Alcott seated at a desk in her bedchamber at Orchard House (ca. 1872). *Used by permission of Louisa May Alcott's Orchard House.*

that Thomas Niles would publish his manuscript, "Tablets." Niles had offered Louisa $500 to write a "lively simple book" for girls, but Louisa had been reluctant. When Bronson approached him, Niles suggested that he would be more likely to publish "Tablets" if Louisa produced the girls' book. Whether Bronson passed this along to Louisa, and, if so, whether that influenced her, we do not know. But she did get to work on the book Niles wanted. She also accepted a job as editor of the children's magazine, *Merry's Museum*, for which she was paid $500 a year. Louisa was at Orchard House, caring for Abigail, who had developed heart disease. It took her nine weeks to write the first half of *Little Women.*[28]

Niles offered Louisa her choice of an advance of $1,000 and no royalties or $300 plus royalties on each copy sold. He recommended the royalty arrangement, and she agreed. That made her fortune. The first printing of two thousand books sold out in two weeks in October 1868. Louisa moved her ailing mother to Anna's house for the winter and was "so glad to be off out of C[oncord] that I worked like a beaver, and turned the key on Apple Slump with joy." In an apartment in Boston shared with May, she began the sequel that became part two of the book we know today, finishing it in January 1869. When she dropped in at Niles's office to see how the book was doing, he was beside himself with excitement: "Nothing to parallel it has occurred in my experience . . . the triumph of the century." Part two had not yet been published, but three thousand copies had been sold in advance, and he expected to sell twenty thousand by Christmas. In fact, there were soon forty thousand copies in print, setting a record. Even Bronson's *Tablets*, published as promised, went into a second printing and was favorably reviewed. Bronson also cashed in on Louisa's fame in his conversations: "Introduced as the father of Little Women, am riding in the Chariot of Glory wherever I go . . . . I have a pretty dramatic story to tell of [Louisa's] childhood and youth, gaining in interest as she comes up into womanhood and literary note." Louisa, back in Concord, told her mother and May, "Hard times for the Alcotts are over forever."[29]

## After *Little Women*

If hard times are defined only by poverty, they were certainly over. But as much as Louisa enjoyed being able to provide for her parents and sisters and to allow herself the luxury of travel and comfortable surroundings, family was more important to her than wealth. Besides, her health—endangered first by her wartime illness, then by the mercury used to treat it, and finally perhaps by an undiagnosed illness—was deteriorating. The two decades that followed the publication of her bestseller were extraordinarily productive, often heartbreaking, and sometimes surprising.

To satisfy the continuing demand for her "stories for girls," Louisa wrote *An Old-Fashioned Girl*, published in 1870, and then traveled to Europe with May and a friend, Alice Bartlett. In December, she learned that Anna's husband, John Pratt, had died. Unable to comfort her sister in person, she took very practical action: she wrote *Little Men* with the idea of using the proceeds to support Anna and her two sons. The novel, set in Plumfield, a school for boys and girls run on progressive principles, is the first to make use of Bronson's educational philosophy. It was published the day she returned from Europe, with fifty thousand copies sold in advance.[30]

Louisa continued to write, living mostly in Boston, while Bronson traveled, presenting his conversations throughout the Midwest and New England. Louisa used her growing wealth to help family members. She paid cousins' tuition at Harvard and Smith and gave other relatives money to buy houses and start a medical practice. In 1876, May—building a reputation as an artist—returned to Europe to study painting, with Louisa's financial help. A year later Louisa helped Anna buy Thoreau's old house on Main Street in Concord, less than a mile from Orchard House.[31]

Abigail's health was failing, and Louisa spent the summer of 1877 caring for her. She wrote much of *Under the Lilacs* in her mother's sickroom. In November, Louisa and Anna moved Abigail to Anna's house, and she died there two weeks later. Louisa told a friend: "She died in the arms of the child who owed her most, who loved her best, who counted as her greatest success the power of making these last years a season of happy rest to the truest & tenderest of mothers."[32] Reading Abigail's diaries, Bronson acknowledged the difficulties of her life and his responsibility for them:

> I copy with tearful admiration these pages, and almost repent now of my seeming incompetency, my utter inability to relieve the burdens laid upon her and my children during these years of helplessness. Nor can I, with every mitigating apology for this seeming shiftlessness, quite excuse myself for not venturing upon some impossible feat to extricate us from these straits of circumstance . . . But it is past now. And it is a sweet satisfaction that in her latter years she found in her daughters, if not in her husband, the compensations that fidelity to principles under the deepest tribulations always brings about and nobly rewards. Under every privation, every wrong, and with the keen sense of injustice present, the dear family were sustained, the fair bond was maintained inviolate, and independence, a competency, honorable name, and even wide renown, was given it at last. And but for herself this could not have been won.[33]

With Abigail's death, Louisa lost all interest in Orchard House: "The old house is to let," she wrote, "as it is no longer home without 'Marmee.'" She wrote in her journal: "I never go by without looking up at Marmee's window, where the dear face used to be." Anna added a study to her house, and Bronson moved in with her and her sons. Bronson told May that his study was "by no means roomy, but where Thoreau has sat and written, a humbler scholar will be content." Orchard House, and later the rustic Hillside Chapel built by

Bronson, became the home of the Summer School of Philosophy and Literature, which kept Bronson and his fellow thinkers active for the next decade.[34]

May was in London when her mother died, and she was beginning a new chapter in the family's story. She had never considered marriage and at thirty-seven believed herself safe from temptation, but Ernest Nieriker, a Swiss banker sixteen years younger than she, proposed. They were married in March 1878. Ernest, she told her sisters, "is a practical, thrifty business man; he is young, ambitious, with real faculty, instead of an impractical philosopher." The couple lived in Paris, where May continued painting. She also wrote a brief, charming, and immensely well-informed book for aspiring American artists: *Studying Art Abroad and How to Do It Cheaply*. In November 1879 she gave birth to a daughter, Louisa May Nieriker. The family's joy at the news was short lived: May became very ill soon after the birth, and on December 31 she died. She had asked Ernest to send the baby to America, so that Louisa could raise her namesake. In September 1880, "Lulu" arrived in Boston. Louisa and Anna became the parents of two teenaged boys and an infant, as well as caretakers of an increasingly infirm father. Even with servants, it was a challenge for a middle-aged woman who had serious health problems. But Louisa adored Lulu, writing that the toddler "seems to have decided that I am really 'Marmar.' My heart is full of pride & joy." Anna said that Louisa was "entirely absorbed in her baby whom she loves passionately & on whom she lavishes all the strength & affection of her generous nature."[35]

Bronson had been in excellent health, touring extensively with his conversations, when in 1882 he had a crippling stroke. Louisa took over his care. She sold Orchard House and took Bronson and Lulu to live in Boston, first in a townhouse on

Chestnut Street and then to 10 Louisburg Square, one of the loveliest residential areas in Boston. Although she had several servants, she once said that when her father and her daughter were both looking for her, she felt "like a nursing ma with twins." Louisa's own health gave way, and she asked Anna to take over the household while she moved to a nursing home in Roxbury. She did not expect to live much longer, and she drew up a new will that would use her very large estate to care for her family. The law then in effect allowed only descendants to renew copyrights, so she adopted Anna's son John. He would hold her copyrights in trust, with the income divided equally among John, Frederick, Lulu, and Anna. On March 4, 1888, Bronson died at 10 Louisburg Square. Louisa, at the nursing home, lost consciousness a few hours later and died on March 6, the day of Bronson's funeral.[36]

In his funeral sermon for Bronson, Cyrus A. Bartol described him as a "childlike man" who was an optimist "because of a God-like incapacity in the purity of his eyes to behold iniquity." At Louisa's funeral, he said that the "little women" and "little men" who read her books should officiate, "but there would not be room for them." In the published version he added: "She unlatches the door to one house, and they all find it is their own house which they enter. She unroofs every dwelling in the land, while she describes the home she is acquainted with and may have been brought up in."[37]

## Marches and Alcotts

With just a little imagination, visitors to Concord can find both the real family and their fictional incarnations. The tour guides point out details from both the book and from the Alcotts' lives. May's drawings can still be seen on the walls, Louisa's desk holds her inkwell, Elizabeth's piano sits in the parlor, Anna's wedding dress is sometimes on display, Marmee's stove awaits her hand, and Bronson's books fill his study shelves. Anyone who has read *Little Women* can see the sisters and their mother in the rooms of Orchard House and Hillside, and readers of "Transcendental Wild Oats" may find traces of the Alcotts at Fruitlands. Bronson does not come as readily into view, though his beliefs—and his failings—dominated the family's life. Perhaps that is because he is nearly absent from his daughter's fiction. He appears only fleetingly in *Little Women*. He had often urged her to write about him in a book that would have been called "The Cost of an Idea." Susan Cheever, one of Louisa's biographers, said the book was to tell the story of "a noble, brilliant, but misunderstood philosopher [who] gave up financial and social success because of his high principles." As Cheever notes, Louisa never started that book.[38]

## To Visit

Orchard House is operated by the Louisa May Alcott Organization (www.louisamayalcott.org) and is open year-round, every day except holidays. Visitors can see the house on guided tours. Hillside, now known as The Wayside, is operated by the National Park Service as part of Minute Man National Historical Park (www.nps.gov/mima/). It is open mid-June through late October, Thursday through Monday. It was home to two additional writers: Nathaniel Hawthorne and Harriett Lothrop (Margaret Sidney), author of the Five Little Peppers series for children. The tour explains how each family lived in and added to the house. The farmhouse at

Fruitlands is part of Fruitlands Museum, operated by the Trustees of the Reservation (www.fruitlands.org). Although it has been enlarged and altered, visitors get a sense of how primitive life there was. The compound includes the Shaker Museum, the Native American Museum, and the Art Museum. It is open from mid-April to early November, every day but Tuesday. The farmhouse is located on a trail from the Fruitlands visitors' center and can be seen on a self-guided tour.

## To Learn More

Although all the Alcotts kept journals, they destroyed many of them. More of Bronson's journals survived than those of other family members, and they are at Harvard's Houghton Library. As Odell Shepard noted in his selected edition, "The paper in these volumes, though bought by a poor man at a time when good paper was expensive, is of excellent quality" (p. xi). He also had them bound in leather. Shepard's edition, *The Journals of Bronson Alcott*, includes entries from Abigail's journals for the Fruitlands period because Bronson's journals for that time were lost. Bronson's journals for 1836–38, edited by Joel Myerson and Larry A. Carlson, were published in *Studies in the American Renaissance* (1978, 1981, 1982, 1993, and 1994). Some of his correspondence was published in *The Letters of A. Bronson Alcott*, edited by Richard L. Herrnstadt. Selected entries from Abigail's journals, along with some of her letters, were edited by Eve LaPlante in *My Heart Is Boundless*. Some of Louisa's letters are available in *The Selected Letters of Louisa May Alcott*, edited by Joel Myerson and David Shealy. Ednah Dow Cheney, who knew the Alcott family, included journal entries and letters in her biography, *Louisa May Alcott: Life, Letters, and Journals*.

The Alcotts have been the subjects of many biographies. Soon after Bronson's death, Franklin B. Sanborn and William T. Harris published A. *Bronson Alcott: His Life and Philosophy*, in two volumes. Sanborn was a student of Bronson's, and the book is focused on his life and works, rather than on the family. Its chronology is somewhat random. Madelon Bedell is far less sympathetic to Bronson in *The Alcotts: Biography of a Family*, which takes the story up to the Civil War. John Matteson's *Eden's Outcasts: The Story of Louisa May Alcott and Her Father*, is a superb group biography and study of family dynamics. Eve LaPlante's *Marmee and Louisa: The Untold Story of Louisa May Alcott and Her Mother* fills in more pieces of the puzzle. In *Louisa May Alcott: A Personal Biography*, Susan Cheever includes comparisons of the Alcotts and the Marches. Richard Francis focuses on the Fruitlands experiment in *Fruitlands: The Alcott Family and Their Search for Utopia*.

# 6

# A Room of Her Own

*The Mary Baker Eddy House, Chestnut Hill*

ON January 26, 1908, Mary Baker Eddy—founder of the Church of Christ, Scientist—moved from Pleasant View, her beloved home in Concord, New Hampshire, into a mansion in Chestnut Hill, near Boston. The move was necessary for practical reasons—proximity to the Mother Church, space for a large staff, and security for an elderly woman who had become controversial. The Chestnut Hill home was elegant, with extensive gardens, carriage roads, and beautiful views— always important to Mrs. Eddy. But Mrs. Eddy did not like it. It was *too* elegant and too modern. It was overheated, and the electric lights were too bright. When she agreed to move to Chestnut Hill, Mrs. Eddy had specified that the rooms for her personal use were to be exact replicas of her rooms in Concord. But when she reached the second floor, she found rooms that were nearly twice as large, with wallpaper and carpeting that were not to her taste. The window in her study was too high for her to look out when seated in her chair. She moved up to the third floor during the extensive renovations she demanded. As Gillian Gill, her most recent biographer, reports: "In three weeks' time the rooms of her second-floor apartment were converted to Pleasant View dimensions, the window frames were lowered, a small elevator was installed, the slope of the driveway was changed to afford more privacy when Mrs. Eddy came out, and a large tree was cut down to allow her to look out on nearby homes . . . Mrs. Eddy had her old gaslight fixture installed at the head of her bed."[1]

Mrs. Eddy's insistence on re-creating Pleasant View may at first seem merely the eccentricity of a woman in her ninth decade, but she had her reasons. She wrote in *Science and Health* that "home is the dearest spot on earth, and should be the centre, but not the boundary of the affections."[2] Yet for a third of her life she had had no secure home. Pleasant View was the place where, at the age of seventy-one, she had finally been able to find the comfort and happiness she had known as a child. She enjoyed its comforts, as well as the beauty of its grounds and views, for fifteen years. Of course she was loath to part with it.

## Childhood Homes

Mary Baker was born in 1821, in the farmhouse where her father, Mark, and her five brothers and sisters had been born. The farm, in the hills of Bow, New Hampshire, had views of mountains, woods, and other farms. The Bakers were hospitable people from large families, and cousins and clergy visited often. It was a small house, and with the children, parents, and Mark's mother, it was probably crowded even without guests. Family life was important to Mary, but she needed to find her own space to read and think. The Baker children listened to lively, often contentious, discussions of religion and politics. Mrs. Eddy later told a church member that she "always wanted to know who won." Mark Baker presided over family prayers every morning and remained a firm Congregationalist, strongly opposed to the Unitarianism rising in New England. He was active in town and church affairs, conservative in politics as well as religion. He was strict with his children: Mrs. Eddy later wrote that her father "kept his family in the tightest harness I have ever known." But he was a busy man, and his rigor was tempered by Mary's mother, Abigail, and her grandmother, Mary Ann. Mrs. Eddy remembered her years at Bow fondly. A church member who was with her when, many years later, she visited the house, recalled that "tears came to her eyes as she gazed on the old familiar scene and saw the field where her childhood home still stood."[3]

The mother of six and the wife of a farmer, Abigail Baker nevertheless had time to discuss religious questions with her daughter. Mary was troubled by the ideas of predestination and eternal punishment, and she probably found her mother easier to talk to about such matters than her strictly Calvinist father. Abigail's patience and occasional indulgence contrasted sharply with Mark's intolerance. As the children grew older, it was she who mediated disputes among them and with their father.[4]

Mary's grandmother softened the impact of Mark's strictness in another way: she shared books and stories with her granddaughter. Mark and Abigail both recognized the importance of education for the next generation. All the children attended school longer than most of their peers, and Albert, the middle son, graduated from Dartmouth and became a lawyer. The girls, too, were well educated for their time. Abigail and Martha taught school before marrying, while Mary aspired to a career as a writer or journalist. Although he allowed his daughters to attend school, Mark drew a line between proper education and "bookishness"—a state that he believed contributed to frail mental and physical health. He often hid Mary's books, but she quickly learned to find them.[5]

Though bookishness probably did not make her sick, Mary was frail. More likely than reading as a cause of her indigestion and frequent colds were the New Hampshire climate, the primitive nature of medical care, and the family's adoption of an extreme form of Sylvester Graham's diet. At first, she remembered, they "ate only bread and vegetables, and drank water." When this proved ineffective, they "partook of but one meal in twenty-four hours, and this consisted of a thin slice of bread, about three inches square, without water." Mary frequently missed school because of illness, but she seems to have spent the time at home reading in her rocking chair, so little was lost. She was a quick study and was able to write fluently at a young age.[6]

In 1835, Grandmother Baker died, and Mark sold the family farm in Bow to buy property in Sanbornton Bridge, a town that provided greater economic, educational, and social opportunity for the family. With a population three times greater than that of Bow and an academy that admitted both boys and girls, it offered the teenaged Baker girls both schooling and prospective husbands. Soon after their arrival, Mary's sister Abigail wrote to her brother George: "We go on finely here, almost as well as we could wish. The people are very kind and hospitable, we find society very agreeable and refined; but we associate with none but the *first* you may depend. We have been treated, since we came to this place, with every token of respect, by all classes of people; but we have not *showed out much yet*, nor do not intend to at present, for we think a gradual rise in the esteem of people, more commendable, than a precipitate ascension. We have some fine young ladies here, brother; I think some of the most refined and accomplished that I ever met with; and they appear very solicitous to render us happy and contented in our new situation. The young gentlemen have not been slow in their attentions."[7]

One of the young gentlemen courting Abigail was Alexander Hamilton Tilton, a son of the town's most prominent

family. (Sanbornton Bridge was renamed Tilton in 1869.)
They were married in 1837, when she was twenty-one and he,
thirty-two. Martha also married at twenty-one; her husband
was Luther Pillsbury, a friend of her brother George. Mary was
twenty-two when she married George Washington Glover, a
building contractor who had been courting her on and off for
several years. They were married on December 10, 1843, and
sailed for Charleston, South Carolina, on Christmas Day. In
February, they moved to Wilmington, North Carolina, where
they joined a circle of young northerners. George was already
popular in the city, and Mary was welcomed not only as his
wife but as a beautiful and witty young woman who wrote for
the local magazine. Mary had become pregnant in the first
few weeks of their marriage. She was flourishing as a wife,
expectant mother, and writer. But that spring, yellow fever
struck Wilmington, and George became infected. He died on
June 27. A pregnant, penniless widow, Mary began years of
uncomfortable and unwelcome dependency.[8]

## The Kindness of Others

With the help of George's Masonic brothers, she returned
in July to her parents' house, where she gave birth to her
son, George Washington Glover II, on September 12. The
delivery was difficult and left Mary unable to nurse her baby
or, possibly, to have more children. When she recovered,
Mary Glover searched for ways to support herself and her
son. She wrote poetry, essays, and short stories and, with the
help of her sister Abigail, opened a school for young children.
None of these attempts brought in enough money to gain her
independence. Life in her parents' house became strained as
George grew older and more active. He was always a difficult

child: Mrs. Eddy later said that he screamed constantly as an infant. Her father no longer had the patience to deal with an active toddler, and little George physically resembled his father, whom Mark had never liked. Mary's mother did her best to smooth things over, but her health was failing. When she died in 1849, Mary's situation became untenable. Tensions in the family home increased when Martha's husband died and she and her two children moved in. In December 1850, Mark remarried and moved his wife to a new house that could not be a home for Mary and George. Abigail Tilton invited Mary to live with her but did not include George in the invitation. Her two children, near George's age, were frail and timid, and the boisterous young boy was more than she could tolerate. In what must have been a wrenching decision, Mary sent George to live with Mahala Cheney, who had been a servant in the Baker home, and her husband, Russell. It was to be, she hoped, a temporary measure. She felt she had no choice: "I had no training for self-support, and my home I regarded as very precious."[9]

Mary Glover was not happy in Abigail's house. As a church member recalled, "Abigail Tilton was a kind enough sister just so long as Mary humbly conformed to the rules of the household . . . after the freedom and happiness of her own home, Mary's position in Abigail's house was far from ideal." Mary had no dependable home or way of supporting herself, and she missed her son, who was not being raised in the way she thought he should be. (Russell Cheney neglected George's education and treated him as an indentured servant.) Mary had had several suitors, and in 1853 she accepted the proposal of Daniel Patterson, a personable and handsome man who worked as a dentist and homeopath. She went to court to have Patterson named her son's guardian, and Patterson signed the necessary bond for the appointment. She later wrote: "My dominant thought in marrying again was to get back my child, but after our marriage his stepfather was not willing he should have a home with me. A plot was consummated for keeping us apart." The Cheneys moved west, taking George with them, and he was told that his mother had died. She was told that he had run away and was lost in the wilderness. She would not see her son again until he was thirty-five.[10]

The pain of this separation was extreme. In 1891, when she was seventy years old, she wrote: "The true mother never willingly neglects her children in their early and sacred hours, consigning them to the care of nurse or stranger. Who can feel and comprehend the needs of her babe like the ardent mother? What other heart yearns with her solicitude, endures with her patience, waits with her hope, and labors with her love, to promote the welfare and happiness of her children?" She did not *willingly* give up the care of her son, but she had nevertheless failed him.[11]

Her second marriage lasted as a legal entity for twenty years, but in reality the relationship was shorter and disastrous. From the outset, it failed to serve Mary's purpose in marrying: to restore the unity of her family. But Patterson also proved to be a poor provider. In 1855 her family helped him to establish a practice and a home in North Groton, near where young George then lived, but Patterson quickly became mired in debt and in 1856 declared bankruptcy. The Pattersons remained in their four-room cottage in North Groton for five years, in poverty and, for Mary, ill health. Patterson told her sisters (to whom he owed money) that his practice was failing because he had to spend so much time taking care of her. Mary was ill, but she was not totally incapacitated. She studied homeopathy, tutored neighbors' children, read, and kept a scrapbook.[12]

In 1860, Mary moved to a boardinghouse in Rumney, New Hampshire, where she lived until she and her husband moved to a small cottage. Mary's illness continued, with diets, fresh air, and homeopathy offering no relief. Her spirits and health revived at the beginning of the Civil War when, in 1861, she received a letter written on behalf of her son telling her that he had enlisted in the Union Army. A neighbor reported that she wept with joy on hearing from him, but she was shocked to find that he was illiterate. She began writing again—patriotic poems that were published in a Portland, Maine, newspaper.[13]

Daniel Patterson, too, had a role in the war. The governor of New Hampshire asked him to travel to Washington with funds for Union sympathizers living in the South. He accomplished the mission but was captured and accused of spying. He spent several months in Salisbury prison, in North Carolina, from which he escaped after a few months. In his absence, Mary tried a water cure in Hill, New Hampshire. When it did not help her, she decided to seek medical help from a new source, Phineas Parkhurst Quimby, a healer in Portland, Maine. She arrived there in October 1862, and a month later she had a letter published in the *Portland Evening Courier:* "Three weeks' since, and I quitted my nurse and sick room en route for Portland. The belief of my recovery had died out of the hearts of those who were most anxious for it. With this mental and physical depression I first visited P. P. Quimby, and in less than one week from that time I ascended by a stairway of one hundred and eighty-two steps to the dome of the City Hall, and am improving ad infinitum." From December 1862 to April 1865, except for a few months with her family in Sanbornton Bridge, she lived in boardinghouses in Portland or with friends she met at Quimby's establishment.[14]

She went from being Quimby's patient to becoming his student and occasional publicist. Quimby's son explained that "she learned from him, not as a student receiving a regular course . . . but by sitting in his room, talking with him, reading his Mss., copying some of them, writing some herself and reading them to him for criticism." A friend reported that Mary had "no money, scarcely comfortable clothing,— most unhappy in her domestic relations." But she was developing the practice and theory of healing that she would explain in *Science and Health*, the foundational text of Christian Science—a process that would occupy the next twelve years of her life.[15]

After Mary left Maine, the Pattersons rented an apartment on the second floor of a house on Paradise Road in Swampscott, Massachusetts. One evening, on her way to a temperance meeting, she fell on the ice and, according to the doctor who attended her, suffered severe internal injuries that threatened her life. But a few days later, after reading a Bible passage about Jesus healing the sick, she was suddenly able to walk across the room. Quimby's teaching had given her a method, and her healing through prayer gave her a revelation—not a flash of insight, but a "gradual process of unfoldment in which she had played an active part," as a historian of religion explains. She had to work to understand what was being revealed to her and then find a way to impart her understanding to others.[16]

When the house on Paradise Road was sold in 1866, Daniel Patterson abandoned his wife, and she stopped using his name—she was once again Mary Glover—although she did not divorce him (on grounds of desertion) until 1873. For the next decade, she lived in more than a dozen rented rooms, boardinghouses, and friends' homes in Lynn, Swampscott, Amesbury, and Stoughton—sometimes for as long as eighteen months, sometimes for only a few weeks. In the mid-nineteenth century, boardinghouses often served as surrogate family homes for young men who came to cities to find work. It was more unusual for women, especially older women, to rent rooms. But Mary Glover had no choice.[17]

The best of her lodgings did provide the warmth of family life; others offered only the barest of shelter. It was difficult for her to find places that provided her with the comfort and quiet she needed to write. In 1867, she boarded with Captain and Mrs. Nathaniel Webster. An early biographer described her situation: "She was given a large, sunny room with a fireplace, and Mrs. Webster's special 'spiritual' desk at which to write, but she had to sit through some of her hostess's séances and a good deal of spiritualistic chit-chat." In 1872, she spent two months with a Mrs. Chadwell, but the room was too cold and Mrs. Chadwell was too talkative. Two years later, boarding with a Mrs. Scribner, she wrote to a friend: "Tired to death, broken down with persecution, no home to rest in, invalids all around me, *one*, room only etc etc to work in This is my present lot." Some of her landlords were hostile to her work or her work habits. When she became absorbed in her writing, she was oblivious to her surroundings. Sometimes, she later told a friend, "after one of these outpourings . . . I would not be allowed to remain in the house. I moved eight times in eight months while writing Science and Health. I would find my trunk and my chair set out on the sidewalk, and sometimes I would find my manuscripts covered with ink by some person in the house through malice. Sometimes people would leave me only the bed slats to sleep on."[18]

Other arrangements worked better. Her longest stay was in the Stoughton home of Alanson and Sally Wentworth, beginning in late 1868. For eighteen months, the Wentworths provided her with room and board in exchange for instructing Sally in healing through prayer. She told a friend that she had "a large pleasant room with trees in front of my window." The Wentworths welcomed her at the dinner table and in the parlor in the evening, and she spent time with their children. She did a great deal of writing in this house, completing teaching materials called "The Science of Man." In 1872, she spent the winter at 78 Chestnut Street in Lynn with Dorcas Rawson and her mother. She wrote: "I have a very nice time this winter everything so quiet pleasant scientific and comfortable I have a better opportunity to write than ever before."[19]

In 1874, Mary Glover was living in rented rooms at 7 Broad Street in Lynn when she saw that No. 8 was for sale. With money she had saved from her earnings as a teacher of healing, she was able to buy the house, although she always needed tenants to help her pay the mortgage. She was fifty-three, unmarried, the future uncertain, but for the first time she owned a home.

## Foundations

The house at 8 Broad Street became the home of the woman we know as Mary Baker Eddy. It is where she completed and published *Science and Health* and *The Science of Man*; founded the Christian Scientist Association; began delivering sermons; and founded the Church of Christ, Scientist. It is also the house where she married Asa Gilbert Eddy, one of her students, on January 1, 1877. And it is the house where she was reunited with her son. But with her success came controversy and litigation. Over the years, Mrs. Eddy found herself embroiled in disputes with former students, usually over money.

The most disastrous falling-out was with Daniel Spofford, one of her tenants as well as a student. Spofford, married and twenty years her junior, had fallen in love with his teacher. In 1875, she asked him to give up his practice to Gilbert Eddy and to devote all his efforts to promoting *Science and Health*. Over the next two years, the business relationship with Spofford deteriorated, and he was undoubtedly unhappy about her marriage. In 1878, Mrs. Eddy sought to settle their dispute in court, but the results were inconclusive. Later that year Gilbert Eddy and another man were accused of conspiring to murder Daniel Spofford. Although the accusation was based on testimony later found to be false, the men were jailed for nearly three months, and newspapers reported the trial as colorfully as they could. Gilbert Eddy's defense was costly, and by the time the lawyer's bills were settled, the couple had become financially strapped. The trial brought unwelcome publicity, took time away from Mrs. Eddy's work, and exacerbated hostility to the Christian Scientist Association.[20]

Christian Science was one of many new religions emerging in response to the social and intellectual developments of the times. The Seventh-day Adventists organized in 1860; the Jehovah's Witnesses, around 1872; Theosophy came to the United States in the 1870s; Spiritualism was on the rise; and the Church of Latter-day Saints was continuing to grow. Traditional churches were grappling with the new discoveries in physics and biology that challenged biblical accounts. Their approach was basically to argue that the Bible was right about the material world. Mrs. Eddy changed the terms: "There is no life, truth, intelligence, nor substance in matter. All is infinite Mind and its infinite manifestation for God is All-in-all. Spirit is immortal truth; matter is mortal error. Spirit is the real and eternal; matter is the unreal and temporal. Spirit is God, and man is His image and likeness. Therefore man is not material; he is spiritual." According to one scholar, she believed "that Christian Science represented both the most genuine Christianity and the most comprehensive science."[21]

Boston was the epicenter of religious change and unrest. One of Mrs. Eddy's biographers offered a landscape of the city's faiths:

> On Good Friday the socially formidable, ostentatiously penitential Mrs. Jack Gardner could be seen scrubbing the altar steps of the Church of the Advent, Beacon Hill beachhead of fashionable Anglo-Catholicism. On a midsummer afternoon Miss Elizabeth Peabody, the veteran virgin of American Transcendentalism, could be found addressing assorted Platonists and Hegelians at Bronson Alcott's Concord School of Philosophy on women's rights, or dozing peacefully on the platform while William James made vigorous forays into the alluring wilds of psychology.
>
> While the Sunday afternoon meetings of the new Spiritual Temple drew large crowds to hear excellent organ music, violins, singers, followed by titillating exhibitions of mediumship, the Sunday afternoon meetings of the Christian Scientists at Hawthorne Hall on Park Street drew more modest numbers . . . On the days when Mrs. Eddy herself preached, an expectant congregation overflowed the attractive little hall.[22]

The Church's growing success generated hostility. According to the *Times* of London, Boston "clergymen of all denominations are seriously considering how to deal with what they regard as the most dangerous innovation that has threatened the Christian Church in this region for many years. Scores of the most valued church members are joining the Christian Science branch of the metaphysical organization, and it has thus far been impossible to check the defection." Jewish leaders worried about the growing numbers of the faithful converting to Christian Science.[23]

Although Mrs. Eddy certainly welcomed the growth of her church, there was a price to pay. As Christian Science became better known, the church and its founder became the targets of hostile press coverage and publicity. Christian Scientists did not experience the degree of violence directed at the Mormons, but they were often ridiculed, as the Spiritualists were. The press relished covering the rifts between Mrs. Eddy and other church members and defectors. These distractions took a great toll on Mrs. Eddy. Not only did they waste time, but they exhausted her. Mrs. Eddy believed that her enemies tried to harm her from a distance with what she called "Malicious Animal Magnetism." One need not share this belief to understand how persistent lawsuits, rumors, defections, and negative press coverage would distract, discourage, and upset her, making it difficult to work.

Christian Science activities were increasingly centered in Boston, and in 1880 the Eddys rented out the house in Lynn and sought rooms in the city. Here they felt the full force of opinion against them. As Mrs. Eddy wrote to a friend that January: "Ever since we came to Boston it has been one line of persecution from those inhumans. Our first residence on West Newton we kept but a few weeks, although the lady agreed to rent us the rooms until spring but after we had got all our furniture boxes etc there and set up, she gave us a notice to give up our rooms, and shut off the heat. We moved to Springfield St. I wrote a lease for our rooms they signed it and after we got all moved and before a week had elapsed they gave us a request to vacate. My husband looked for his lease and lo! it was gone, he had left it in his coat pocket and hung his coat on the hat-tree in the lower hall! So it has gone on from one step to another. We are now looking for rooms, all our time is taken up in this way." Finally the Eddys, together with fellow Christian Scientists George and Clara Choate, rented a house at 537 Shawmut Avenue. The Eddys had two rooms on the second floor.[24]

In the winter of 1882, the couple traveled to Washington, where for a month Mrs. Eddy lectured and saw the sights, while Gilbert investigated copyright issues. Then they moved on to Philadelphia, where she again lectured and promoted Christian Science. They returned to Boston, where Mrs. Eddy became president of the Massachusetts Metaphysical College and pastor of the Church. Both the college and the Eddy residence were at 569 Columbus Avenue. The Eddys and their close associates were poised to expand the Church and reach a larger audience, but that spring Gilbert grew seriously ill. On June 3, 1882, he died of heart disease. He was buried in Tilton, next to Mark and Abigail Baker. Now sixty-one, again widowed, Mary Baker Eddy was about to enter the most successful and productive period of her life.[25]

## Home and Work

From 1882 to 1889, Mrs. Eddy lived and worked in Boston. She continued to teach and give sermons and lectures, but as the Church grew, so did her administrative duties. The Massachusetts Metaphysical College alone demanded much of her time, with students to be housed and fed as well as taught. She hired Calvin Frye, a former student, who over the years performed a range of duties—bookkeeper, secretary, housekeeper, even carriage driver. And, of course, she continued to

FIGURE 20. Mary Baker Eddy in carriage. *Courtesy of The Mary Baker Eddy Library.*

expand and revise *Science and Health,* with a sixth edition—*Science and Health with Key to the Scriptures*—issued in 1883. She also launched a periodical, the *Christian Science Journal,* which quickly gained thousands of subscribers well beyond New England. Subscriptions and book purchases, as well as tuition, provided enough income that in 1887 she was able to buy new quarters for living and working, at 385 Commonwealth Avenue, which was more elegantly furnished and in a better neighborhood.[26]

She took great pride in her new home. One of her former students visited Mrs. Eddy there and recalled that Mrs. Eddy "showed her caller all over the new residence. She went with her from cellar to attic. She showed her the kitchen and the pantry. She took her into the sleeping rooms and commented on the spacious wardrobes . . . as they were coming down the front stairs, Mrs. Eddy placed her arm around the waist of her student and said: 'I want every one of my students some day to have a home of their own.'"[27]

Success also bred internal criticism, rivalry, defections, and new legal problems. Former students set up their own practices, departing—sometimes drastically—from Mrs. Eddy's teachings. Former associates accused her of plagiarizing the work of P. P. Quimby, with whom she had studied in Maine, generating a great deal of adverse publicity that ended only when Mrs. Eddy sued them and won. Finally, in 1889, she chose to deal with dissension by leaving Boston and limiting her public role. She closed the college and dissolved the Christian Science Association. She bought the Boston property that would become the site of a church building and established a trust to oversee the project. The building, known as the Mother Church, belonged to all Christian Scientists—not just the Boston members. At Mrs. Eddy's insistence, construction was completed in an astonishing eight months. Various boards were appointed to manage Church activities and publications. As one historian summarized, she "presided over the transformation of her church from a charismatic into a bureaucratic institution." She had founded the Church; now she was ensuring that it would survive after her death.[28]

## "The Strongest Tie"

When she left Boston, Mrs. Eddy rented a house at 62 North State Street, in Concord, New Hampshire. It was a pleasant house, but it was noisy and on a small lot, making the privacy she needed all but impossible. In the fall of 1891, she found a small farmhouse on a hill, with a view of sloping fields and meadows. She bought the property and some adjoining land and remodeled the house. According to a church member who oversaw the project, she "inspected the work every day, suggested the details outside and inside from the foundations to the tower, and saw them carried out." She also built lodgings for her staff. She changed the landscape, draining wetlands and digging a fish pond. "Pleasant View" was a working farm, with horses, cows, pigs, orchards, fruit and vegetable gardens, barns, and stables. The house, after renovations, was comfortable and offered a choice of views. A biographer described the changes: "The improvements to the house were designed to make the most of the scenery, with a veranda built on at the back . . . a porte-cochère built onto the front so she could easily embark in her carriage every day, and a side tower built to house her own apartment from which she had a clear view in several directions. Living in a setting of natural beauty was an important thing for Mary Baker Eddy . . . Having ample space around her and almost no uncontrollable ambient noise had also become vital requirements." She brought familiar furniture with her and decorated the parlor with gifts she had received. Beloved but worn chairs were replaced with exact replicas. Her living quarters were typically Victorian—"cluttered, haphazard, highly patterned tightness, full of knickknacks and whatnots and antimacassars."[29]

Pleasant View was also Mrs. Eddy's workplace. She had entrusted most of the administrative responsibilities to others, but she continued to make major decisions. It was she, for example, who decided in 1908 that the Church should publish a newspaper, the *Christian Science Monitor*. The staff of the Mother Church visited frequently, and Mrs. Eddy

FIGURE 21. Pleasant View, photo by J. C. Derby & Co. *Courtesy of The Mary Baker Eddy Library.*

maintained a large staff of her own. In addition to permanent staff, Christian Scientists came for six months to a year to help with correspondence, household and farm tasks, and "watching" to avert negative influences. Calvin Frye remained in her service until his death. Mrs. Eddy was an exacting mistress, and the house was not merely immaculate. Everything was kept in precisely the order Mrs. Eddy required, down to the position of the pins in her pincushion.[30]

Pleasant View was the house that Mrs. Eddy had always wanted—comfortable, simple, with beautiful views in a welcoming community. She was surrounded by people who loved and admired her. She could read, write, pray, and think in peace. But family problems, dissension within the church, and hostility from the world outside intruded on her quiet and privacy. George Glover and his family had reentered her life, but this was not an unalloyed blessing. George was always in need of money, and as his mother's prosperity became apparent, he sought to involve her in his business dealings. She did give him money, especially for his children's education, but it never seemed to be enough. Their communications grew increasingly unpleasant, and Mrs. Eddy worried that George would seek more money from her estate than she planned to leave him.

Church members were also creating problems. Josephine Woodbury had been a prominent member of the Church for several years. When she became openly involved in an extramarital relationship in 1889, Mrs. Eddy told her to end it. Even worse, Woodbury began to threaten the people she treated with illness, bankruptcy, or other difficulties if they did not do as she told them. The last straw came in 1890, when Woodbury gave birth to a child that was not her husband's. She claimed that the baby had been immaculately conceived and was a second Christ. Mrs. Eddy expelled her from the church and condemned her actions, including references to her in her 1899 Communion message. Woodbury responded by suing Mrs. Eddy and other Church officials for libel. Mrs. Eddy won easily in court, but the press loved the story, and the publicity was painful. After his defeat in court, Woodbury's lawyer published a pamphlet, *Complete Exposure of Eddyism or Christian Science*, which remained in print in one form or another into the 1920s. He was probably the author of a long anonymous article in the *New York Times* in 1904 reviving the claims that Mrs. Eddy had plagiarized from Quimby.[31]

As the Woodbury suit was beginning, Mark Twain wrote a series of articles attacking Mrs. Eddy. He claimed that "I am not combating Xn Science. I haven't a thing in the world against it. Making fun of that shameless old swindler, Mother

Eddy, is the only thing I take any interest in." Indeed, the articles were personal attacks, focusing on the "cult of personality" that had grown up around the founder. Mrs. Eddy took them to heart. She insisted that she be called "Leader," instead of "Mother" and had her private "Mother's Room" in the Mother Church closed.[32]

Then, in 1904, two publishing giants launched rival efforts to discredit Mrs. Eddy and the Church. Sam McClure, the publisher of *McClure's Magazine*, and Joseph Pulitzer, publisher of the *New York World*, commissioned investigators to look into the Church's finances and sent reporters to Concord to dig up whatever dirt they could find. (They may have been spurred on in their efforts because their competitor William Randolph Hearst supported Christian Science.) Reporters interviewed disaffected students, gathered local gossip, and spied on the house. Despite having been granted an interview in which they found her healthy, they reported that she was dead, or at least dying. Other reports suggested that she was being held prisoner at Pleasant View.[33]

Pulitzer went beyond reporting. He recruited Mrs. Eddy's son and her nephew, George Waldron Baker, to sue Church officials in what became known as the Next Friends Suit. The suit, filed in 1907, demanded that the defendants provide an accounting of Mrs. Eddy's assets and return to her any that they had wrongfully taken from her. It also asked that a receiver be appointed to handle her property. To win, they would have to demonstrate that Mrs. Eddy was incompetent to handle her own affairs. What the "Next Friends" did not know was that Mrs. Eddy had placed her assets in a trust earlier that year. If she was competent at that time, there was no complaint to answer. While awaiting trial, Mrs. Eddy and her lawyers conducted a magnificent public relations campaign, granting interviews to friendly journalists, permitting doctors to examine her state of mind, and writing letters to the judge explaining why she handled her money as she did and why she limited access to visitors. The judge and the attorneys met with Mrs. Eddy at Pleasant View, and the outcome was never in doubt. A witness reported that the men "were greeted by a slim, frail, slightly deaf old lady, charming, polite, authoritative, who answered their questions of fact, insisted, despite their demurrals, upon giving a brief and lucid history of Christian Science and its doctrine, and begged them to take the time to listen to her marvelous new gramophone before they left the house . . . [Judge] Aldrich was reminded of his mother." The plaintiffs' attorney, William Chandler, was overheard to say that Mrs. Eddy "had a mind like a steel trap." The Next Friends went down to defeat.[34]

The trial, and the preparations leading up to it, had taxed Mrs. Eddy's patience and resilience and had made her aware of how vulnerable she was in her home. She feared that George could force his way into her house and kidnap her. In fact, strangers had broken into the house from time to time, and reporters had besieged her. With her privacy gone and unable to enjoy her grounds and views, Mrs. Eddy decided to return to Boston. Church officials, operating in secrecy, located, purchased, and remodeled the house in Chestnut Hill, where this chapter began.

Mrs. Eddy agreed to the move but required alterations to make her personal space as much like Pleasant View as possible: "I do not want to look at anything strange." The assistant assigned to oversee the move arranged "to have the reproductions of her Pleasant View furniture made for her new quarters" and "arranged with Paine's Furniture store to do this work." Twenty-two pieces of furniture were replicated and in their places when Mrs. Eddy arrived. But the furniture was the only thing that was right. Her maid recalled that "it was terribly hot everywhere; that there was a blaze of light from the top of the house to the bottom, and that the rooms were filled with flowers." Mrs. Eddy remarked that her study was "a *great barn* of a *place*" and complained, "Just see what has been done to me. The rooms are so large that it is really a great deal of exertion for me to walk the distances." Her maid recalled: "There is no doubt that a belief of homesickness tried to tempt Mrs. Eddy during the first months after she left Pleasant View. She missed the old scenes, the view, and the familiar houses which she had looked out on for so many years."[35]

When the second round of renovations of Mrs. Eddy's rooms at Chestnut Hill had been completed, she went out for her daily drive while the staff moved her furniture into the precise positions she had specified. The standard of cleanliness and order established at Pleasant View was maintained in the new house, and Mrs. Eddy had the companionship of trusted staff members. Reporters still stationed themselves near her home, but their view was limited to her daily drives. The lesson Mrs. Eddy drew from the power of the press to shape opinion about the Church was that she should take advantage of it, and in 1908 she instructed the trustees of the Publishing Society to begin publishing a daily newspaper. In four months, the *Christian Science Monitor* was reporting the news. She also resolved family problems by reaching an agreement with her son that gave him a substantial sum in exchange for giving up any right to contest her will.

Mrs. Eddy lived in the Chestnut Hill house for the last three years of her life. Like Pleasant View, it offered a genuine feeling of home to her staff. Each had a bedroom and bath, they dined together, and they often spent evenings together in the parlor or on the roof, viewing the heavens through a telescope. Despite its size and grandeur, it feels even now like a family home. It was the largest, most expensive, and most luxurious house she had ever had, but she told one of her staff members, "This is not my home. Pleasant View will always be my home." For Mrs. Eddy, "the strongest tie that I have ever felt next to my love for God has been my love for home."[36]

## To Visit

Philanthropist Mary Beecher Longyear understood the importance of home. When she and her husband moved to Brookline in 1903, she did not want to give up her house in Marquette, Michigan. They had the building disassembled, put on railroad cars, and taken to its new site for assembly. Mrs. Longyear founded the Longyear Museum in Chestnut Hill (1125 Boylston Street) and collected documents and artifacts relating to Mrs. Eddy's life. She also purchased and restored four of Mrs. Eddy's residences, and four more have been added to the museum since. The houses open to the public are those in North Groton and Rumney, New Hampshire; Swampscott, Amesbury, Stoughton, Lynn, and Chestnut Hill, Massachusetts; and the house at 62 North State Street in Concord, New Hampshire, where Mrs. Eddy lived before moving to Pleasant View. Pleasant View was razed in 1917. Information about visiting the houses and museum is available at www.longyear.org.

## To Learn More

Mrs. Eddy's life is richly documented. The two repositories are the Historical Manuscripts Collection at the Longyear Museum and the Mary Baker Eddy Library, in the Church complex at 200 Massachusetts Avenue in Boston. As biographers have noted, access to these documents used to be severely limited, but since 2000 the library has welcomed researchers. Particularly useful for me were the reminiscences of people who knew Mrs. Eddy, which are available as typed transcriptions. Some of them have been published as *We Knew Mary Baker Eddy*, 2 vols. (Boston: Christian Science Publishing Society, 2011). The Eddy Library has put finding aids, sermons, some correspondence, and other material online in an ongoing digitization program: https://mbepapers.org.

The best and most thorough biography is Gillian Gill's *Mary Baker Eddy*, a volume in the Radcliffe Biography Series. Gill deftly untangles episodes in Mrs. Eddy's life that had been obscured by conflicting, highly politicized accounts. She also provides excellent evaluations of earlier biographies. Her book was fact checked, but in no way censored, by the Church History Department. (Her "Research Note," 557–62, explains this relationship.) Despite its length (more than seven hundred pages), it is the place to start. A second, earlier biography is Robert Peel's *Mary Baker Eddy*, in three volumes. Mrs. Eddy's own writings are widely available in print and online. All Christian Science Reading Rooms include her works, the Church's own publications, and many other resources. For an account of the publishing history of *Science and Health*, see William Dana Orcutt, *Mary Baker Eddy and Her Books*. Orcutt printed most of her work. An excellent explanation of the place of Christian Science in American religion, as well as a clear discussion of the Church's theology for non–Christian Scientists, is Stephen Gottschalk, *The Emergence of Christian Science in American Religious Life*.

# 7

## Greater Than the Sum of Its Parts

*Beauport, Gloucester*

IN June 1900, Harvard University awarded Abram Piatt
Andrew a Ph.D. in political economy. His parents and sister
had traveled from Indiana to Cambridge for the commence-
ment, and afterward they vacationed in a rented cottage at
Eastern Point, in Gloucester—on Cape Ann, in the north-
ernmost part of the Massachusetts coast. At twenty-seven,
Andrew was launched on a brilliant academic and political
career, and he had fallen in love with this small seaside resort.
It was to become not only *his* home but also the home of the
friends who were most important in his life. Over the next
few years, he founded an astonishing community of creative,
accomplished, fun-loving friends—young and old, men and
women, gay and straight.

### Dabsville: The Parts

Eastern Point was the farm of Thomas Niles from the eighteenth century until 1889, when Niles's heirs sold four hundred acres for summer cottages. In 1901, Andrew bought land
there and, a year later, began building the house that would
come to be known as Red Roof. Joseph Garland, a Gloucester historian, described it as "a comfortable, tasteful, shin-
gled and shuttered, three-story villa under a steep roof, flared

distinctively at the eaves . . . Inside all was white stucco, rich dark beams and panels, floors of hardwood or tile, mitered windows . . . tucked-away window seats, more nooks, steps and stairs and hidden rooms, cloisters, clever closets, trap doors, sliding panels and secret passages." He invited friends and students—including Franklin Delano Roosevelt, who enrolled in his introductory economics class—to visit. He sometimes called the house his wife, sometimes his shanty.[1]

Andrew made a friend of Joanna Davidge, who was staying with her mother at the nearby Fairview Inn in 1900. When her father died, she had been left a "modest fortune" and, in the tradition of fictional heroines in similar circumstances, became a governess/companion to a wealthy young woman. Davidge had been a friend of Flora Payne Whitney, the wife of William C. Whitney, a former secretary of the Navy and successful businessman. When Flora died in 1893, Davidge (then in her early forties) became the companion of Whitney's nineteen-year-old daughter, Pauline. In March 1895, she was rumored to be engaged to Whitney. Newspapers described her as "a tall and stately brunette . . . a most beautiful woman" and "the possessor of many accomplishments of grace . . . highly intellectual and in every way a worthy mate for the distinguished ex-Secretary of the Navy." They also said she was generous and charitable: "Every poor beggar in New York has a feeling of personal regard for this lady, as she never refuses a petition for alms." By the end of the year, however, the rumors were put to rest when Pauline became engaged and Davidge left the household. She used her intellect, grace, and social connections to establish an elite New York school for socially prominent young women. In 1902, Davidge became Andrew's guest at Red Roof, while her own cottage, Pier Lane, was being built next door. Her future husband recalled Davidge's house as a "charming little villa in Italianate style . . . the true home of her spirit."[2]

Another guest at the Fairview Inn in 1900 was Cecilia Beaux, a renowned artist from Philadelphia, recipient of many awards, including the gold medal presented at the 1900 Paris Exposition Universelle. In 1902 she, too, was Andrew's guest at Red Roof, and in 1904—with Andrew's encouragement and advice—she bought land nearby to build a house and studio that she named Green Alley. Her house, hidden from the road, was finished in stucco, with a gray roof and a loggia of pink bricks studded with terra-cotta bas-reliefs. A biographer claimed that the large, separate studio "reflected her 'sacred calling' as an artist." Andrew and his young friends were undoubtedly part of what attracted Beaux to Eastern Point. Although she avoided marriage as a distraction from her work, she enjoyed male companionship and admiration. Her niece remarked that these "noticeably good-looking . . . willing followers" were usually "ten or twenty years her junior." The friendships she developed were also good for business: many of her neighbors' affluent guests commissioned Beaux to paint their portraits.[3]

A year later, Caroline Sidney Sinkler, a wealthy socialite from South Carolina, moved into a house she called Wrong Roof, which she filled with a stream of visiting friends and relatives. In 1895, when Sinkler was thirty-five, she had been engaged to John Stewardson, a Philadelphia architect. Shortly before their wedding, Stewardson went skating on the Schuylkill River, fell through the ice, and drowned. Sinkler never married and, in her fiancé's memory, always dressed in lavender. Her niece said that "Aunt Cad, with her extraordinary charm, her enormous appetite for life, would put up with absolutely anybody if they entertained her . . . She had no formal education, but she could pick up a book just out, thumb through a few pages beforehand and then flatter the author to pieces."[4]

In 1906, Andrew invited Henry Davis Sleeper to visit Red Roof. With his brother Stephen, Sleeper managed their family's trust and real estate holdings. He had been a sickly child, taught at home, and he enjoyed antique hunting with his mother. After she died, he wrote, "So many of the things I care most for in my house are the fruit of hours of pleasant searching, with mother, among old shops & houses." Garland described "Harry" Sleeper as "impeccably tailored, slope-shouldered, soft-spoken and gentle in appearance," a man of "penetrating intelligence, devastating wit, passionately loyal," and "a connoisseur gifted with a sheer virtuosity of creative taste." He was a tall, handsome man with warm brown eyes. Henry James described him as a "dear young man, the Newfoundland dog, the great St. Bernard nosing-in-the-snow neighbor."[5]

A close relationship with the poet Guy Wetmore Carryl had ended in 1904, when Carryl died after a fire in his home. Carryl's book *Far from the Maddening Girls*, dedicated to Sleeper, advised that a bachelor "must have a house, and equip and order this in such a fashion that all the married couples for ten miles around will fall down with one accord and grovel." Sleeper took the challenge seriously. A year after his visit he bought a one-acre lot at Eastern Point and began building a house he named Little Beauport.[6]

In 1907, the colony of friends was complete. It was known informally as Dabsville, a rough acronym of Davidge, Andrew, Beaux, Sinkler, and Sleeper. Davidge was fifty-seven, educated and accomplished; Andrew was thirty-four, a nationally recognized economist; Beaux was fifty-two, an internationally acclaimed artist; Sinkler was forty-seven, with a quick intelligence and endless effervescence; Sleeper, the youngest at twenty-nine, was interested in antiques but uncertain about how he wished to use his talents. Beauport set him upon his path.

Dabsville had one honorary member. On April 15, 1903, Andrew wrote to his parents: "Today has been a gala day for me! . . . I was made assistant professor of economics [at Harvard] . . . I think I am about the youngest professor in the University . . . Today I had another delightful experience. Through Miss Beaux's ingenious machinations, I was invited by Mrs. Jack Gardner to visit her new Fenway Court . . . received at the entrance by Mrs. Gardner herself who showed us the wonderful place from top to bottom." Andrew said he had "never seen any house in the world as beautiful" as the Venetian palazzo now known as the Isabella Stewart Gardner Museum. Gardner, then well into her sixties, had always enjoyed the company of attractive, interesting younger men. Andrew and Sleeper became frequent visitors to Fenway Court and often joined Gardner at the opera, symphony, and theater. In 1908, Andrew invited Gardner to Red Roof, and she returned often. She brought others—John Singer Sargent, Henry James, Childe Hassam, Henry F. du Pont, Helen Hayes, John D. Rockefeller Jr.—widening the colony's network of wealth and talent.[7]

Gardner and Caroline Sinkler also became good friends. In March 1919, Sinkler sent a gift of perfume. Gardner thanked her enthusiastically: "How dear of you to send me such a fragrant gift. It makes me think you must almost be in the room with me." At Christmas, Gardner was "so humiliated, dearest friend, I can hardly write. Was there ever a stupider thing done? One of my myrmidons blundered over wrapping your package & another, and gave the wrong one to send to you." A week later, she thanked Sinkler for her gift: "You are never forgetting, always loving. May the dear blessed Lord keep you & bring sweet things into your life. My deepest love to you & gratitude for all you are to me."[8]

Although there is no letter *h* in "Dabsville," the Gloucester architect Halfdan Hanson was an essential part of the group. He and Henry Sleeper became close friends as well as colleagues. Sleeper promoted Hanson's career in Gloucester and beyond, and the two worked together apparently without friction—not always the case for architects and their clients or designers. Like Sleeper, Hanson had serious health problems. In 1918, he was drafted and sent to Washington, D.C., where he designed military installations and continued to work on private commissions. He developed tuberculosis, exacerbated by the Washington climate. In March 1921, Sleeper recommended that Hanson move to Colorado, but he could not afford to do so. Sleeper continued to promote Hanson's career, and the architect told him, "I appreciate very much your writing to get work for me, it means more than you perhaps realize to have you take such interest in me always and the courage that it gives me is more beneficial than gallons of medicine." With a March 18 letter, Sleeper enclosed two checks. The first was for $250 "with much gratitude for the genius with which you drew the plans. It was awfully clever of you (and like you, and no one else!) to think of making so many notes that a contractor could not blunder much." The second was for $50 "to go to Baltimore to see Dr. Hamman" at Johns Hopkins. Sleeper added, "Don't bother to write me a long letter . . . Don't waste your energy on manners or politeness." Hanson did move to Denver and stayed for ten years, continuing to work with Sleeper. Sleeper missed him, though: "How very often I wish you were here with your swift and excellent way of solving apparently insuperable obstacles."[9]

Like the other residents of Dabsville, Sleeper and Hanson exchanged gifts and gossip. Sleeper thanked Hanson for a Christmas gift: "I am perfectly enchanted with the little candlesticks . . . I know you must have made them for they have, I think, just your ingenuity, and so I value them particularly." And Hanson must have enjoyed Sleeper's local news: "Did you hear that Miss Mary Davison, my neighbor here out on the point, who is fifty-five years old, has red hair and flat feet, has just married Anatole Le Braz, one of the greatest poets in France!—so one never knows what is next."[10]

Dabsville also had a supporting cast: the servants who maintained the houses and grounds, fed the guests, and made the residents' work and play possible. Cecilia Beaux's home was maintained with the help of her cousin, May Whitlock; Anna Murphy, who worked for her for forty years; and Natale Gavagnin, a former Venetian gondolier. According to a biographer, Murphy "cooked, cleaned, and fixed her mistress's hair, while Natale chauffeured, gardened and generally added an exoticism to life at Green Alley." Natale was a favorite of Isabella Gardner's. She spoke to him in Italian and admired his biceps; Beaux feared that she would lure him away. Gardner usually stayed at Red Roof and never visited without her maid Ella Lavin. Caroline Sinkler's servants included a maid and a page. At Red Roof, Andrew hired Austin Wonson as caretaker and his wife, Virginia, as cook. George Wonson succeeded his father as caretaker in 1913, and his brother Roland was the chauffeur.[11]

In 1919, Sleeper hired George Wonson's wife, Mary, as cook and housekeeper, and later their sons also worked for him. In the summer, the family lived in small, simply furnished bedrooms and a bathroom above the kitchen. Life at Beauport would have been impossible without the Wonsons. They opened Beauport in March and closed it when the season ended. Mary's cooking was an added attraction. Her son "remembers Sleeper hovering in the kitchen, waiting for Mary's pastry to emerge from the oven . . . Guests raved about Mary's lobster curry." She spent days preparing the traditional Thanksgiving dinner that Sleeper served in the Pine Kitchen. When she needed extra help, Sleeper hired Anna Murphy and Natale Gavagnin. Austin and Virginia Wonson's daughters also helped out at parties; once, Sleeper recalled, they "waited on table dressed as rabbits."[12]

Beauport contained thousands of objects, each meticulously placed by Sleeper. A historian described how they were cared for: "Each year before opening the house for the summer, Mary and her hired helpers (usually Wonson relatives) cleaned each object in the collections and recreated the arrangements. She often drew maps and diagrams to be sure she replaced each item in its exact position . . . Every spring she worked through the entire house, one shelf at a time." Every year, Sleeper returned to a house that looked exactly as it had when he left.[13]

Much of the early writing about Dabsville focused on rumors about wild parties and speculated about the sexuality of its residents and the relationships among them. They did enjoy a good party, especially if it involved wearing costumes. Certainly their sexual identities were integral to their lives and relationships, as were their careers, intellectual interests, commitments to causes, and friendships. Andrew and Sleeper were gay, but as one historian has pointed out, they "would not have identified themselves as either 'heterosexual,' 'homosexual,' or 'bisexual' since those categories only gained currency late in their lives or after their deaths. Nor would the modern terms have captured how they thought about love and sexuality." We do know that all these people were devoted friends who enjoyed one another's company and enhanced one another's lives.[14]

As their careers and personal lives developed, they created a network that extended well beyond Eastern Point.
Andrew's grandnephew, Andrew Gray, said that "the nucleus
they formed on the Point appears to have expanded to
absorb people according to their wit, good looks, vivacity,
and capacity for self-dramatization . . . They all drank very
little—most worked rather hard, even when playing—and
took great pleasure in each other's success . . . They were
hospitable to outsiders . . . but surely rather snobbish toward
people less verbally adept than they. They were very private people." In a letter to the mother of a friend who had
been with the AFS in France, Sleeper was explicit about the
kinds of people he invited to his home: "the men & women
who, irrespective of age, were fitted by character & fine living to prove worthy of long friendship." The magnetism of
the group brought hundreds of people to the colony, but the
architectural lodestone was Sleeper's house.[15]

## Beauport: The Parts

The houses on Eastern Point were built at a time of transition in the styles of American architecture and interior
design. The Arts and Crafts movement, international in
scope, emphasized the value of handcrafts over machine-
made objects and simple, organic design over the ornate
and artificial. The Colonial Revival, an American variant,
had brought back styles associated with the colonial and
early national periods of America's history. Some designers,
such as the antiquarian Wallace Nutting, tried to reproduce
exactly the domestic interiors of the past with period furniture or reproductions, creating an effect that often seems
artificial. A parallel movement sought to preserve historic

houses. Both American movements were initially nostalgic, nationalistic reactions to the machine age and the arrival of large numbers of immigrants from Ireland, Italy, and other (generally Catholic) countries. Esthetically, the movements were a reaction against the overstuffed fussiness of Victorian interiors, a principle most famously expressed in *The Decoration of Houses*, by Edith Wharton and Ogden Codman, published in 1897.[16]

Sleeper was connected to architects and amateurs in the Colonial Revival movement. Arthur Little had designed his parents' summer house in Marblehead. Little, his partner Herbert W. C. Browne, and his close friend Ogden Codman were known as the Colonial Trinity. Codman and Little, like many of the men involved in historic preservation at the time, were gay. They were of an earlier generation than Sleeper, but the place of gay men in Boston society had not changed a great deal: they were accepted—that is, their sexuality was overlooked—as long as they were discreet and not effeminate. But belonging to a circle where one could be honest about one's sexual identity was important, even if not completely liberating. For Sleeper, both his professional connections and Dabsville offered such circles.[17]

Arthur Little had written in 1877 that Americans "should revive our Colonial style, which is everywhere marked with peculiar dignity, simplicity and refinement." Sleeper would certainly have read Little's work as well as *The Decoration of Houses*. But, as modern critics have noted, "he showed little of their concern for historical accuracy. Panache was what he was after."[18] At Eastern Point he was not restoring or replicating a colonial house: he was building a new house, creating interiors that would incorporate artifacts from various periods of American and European history in imaginative, even provocative, ways. Equally important, although he was passionate about American history, he was not provincial. He had traveled in Europe, and those experiences influenced his aesthetic choices.

Sleeper could have hired Little or another established architect to build his house. Instead, he entrusted the work to Halfdan Hanson, who at twenty-three had recently completed a correspondence course in architecture. Their collaboration lasted nearly forty years, as the house grew from a small cottage to more than forty rooms. Hanson shared Sleeper's perfectionism. In 1917, hospitalized in Rhode Island during construction at Beauport, Sleeper wrote to Hanson: "I know how harrassed you are these days with clients who don't know what they want (but want it right away!) and therefore I hesitate to add to your burden . . . Will you for friendship's sake make trips there [Beauport] at least once a week & straighten out any trivial difficulties—Frankly I shall not be able to afford to 'do things over'—Nor do I want to see them wrong all my life." Arthur Little visited the house in September 1908 and, as Sleeper told Hanson, he sent "a very laudatory letter—offering me the services of his draughtsmen, superintendents, contractors, etc. if I should want to build a house for anyone else! . . . & he adds that if it turned out as well as this house has in every detail, he should be only too glad to have his office affiliated with the making of it."[19]

Sleeper's vision for the house began with two expeditions—the first with Andrew and Beaux, the second with Andrew, Davidge, and Gardner—to the eighteenth-century William Cogswell house in Essex in 1907. The building was going to be demolished, and Sleeper bought its pine paneling and shutters, which he installed in his front hall and three other rooms. Throughout Beauport, Sleeper would integrate pieces salvaged from older houses to create a feeling of antiquity, but there was nothing antiquarian about his designs.

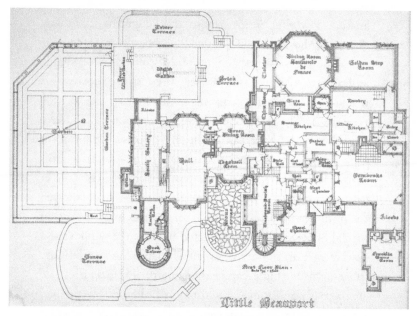

FIGURE 22. Floor plan of Beauport, the Sleeper-McCann House, attributed to Halfdan N. Hanson. *Courtesy of Historic New England.*

As one architectural historian suggested, "At the same time that Braque and Picasso were developing their technique of collage, using artifacts of everyday life to create two- and three-dimensional works on canvas of great plastic and narrative complexity, Sleeper proceeded to develop similar techniques on the architectural level. For Sleeper, architecture was but the canvas for an assemblage of precious objects that were not only inherently beautiful but also rich in historic association."[20]

Only one room came close to being a reconstruction. The Pembroke Room, or Pine Kitchen, was assembled from the doors, paneling, chimney, and ceiling beams of the family homestead of Sleeper's mother. The furnishings had been auctioned off, but Sleeper traced and bought back as many objects as he could. He added floorboards from another house, newly fashioned adaptations of colonial wing chairs, and antique redware and pewter. The Colonial Revivalists would have been at home in this room.[21]

Some of Sleeper's rooms were built around his collections, but he did not create traditional displays. Collectors of nineteenth-century pressed-glass cup plates—clear or brilliantly colored small round dishes on which the tea drinker rested a cup while drinking from the saucer—usually showed them in custom-made cases or stored them away except on special occasions. Sleeper soldered his into the window of a display case and into a door frame, depriving them of any monetary value but greatly enhancing their visual effect.

There is no shortage of whimsy at Beauport. Sleeper had found a cast-iron stove in the shape of George Washington wearing a toga. In the fall he would light it. The historian Paul Hollister recalled Sleeper telling a guest, "You must come some time in Autumn . . . George's whole body is the heat-chamber of the contraption. It's wonderful to sit here and see him get hot. He is slow to anger." The stove is one of nineteen images of Washington in the house. Hollister said that Sleeper told people he had included a secret staircase "so that when the mob comes to seize Aunt Imprudence, to duck her for a witch, we can spirit her upstairs." The way he actually used the staircase was almost as dramatic: When guests arrived, a servant led them into the hall and called their attention to something at the other end of the room. Sleeper emerged from the hidden staircase while their backs were turned, appearing as if by magic.[22]

Gloucester is a fishing port, and the residents of Dabsville mingled happily with the local sea captains. Andrew joined the Master Mariners Association in 1910 and entertained the group at Red Roof every year; two fishing boats were named after him. Sleeper devoted a room to maritime artifacts—a whaling log, scrimshaw, spyglass, charts, and navigational instruments. A cribbage board invited the mariners to play their favorite game.[23]

Many of Gloucester's fishermen were of Portuguese descent, and in 1914, when their church burned, Andrew wrote to Isabella Gardner: "Harry and I ran into the fire as we returned to Gloucester, and it was so full of pathos, the smoking ruins, the charred and headless virgin and half burned figures which had been 'rescued,' the silently weeping priest and the scores of anxious parishioners who had worked so hard for and take so much interest in the church,—that we decided that we would help them to get a new 'Lady of Good Voyage' from the old world. Can we use your name on the list of subscribers?" Andrew and Hanson oversaw the reconstruction. After the church had been rebuilt, Andrew gave the congregation a statue of Joan of Arc as a World War I memorial, and Gardner gave them money to add a carillon tower—the first in the United States. She came to Gloucester to hear the bells, cast in England, played for the first time.[24]

Sleeper sometimes created a room around an especially spectacular antiques find. In the attic of the Elbridge Gerry House in Marblehead, he found boxes of wallpaper, more than a century old, in its original wrapping. Robert Morris, the financier of the American Revolution, had ordered it from China for a house that he was never able to build. In three sets, it illustrated the making of porcelain, rice, and tea. Sleeper bought the wallpaper, which became the inspiration for the China Trade Room. Another room was inspired by a set of red "curtains" made of painted pine. Sleeper paid twelve dollars for them, designed windows to accommodate the sham curtains, and then built an astonishing two-story round book tower around the windows. Still other rooms were built to honor people Sleeper admired: Benjamin Franklin, Percy Bysshe Shelley, Lord Byron, Admiral Horatio Nelson. Almost anything could be an inspiration—or an excuse—to envision and build a new room.[25]

All the rooms were used. Guests were greeted in the hall and could sit comfortably for casual conversations in many of the ground-floor rooms. Sleeper could choose to have dinner served in any of five dining rooms, depending on the nature of the meal. His widowed mother had a three-room suite, including a music room. His brother Jacob often stayed between assignments for the Foreign Service and lived at Beauport during a serious illness. Games were played in the Franklin Room, and the China Trade Room accommodated large gatherings. Many of the rooms opened onto spectacular views of the harbor and, because they faced west, dramatic sunsets. The large west-facing window of the Golden Step Room, named after a model ship on display, could be lowered into the wall so that guests dined in the open air without setting even a toe outdoors.[26] If you imagine the house full of people, it quickly looks less like a museum and more like a home where you would love to be a guest.

## The Rest of Life

The residents of Dabsville were doing more than building and partying. Cecilia Beaux's portraits became so popular that by 1915 she was turning down commissions. Joanna Davidge was teaching her classes and, at sixty, enjoying a new romance. Caroline Sinkler had invited David Randall-MacIver, an archaeologist in his late thirties, to Wrong Roof. Randall-MacIver was an Oxford Egyptologist, leader of several expeditions, curator of Egyptology at the University Museum in Philadelphia, and an heir to the Cunard fortune. He and Davidge fell in love and were married in New York in March 1911.[27]

Andrew taught at Harvard until 1909, but his talents were needed beyond the academy. From 1908 to 1911, he was an expert assistant and editor of publications of the National Monetary Commission, which had been created to study financial systems in other countries and structural problems in the U.S. system. His departure for Europe in 1908 was the occasion for a week of farewell dinners, including what Isabella Gardner described as a "great fête" at Beaux's studio. The eighteen guests wore elaborate costumes: Andrew was a Roman emperor, seated on a red velvet throne. While Andrew was away, Sleeper took care of Red Roof—duties that included hosting visitors and dealing with mice and moths.[28]

In London, although busy with Monetary Commission business, Andrew occasionally ventured into expatriate society. One visit generated an extraordinary social misunderstanding—or perhaps gender confusion. He wrote that he had been taken "to see some 'artistic' American woman" with a collection of works by Matisse, which he judged to be "Gawd awful." Their hostess, "a Mrs. Stein, sat raptly wrapped in a sort of artistic mixture of kimona and maternity gown in the midst of all these horrors . . . The hostess, who is a pupil of Matisse, remarked as we were leaving that her husband arranged the flowers in the studio and that he was 'a perfect wife.'" In 1909, President William Howard Taft appointed Andrew director of the U.S. Mint and, a year later, assistant secretary of the Treasury. That same year, Andrew attended a secret meeting of six men on Jekyll Island, Georgia, where the foundations were laid for the Federal Reserve System.[29]

And Harry Sleeper found his vocation. Arthur Little had encouraged him to work as a professional designer, and his house was being noticed in magazines. He received his first commissions from his Gloucester neighbors, and his reputation was growing. Henry Francis du Pont and his wife visited Beauport—a connection that would later lead to major commissions. He traveled to Williamsburg, Jamestown, Monticello, Mt. Vernon, and the University of Virginia, broadening his knowledge of the restoration of colonial sites. In 1911, the Society for the Preservation of New England Antiquities (now Historic New England) appointed him its museum director.[30] But in 1914, the friends' domestic and professional lives took a sharp turn. They were alarmed by the outbreak of war in Europe and, despite U.S. neutrality, were determined to become involved.

## War

The United States was neutral in World War I until April 1917, but many Americans, especially young people, sided with the nations allied against Germany. They could not participate as combatants without losing their citizenship, so they needed another way to serve. Andrew was devoted to France, where he had traveled and studied. In 1914, he volunteered with the American Hospital at Neuilly as an ambulance driver. He sailed from New York on December 20, with Cecilia Beaux and Harry Sleeper at the dock to see him off. Throughout January and February, he transported wounded soldiers and witnessed the human toll of war firsthand. He was older than most volunteers and had considerable administrative experience. On March 2, he was promoted to general inspector of the field service: "the most interesting job I can imagine . . . It is a new place just created, and I am to make of it what I can."[31]

Andrew quickly developed an ambitious goal: to supply enough ambulances and American drivers to carry wounded soldiers quickly from the battlefield to field hospitals. This required overcoming what he later described as "certain preliminary and somewhat formidable obstacles in France." By April 1915, Andrew had negotiated an agreement under which candidates would provide reference letters from "men of standing in their communities, testifying to their character and unquestioned loyalty to the Allied cause" and would agree to serve for at least six months. Men with German parents would be rejected. This agreement established the American Ambulance Field Service, later known as the American Field Service (AFS).[32]

Andrew now faced the challenges of recruiting drivers, raising money, and designing and outfitting ambulances that would work best under the conditions of trench warfare. Back in Gloucester, Harry Sleeper, who had been looking after Andrew's house and finances and visiting his friend's mother daily, took on the recruitment and fund-raising efforts. Sleeper had little experience in raising money or recruiting, but he was working for an appealing cause that he believed in, and he was charming. Even before Andrew started the AFS, Sleeper wrote, "I have been doing my little toward war charity effort—& helped make quite a bit of money. The requests in that direction for monetary—or social effort are limitless as soon as people discover one is vulnerable." Sleeper was committed: "If it were not for mother I should go over—for the part this country has played so far (or lack of part, rather) makes me feel that every decent individual should do his share toward saving civilization." For the ambulance effort, he began at home, quickly raising $1,100 for a "Gloucester ambulance." Isabella

Gardner also donated an ambulance that went into service in November 1915. Andrew sent her several photographs of it and told her that it was "being driven by a young fellow named Samuel G. Dayton of Philadelphia, a graduate of Princeton, exceedingly nice fellow."[33]

Sleeper soon learned to extract larger amounts from wealthier donors. The first, and most important, was Edward J. de Coppet, a New York financier and patron of the arts, who after two minutes' conversation gave him $1,100 for an ambulance. Sleeper wrote to Andrew: "He did not want to have the ambulance named after him, but I told him that if he did he could have a record of its service sent him from time to time (I thought this would prove worthwhile). He was so pleased with this possibility that he exclaimed: 'Oh! how good that would be to hear of!–I should want to give *another* I am sure!' De Coppet soon gave several ambulances, $1,000 a month for maintenance, and funds for organizational costs. When he died less than a year later, his son continued the gifts. Boston lawyer and banker James Storrow gave the same amounts as de Coppet and provided office space for the American headquarters. New York office space was provided by J. P. Morgan. By the end of 1915, eighty ambulances had been purchased. By the end of the war, a thousand were in service.[34]

Sleeper published and distributed pamphlets about the AFS. He organized committees in more than a hundred cities that raised money and recruited volunteers, often by giving lectures illustrated with films that the French Army had made of the volunteers at work. A single lecture in Cleveland raised $87,000 and sponsorships for more than a dozen ambulances.[35]

The booklets and publicity also helped with recruiting, which focused on college campuses. Numerous colleges and prep schools sent volunteers. Stanford, Harvard, Princeton, and Dartmouth sent several units each. Harvard alone sent

325 volunteers. Several cities, including St. Louis, Cleveland, Chicago, and Buffalo, provided complete sections of vehicles, volunteers, and funds. The AFS, with approximately two thousand drivers in France at any one time, cost nearly a million dollars a year to operate. Sleeper helped to raise the funds year after year until the end of the war.[36]

When the United States entered the war, the AFS was integrated into the U.S. Army, to function as it had before, and was expanded. Most of the volunteers enlisted, and Field Service officers were given commissions. By the end of the war, more than a hundred sections were serving in France. Andrew was commissioned a major, then a lieutenant colonel, and was awarded the Distinguished Service Medal. The French government awarded the Croix de Guerre, the Légion d'Honneur, or the Medaille Militaire to 250 volunteers. Andrew and Sleeper both were awarded the Légion d'Honneur and the Croix de Guerre.[37]

In 1917, Sleeper's mother died, and he was able to go to France in October. He became the director of AFS headquarters, located in an elegant mansion on the Rue Raynouard in the Parisian suburb of Passy, donated by the owners for the duration of the war. The job was both administrative and pastoral, because the headquarters was also a hospital and a club where volunteers could congregate between ambulance assignments. Sleeper proved adept at resolving disputes among the staff and solving problems for the volunteers. He wrote to Mrs. Gardner that as soon as he arrived, the office and household staff gave notice, and he "spent three busy days convincing them how valuable, indispensible and important they all were!" Throughout his tenure, he had to deal with food shortages and bad tempers.[38]

His favorite part of the job was helping the volunteers with what he called their "monetary, military, or moral" problems in a low-key but effective way. A reporter for the *AFS Bulletin* wrote: "If difficulties could be straightened out, Mr. Sleeper was the man who could straighten them . . . You might find him at most hours of the day moving around within the clubrooms, apparently with nothing more to do than the men with whom he was talking. But somehow if you mentioned to him some difficulty that you couldn't untangle he would tell you he'd look into it; and probably the next noon would casually tell you that he had fixed it up . . . Where he got the time for all these things, nobody knows."[39]

Predictably, Sleeper lost no time improving the interior of the mansion. He told Mrs. Gardner: "The lower floor of this house really has wonderful possibilities . . . I have got a number of people around here to contribute various rather fine things, so that it really will be very good looking." Within a month, he had it "pretty well furnished. The lower floor is deliciously cozy and cheerful." Nor could he resist collecting: "I have been asked out a great deal to lunch and dine with delightful people here, most of whom have enchanting places of abode (!), with walled gardens and rooms, filled with the delightful products of the hundreds of antique shops of Paris. Alas, the antique shops are not for me at present, *but* I stopped in one the night before last." By the time he left France, he had acquired an extensive collection of toleware, "red painted tin," that he later displayed in the Octagon Room at Beauport. Despite the light tone of Sleeper's letters, Gardner knew that he, Andrew, and other young friends were in danger. She wrote to Caroline Sinkler that "H.D.S. sent a letter which came today. I am worried about him & pray to have him strong & well. If they would only all come home."[40]

It is impossible to know how many lives the AFS saved. Jean Jules Jusserand, the French ambassador to the United States, spoke of "lives saved by the thousands, suffering attenuated, amputations avoided, families spared their fathers for after the war; these form only a part of the French debt toward the American Field Service." Andrew and Sleeper were also proud of the way the AFS influenced opinion at home, helping to bring the United States into the war. Theodore Roosevelt was blunt in his praise: "The most important thing that a nation can possibly save is its soul, and these young men have been helping this nation to save its soul."[41]

When the war ended, Andrew and Sleeper transformed the AFS into a foundation to fund educational exchanges between France and the United States. The volunteers returned to work or college. Sleeper wrote of the psychological challenges they—and he—faced: "The spirit which led them to France by inclination, before the time of obligation, is the same that in considering the future makes them hesitate to dedicate themselves permanently to a purpose with little human interest. In the maze of possibilities they have come home to face, some may be fortunate in finding their desire; but very many will have to be content with small monotony, unless those of us whose lives are more established can serve them to finer purpose."[42] Like the volunteers, Andrew and Sleeper sought careers that would be more than "small monotony."

## Peace

After returning home, Andrew and Sleeper began work on the scholarship project and a three-volume collection of memoirs by volunteers, *History of the American Field Service in France*, published in 1920. Andrew told Isabella Gardner that he had "*no plans* at present. I am busy with the book, and arranging about the fellowships in French universities, and many other

FIGURE 23. Henry Davis Sleeper and A. Piatt Andrew. A. Piatt Andrew Archive. *Courtesy of Historic New England.*

little things, and expecting that sometime, the right thing for a long pull will turn up." In the summer of 1921, "the right thing" did turn up. A special election was held for the Gloucester district seat in Congress. Andrew entered the race, as he told Mrs.

Gardner, "without really intending to do so, and although I said to you that I would not. I have been swept along by a kind of fate that could not be resisted." She drafted a response: "I'm awfully sorry but I think you must have wanted it or you really wouldn't have succumbed." Andrew won the Republican primary almost two to one; in Gloucester itself, the vote was 4,758 to 207. In the general election two weeks later, Andrew defeated Democrat Charles I. Pettingill 22,545 to 6,792. He was reelected again and again, serving until his death. In Congress, he worked to provide aid to France in paying its war debts. Whenever possible, he returned to Eastern Point in the summer and for Thanksgiving, and he often entertained visiting French dignitaries at Red Roof.[43]

Harry Sleeper returned to the career and the house that he had begun before the war. He completed the Pine Kitchen and Franklin Game Room. In 1921, he finished the Octagon Room, sometimes called the Souvenir de France, inspired by his time with the AFS. Lafayette's portrait hangs on the wall, and the nineteenth-century red toleware he collected is displayed around the eight sides. He also added the Golden Step Room, designed around a model ship, and the Indian Room—an enclosed porch with Native American artifacts and folk art figures.[44]

Sleeper's work on Beauport and his friends' houses in Gloucester now became the basis of a profession. He built a town house on Beacon Hill for himself and opened an office in Boston, where he began receiving important commissions. His first big project was for his friend Caroline Sinkler, who had bought The Highlands, outside Philadelphia, in 1917. The house, built in 1796, was in need of restoration. It was very much a Colonial Revival project, with the floors painted as checkerboards and the walls covered in a replica of an 1834 wallpaper, "Les Vues de l'Amérique du Nord."[45]

Beauport was featured in such magazines as *House Beautiful*, *Architect*, *Architectural Record*, *Antiques*, and *Country Life*, where architects and potential clients could see Sleeper's work. He was soon receiving commissions beyond the circle of his friends. The first was to design a ballroom for Gull Rock, E. Bruce Merriman's Providence mansion. Sleeper may have met Merriman in France, where he had served with the Red Cross in 1918 and 1919. In 1922, Sleeper began work on both the China Trade Room at Beauport and a Chinese ballroom at Gull Rock. He used two of the wallpaper series at home and the third for the Merriman house. This was soon followed by another Newport commission: Eagle's Nest, built in 1924 for Ferdinand Frazier Jelke.[46]

Some of Sleeper's commissions began when people visited Beauport: the house was becoming a showplace for prospective customers. Henry F. du Pont had visited before the war, and he returned in 1923. He greatly admired the house, especially the Pine Kitchen, and he commissioned Sleeper to design the interior of Chestertown, the fifty-room summer house he was building in Southampton, Long Island. Sleeper's influence is evident not only in the overall design of the rooms but also in the details: the pine and maple furniture, hooked rugs, ship models, ceramics, and pewter. Sleeper later advised du Pont on a new wing for Winterthur, in Delaware.[47]

In 1926, Mabel Choate acquired the house on Prospect Hill in Stockbridge that the Reverend John Sergeant had built in 1739, when he was a missionary to the Mohicans. The house was in disrepair, and she had it disassembled, moved, and reassembled on Main Street. One of the people she hired to work on the project was Henry Sleeper. The *New York Times*, in announcing her decision, described him as "an architect and specialist in early Colonial homes." The official description of the house explains that Sleeper furnished the two-story Georgian structure, known now as the Mission House, with what the restorers called "pieces appropriate to Sergeant's economic status and his wife's taste, many of them dating from the 1750's or earlier. A few original pieces . . . were returned to the house."[48]

In Beverly Hills, Sleeper and Hanson were designing the interior of Nine Gables for Johnny Mack Brown, a college football star whose picture decorated Wheaties boxes and who starred in numerous western movies. At least one Beauport feature caught Brown's fancy: the book tower, which Sleeper re-created for him. An architecture magazine described the feature that is perhaps most like Beauport: the house, though "practically new . . . already has that indefinable stamp of possession and personality generally found only in rooms long lived with." In 1933 Sleeper and Hanson began work on another Beverly Hills mansion, this one for the actor Fredric March. Also half-timbered, it was designed by Wallace Neff, unofficial architect to the stars. A newspaper described Sleeper's European interiors for the March house: a playroom reminiscent of a Normandy kitchen, a living room like an eighteenth-century salon, with "laurel green painted walls . . . 18th Century furniture in deep yellow brocade and a dark brown chintz on the couch." A year later, he created designs for Joan Crawford's Hollywood home.[49]

Several of Beauport's features are echoed in Indian Council Rock, a sixty-room French Norman Revival estate in Newtown, Pennsylvania. It was built by architect Charles Willing for George Frederick and Stella Elkins Tyler in 1930. The house has an octagon room and a near replica of the Pine Kitchen, as well as a room designed to display the Tylers' collection of Dutch, English, and French pewter on shelves that look like frames.[50]

In 1924, when Isabella Stewart Gardner died, Sleeper was named a trustee of the Gardner Museum. He was later named vice president of the Essex Institute in Salem and served on the Committee for the Preservation of the Peirce-Nichols House in Salem. And in 1934, he was made an honorary member of the American Institute of Architects. Harry Sleeper's health had always been precarious. As a child, he was too sickly to attend school, and he was unable to join the ambulance service as a driver. While working on the Fredric March house in Beverly Hills, he learned that he had leukemia. He died in Boston on September 22, 1934, at fifty-six. His brother Stephen was unable to maintain Beauport, and in 1935 he sold it to Charles Edward Francis and Helena Woolworth McCann, who left the house nearly unchanged. In 1942, the McCann heirs transferred Beauport to the Society for the Preservation of New England Antiquities in memory of Helena.[51]

## Dabsville: The Whole

Isabella Stewart Gardner had died in 1924, Joanna Davidge in 1931, and Harry Sleeper in 1934. When Piatt Andrew died two years later, his body was cremated and the ashes scattered from an airplane flying over Red Roof.[52] Cecilia Beaux died in 1936, and Caroline Sinkler in 1949 at the age of 89. Dabsville was gone, leaving individual legacies of great accomplishment and a communal legacy of friendship.

Isabella Gardner, though only occasionally a resident of Eastern Point, was a close friend to the members of the community. Andrew visited her several times a year in Boston and wrote frequently. The few surviving letters show him seeking—and receiving—her advice and help, whether money for the Portuguese church or the AFS, political support, or just a sympathetic ear. Soon after he was elected to Congress, he told her, "It is all right being a Congressman, I suppose, but I often sigh for the old care free, sunny days and freedom, and the intimate joyous times that you and I have together." Shortly before her death, he wrote, "I hope you are happy always in thinking of all that you have given of friendship and counsel and encouragement and delightful companionship to those who love you." And Sleeper, on the train to New York to set sail for France, wrote to Gardner: "For so long now I have brought you joys & sorrows to weigh. And in return you have given me encouragement to accomplish another day's work & whatever crisis has come. It will be good to remember always wherever I am. I shall think of you many an hour these next few days. Please be sure of my constant love & gratitude." Gardner welcomed Sleeper's mother and Andrew's parents at Fenway Court, and she advised and encouraged young people, especially musicians, whom the two sent her way. She received, in turn, their affection, gratitude, and hospitality.[53]

Caroline Sinkler knew how the friends valued one another. When they learned of Andrew's dining in distinguished company at the American Embassy in London, she said that "the best part is that he would just as lief be dining here with us." Sinkler had nearly constant hordes of relatives and friends visiting, and Sleeper often helped out by entertaining them. To complement her wardrobe of violet shades, he planted lavender on the side of Beauport facing Wrong Roof and displayed his collection of amethyst glass on that side as well.[54]

A small portion of the correspondence among the friends remains—not as much as we would like, but enough to get a sense of what they meant to one another. There are frequent thank-you notes for thoughtful gifts—books, pictures, small house decorations, and the like. Cecilia Beaux wrote effusively to Andrew about the volume of Whitman's poetry he had sent her in 1904—"what I would have asked for if I had known how"—and about an unnamed book given in 1906—"I feel as if you had provided me with a volume of notes and commentaries on 'myself.'" In 1907, Beaux thanked Sleeper for his Christmas gift of a calendar—"an owl which flapped its wings & blinked"—and sent him an autographed copy of Richard Watson Gilder's poetry collection, *Fire Divine*.[55]

Sleeper received numerous gifts that year, "but nothing has come—or will come—which could please me like what I got last Thursday": a Napoleon medal from Andrew. "I haven't had it off for an hour since I put it on that afternoon—and I shan't—even when I have it marked—for I shall wait for it—as I did for your pencil Saturday morning. I haven't loved a present so much since I was a child. Every night it goes into the pocket of my pajamas!" In 1911, Andrew sent Sleeper a number of books for Christmas, and he "lay reading in bed, with all of them around me." He wrote that he would not lend them to anyone. "I shall love them for their own qualities of interest—& for other good reasons—more than any of the other books in the round-room at Beauport." (No thank-you note remains for the strangest gift, the two somewhat tame bear cubs that Sleeper gave Andrew and that lived at Red Roof in the summer and a Boston zoo in winter.)[56]

Andrew always found time to write to his friends in Gloucester—perhaps just a postcard or photograph with a brief note. From France, he wrote long letters to his parents that they passed along to Sleeper, who—at Andrew's request—copied them to circulate among his friends. In 1915, he sent Sleeper two photographs of himself in uniform. Sleeper told Andrew that he "loved them—but C[ecilia]

B[eaux] . . . had such a look of longing in her eye when I showed them to her that I gave her one—on impulse—& now must be content with the one left."[57]

We do have numerous letters from Sleeper to Andrew—wonderful gossipy letters about friends and scandals, informative letters about Gloucester events, detailed accounts of AFS activities—that show how deeply Sleeper valued his friend. In 1912, when Andrew was living in Washington and traveling for the Treasury Department, Sleeper had been taking care of Red Roof, financial matters, and other business. When Andrew apologized for the imposition, Sleeper responded:

> For a good many years, now, I have given a service which, whatever its value, must obviously have been sincere—by its voluntary—and insistent—character—and I can truly say that I have never had—& have not now—any wish "to be relieved," in the least degree of the welcome labor your friendship involves.
>
> You have never asked very much of me—but, as I have always been fonder of you than of any other friend I've had, such few things as you have accepted from me have been a very potent factor in my happiness.
>
> In a world where each man is really so solitary—and inwardly on the defensive—by lack of faith in those about him, it would compensate for many disappointments if I knew you believed in my stability.
>
> I have no less an admiration now, for your fineness, than I have ever had—and am as eager now as I have ever been for your approval and affection—so please keep what is yours by virtue of long possession! & believe me, as always, faithfully, H.D.S.[58]

## Beauport: The Whole

Beauport comprises more than forty rooms that grew over the years. Sleeper had no initial plan, yet certain design innovations unite the house. Most often noticed is his use of color. Colonial Revival designers assumed that the houses they were emulating were generally colorless: walls were generally wood paneled, possibly painted white; plaster would have been white, perhaps with some colored stenciling. Sleeper disagreed. Using the technique that today's preservationists endorse, he removed layers of paint from woodwork until he reached the first layer. That did not necessarily mean that he would reproduce the color on that particular panel or door. Rather it authorized him to use the full range of colors he found—a variety of greens, dark browns and reds, yellows, oranges, and blues. In his own words, "Once our ancestors had struggled out of their early harsh life, they cheered up and slapped color on everything in reach."[59]

Sleeper used color to create atmosphere, to bring a room together, to distinguish it from its neighbors, to lead the eye, or to call attention to a specific item or collection of items. The Octagon Room, for example, is painted a dark purple to set off the red toleware on display. A Chinese screen and japanned camera obscura echo the red, as does the coat Lafayette is wearing in the portrait over the fireplace. Even the books on the table and mantel are bound in red leather. The room is further drawn together by the repetition of its eight-sided shape in the table and rug. As a transition from the dark purple, visitors are led through a small room exhibiting amethyst glass to the Golden Step Room—a dazzling space in white and green with brilliant light from a wall of large windows. The furniture—dining tables, Windsor chairs, and a bench—is painted light green. The porcelain on display and on the table is green as well.

The amber window shows off Sleeper's remarkable talent with light. Most rooms at Beauport have exterior windows on only one side. Sleeper created ingenious ways of bringing in natural light, including skylights, interior windows, light shafts, and mirrors. The amber glass collection stands in a case made from a doorway of leaded glass, and a hidden mirror reflects natural light onto frosted glass. Sleeper was equally ingenious in using artificial light. Every fixture is perfectly suited to its room. The colonial-era rooms have pierced-tin fixtures that light the surrounding walls and furniture with sparkling designs. Other rooms have lamps, candles, sconces, ship and railroad lanterns, and ceiling fixtures, all chosen and placed with great care.[60]

What visitors notice most often is the ingenuity and sometimes whimsy with which Sleeper showed off his collections. The displays of amber and amethyst glass, already described, are the most striking, but smaller groupings also attract and hold the eye. Visitors to the Pine Kitchen are first struck by the paneling and wood, but what keeps them looking are the pottery jugs and bowls; the wooden salt box, cheese press, cranberry rake, and mortar and pestle; the row of bone-handled knives; and the iron kettles and other cooking utensils in the hearth. When in use, the room acquired added color from dried corn, pumpkins, squash, and apples. The wood fire added decorative aromas. Contemporary writers have described the rooms as "three-dimensional still lifes."[61]

Books were an important element of Sleeper's collections and design. They are the dominant objects in the Book Tower, of course, and their bindings are used as color accents in other rooms. Sleeper found a brilliant way to exhibit one of his finds: William Jardine's *Naturalist's Library*, a heavily illustrated forty-volume set published between 1833 and 1842. Fourteen volumes are devoted to birds, and many plates are in full color. Sleeper installed a false window with panes sized to fit the pages and then placed the open books behind them, allowing visitors to see many images at once without leafing through the volumes—vicarious bird watching at its best.[62]

Sleeper's impulse to collect came from a love of beautiful things and a desire to share his pleasure in them with others. Finding the exact lamp or vase to perfect a room brought him joy. The house is playful and entertaining. George Washington, after all, is a stove; Ben Franklin's room is the game room. One display of green glass, almost all valuable antiques, includes two Heinz pickle jars that no one would notice if the docent didn't point them out. The house has a sense of humor.

Writers have used many adjectives to describe Beauport: "provocatively unusual," "eccentric," "mazelike," "labyrinthine," "inner-directed," "innovative," "beguiling." The word I find most apt is *theatrical*. Each room can be seen as a stage set, and it is easy to imagine the characters in Beauport's story entering, speaking, laughing, and exiting. The play might begin with Mary Wonson opening the house for the season. Halfdan Hanson stops by with drawings of a new room. The residents of Dabsville celebrate Thanksgiving in the Pine Kitchen, Gloucester's sailors play cribbage in the Mariners Room, and elderly guests muddle through musical chairs in the Golden Step Room. Mrs. Sleeper is seated at her spinet. Harry Sleeper appears magically in the Hall as the du Ponts come calling. Andrew and Sleeper sit at the table in the Octagon Room, reminiscing about their years in France. Cecilia Beaux drops in to relax after a day of painting, and Caroline Sinkler interrupts her peace by bringing her countless cousins to tea. A young FDR and his fellow students sun themselves on the terrace. Joanna Davidge and her fiancé announce their engagement. With Ella Lavin's help, Isabella Gardner dresses for a costume party. Mary Wonson takes cakes from the oven while a crate of lobsters awaits her attention. Helen Hayes, Fredric March, Joan Crawford, and Johnny Mack Brown play cameo roles. Harry Sleeper wins the Tony for best set design.

## To Visit

Beauport is owned by Historic New England and is open from late May to mid-October for hour-long tours. The website (www.historicnewengland.org) provides details. Special events include lectures and a three-hour "Nooks and Crannies" tour. The original houses that remain standing—Green Alley and Pier Lane—are not open to the public. However, Hammond Castle, built across the harbor by Sleeper's friend John Hays Hammond Jr., is open (www.hammondcastle.org). Our Lady of Good Voyage remains an active church.

Sleeper's commissions outside Gloucester are mostly private residences. The exceptions are The Highlands, in Fort Washington, Pennsylvania (www.highlandshistorical.org/); the Mission House, in Stockbridge (www.thetrustees.org/places -to-visit/berkshires/mission-house.html); and Winterthur, in Delaware (www.winterthur.org).

## To Learn More

Archival sources for Beauport are extensive. At the Historic New England Library and Archives, located in the Otis House in Boston, the Beauport Collection includes original documents, extensive research on the house and the residents of Dabsville, newspaper and magazine articles, and photographs. The Halfdan Hanson Architectural Collection includes correspondence between Hanson and Sleeper as well as Hanson's drawings and plans for his many commissions. Isabella Stewart Gardner's papers have been microfilmed and are available at many research libraries. Cecilia Beaux's papers are available online through the Smithsonian Institution's Archives of American Art (www.aaa.si.edu). Piatt Andrew's official correspondence is at the Hoover Institution Archives (www.hoover.org/library-archives). Some of his personal correspondence is in the Beauport Collection at Historic New England, and some has been published.

Published sources about Beauport and Dabsville include the lavishly illustrated volume *Beauport: The Sleeper-McCann House,* by Nancy Curtis and Richard C. Nylander, and *Eastern Point: A Nautical, Rustical, and Social Chronicle of Gloucester's Outer Shield and Inner Sanctum, 1606–1950,* by Joseph E. Garland, who interviewed people who knew Sleeper. Articles published during Sleeper's lifetime in such magazines as *Country Life, Antiques,* and *House Beautiful* are also useful. Published document collections are *Beauport Chronicle: The Letters of Henry Davis Sleeper to Abram Piatt Andrew, Jr., 1906–1915,* edited by E. Parker Hayden Jr. and Andrew L. Gray; A. Piatt Andrew, *Letters Written Home from France in the First Half of 1915;* and *History of the American Field Service in France,* in two volumes edited by Andrew and Sleeper, which includes introductions by the two men and first-person accounts by volunteers. The Historic New England website provides many photographs and a great deal of historical and biographical information.

# 8

## A Book by Its Cover

*The Edward Gorey House, Yarmouth Port*

MOST readers are curious about the authors of books they like. How did they write? What were they like? Who were their friends? What kind of childhood did they have? When writers are private or even elusive, it is tempting to look for the answers in their books. Edward Gorey wrote and illustrated dozens of books, illustrated other authors' books, and designed dust jackets and paperback covers for still more. His books have been described as eerie, macabre, disconcerting, ghoulish, unsettling, surreal, and gothic. He described them as "nonsense." His characters are sometimes the victims or perpetrators of dastardly crimes but more commonly the hapless victims of circumstance. Some of them—the tall, bearded ones with fur coats—look a great deal like their creator. But Edward Gorey was not eerie, disconcerting, ghoulish, or unsettling. He was eccentric but astonishingly sensible. He never committed a crime, and he managed to get through a long life without having heavy objects fall on his head or being mauled by a bear. His house, as well as the stories told by his neighbors and friends, bring us much closer to him than his books do. As he said, "What you publish and who you are are two different things."[1]

For Gorey, 8 Strawberry Lane in Yarmouth Port, on Cape Cod, became the house that perfectly accommodated his life. It was not a gothic castle, an Edwardian country house, or a haunted Victorian monstrosity but a very traditional (though much enlarged) Cape Cod cottage. As John Updike observed, "The odd miniature worlds of his books were ones he somehow wanted to inhabit; here is the world, equally personal and creative, that he did inhabit."[2] Driving by the town green in the summer of 1979, Gorey saw a For Sale sign on a two-hundred-year-old house that had seen better days. The scaling shingles brought to mind an elephant's hide, and he later named it Elephant House. He looked in through the dirty windows. Without checking on its structural soundness or the plumbing, wiring, and heating (there was none), he bought his first house. Over the years, he changed it to suit his needs and taste without altering its basic character. He lived there for the rest of his life.

## Childhood

In Gorey's books, childhood is fraught with peril. Even infants are not safe. When his friend Alison Lurie complained that she could not go to the movies because she had to tend to her "beastly baby," he wrote a book dedicated to the child called *The Beastly Baby*. In his imagination, the beastly baby is "bloated," "damp and sticky," making noises like "faulty drains" and "fingernails on blackboards." Rather than taking care of it, the parents scatter knives, acid, and other weapons around, try to abandon it on doorsteps, and finally take the time-honored step of exposing it on a rock, where an obliging eagle carries it off. Characters who survive infancy rarely make it through their first decade. They fall down stairs, waste away, die of ennui, or are "sucked dry by a leech." As Gorey explained, children "are the easiest targets."[3]

Gorey was an unusual child—far more bookish than most—apparently because of who he was more than how he was raised. He was an only child, and he recalled that he "loved reading nineteenth-century novels in which the families had twelve kids. I think it's just as well, though, that I didn't have any brothers or sisters. I saw in my own family that my mother and her two brothers and two sisters were always fighting." His parents divorced when he was eleven, though they remarried when he was an adult. His mother doted on him, and they "were far closer than I really wished most of the time." She photographed him every month until he was twelve and kept every drawing he made. And he made many: he began drawing when he was eighteen months old and never stopped. His mother kept his shoes and other keepsakes and every letter sent from his school. He attended five different grade schools in six years because his parents, for no apparent reason, often moved from one Chicago apartment to another.[4]

Gorey graduated from the eighth grade at eleven and then attended a progressive private day school. It allowed him more freedom than most, but even there his interests did not always match the curriculum. The head teacher wrote to his mother:

*Dear Mrs. Gorey:*

*Ted seems to be slipping a little. Last Friday Mr. Negronida reported that his Spanish was incomplete, and he has a disconcerting way of being absent from gym which Mr. Long does not like. Perhaps if you talked to Ted.*

*Dear Mrs. Gorey:*

*Do see that Ted does some work on his French during the holidays. He is again reported for inadequate daily preparation, and this is a fine time for him to turn over a new leaf . . . I might add that Ted has also been reported creating a disturbance in music.*

He had an excellent art teacher in high school and attended classes at the Art Institute of Chicago, but mostly he taught himself to draw. He claimed that the only thing he regretted about his early education was that he never learned how to make papier-mâché.[5]

When not drawing, he was reading. He taught himself to read when he was three and read whatever he chose: "I can remember reading *Dracula* when I was about seven, and it scared me to death, but I can't imagine what I was getting out of it. A lot of it must have been totally over my head . . . I still remember Victor Hugo being forcefully removed from my tiny hands when I was about eight, so I could eat my supper." He read *Alice's Adventures in Wonderland* when he was six or seven, and both Lewis Carroll's text and John Tenniel's illustrations made their way into his brain. He "loved *The Secret Garden* and the A. A. Milne books. One awful summer my parents sent me to camp, and I spent all my time on the porch reading the Rover Boys. I still reread them now and again. If I liked a book as a child, I assume I would still like it. Both my parents were mystery-story addicts, and I read thousands of them myself." He read widely and voraciously throughout his life.[6]

Gorey often wrote for children, though he had none of his own and knew very few. "I really don't know any children except my cousin's little boy, Kenny. He goes around imitating *Star Wars* all the time and it's very tiresome. He's everything I was not as a child." (To buy some respite from *Star Wars*, Gorey used to give Kenny five dollars to spend at the arcade in town.) Yet children love his books, even those that he clearly did not intend for them, such as *The Curious Sofa, a Pornographic Work*. "Some fan letters," he said, "come from children . . . People have come to me and said, 'My child just adores *The*

*Curious Sofa.*' At first this baffled me, but apparently they find it funny. For example, I purposely made personal names in *The Curious Sofa* practically indistinguishable one from the other. And there are gimmicks to flatten the prose, like the constant reiteration of the 'well-endowed young man.' A kind of poetry may come through to the child even though the phrase was put in as a parody on pornography where everybody is faceless, undifferentiated." Perhaps believing that what he loved to read as a child would still appeal to him as an adult led him to avoid making sharp distinctions between writing for children and writing for adults.[7]

## Growing Up

Gorey was admitted to Harvard after high school but was drafted into the army before he could attend. He served from 1944 to 1946 as a clerk at the Dugway Proving Ground in Utah, which had been established two years earlier as a place to develop and test chemical and biological weapons. His memories suggest that Gorey had little idea what was going on there: "It was a ghastly place, with the desert looming in every direction, so we kept ourselves sloshed on tequila, which wasn't rationed. The only thing the Army did for me was delay my going to college until I was twenty-one, and that I am grateful for." With his service complete, his Harvard acceptance in hand, and the GI Bill to pay his tuition, he set off for Cambridge.[8]

Harvard was Gorey's first opportunity to give his eccentricities room to blossom. He accentuated his height (more than six feet) and thinness by wearing a long canvas coat lined with sheepskin and adopted his signature rings and white sneakers. Those are hardly the clothes of an Edwardian dandy, but he realized that fellow students recognized him as "a campus aesthete." He and his roommates decorated their suite with "white modern garden furniture, including several chaise longues" and a coffee table made from a tombstone. What others perceived as a sort of *Brideshead Revisited* atmosphere, Gorey remembered carrying off "only in a tacky sort of way."[9]

What mattered most to Gorey at Harvard was not the classes but the creativity and friendships. He majored in French but told an interviewer that "Harvard had a perfectly god-awful French department at the period. And most of my survey courses used to come right after lunch, in which I would have a nice nap." He described his attitude toward courses as "frivolous." One of Gorey's roommates convinced him to take a course in symbolic logic, which seems to have made little impression. Driven by intellectual curiosity, Gorey and his friends sought experiences beyond Harvard's somewhat stodgy curriculum. He recalled that they "were exploring French surrealism, Japanese Kabuki and Noh, Hollywood's 'guilty pleasures,' and, above all, the perfumed, semi-satirical fictions of English novelists like Ronald Firbank, Evelyn Waugh, Ivy Compton-Burnett, C. Day-Lewis, and Henry Green"—all influences easily visible in Gorey's later work and life.[10]

In creative writing courses, Gorey quickly found his own voice. He said that he "wrote short stories and long poems in unrhymed tetrameter." One class required students to imitate various authors' writing. No matter whom he was supposed to imitate, "they all ended up sounding like me." Some of the writing courses were taught by the poet John Ciardi, whose children's books Gorey would later illustrate. The poet, playwright, and art critic Frank O'Hara was Gorey's roommate for two years. Ciardi described the two as "beautiful and

bright," with "unlimited prospects." Other friends included
the novelist Alison Lurie, the journalist George Plimpton,
and the poets Adrienne Rich, John Ashbery, and Robert Bly.[11]

In his senior year, Gorey joined some well-known writers and several of his friends in founding the Poets' Theatre,
which offered readings and performances by poets and play-
wrights. Richard Eberhart and Richard Wilbur, both future
poet laureates, took part, as did Thornton Wilder and William Carlos Williams. The first play the theater produced
was Frank O'Hara's *Try, Try,* and Gorey's illustration for
the poster became the theater's logo. Gorey also designed
sets and tried his hand at writing and directing. He said he
enjoyed "the variety of people who were involved—faculty,
faculty children, graduates, undergraduates, and strange
people." Alison Lurie described Gorey as "one of the sanest
and calmest people" in the group.[12]

The theater and part-time work at a bookstore kept Gorey
in Boston until the end of 1952, but he was beginning to
feel the need to earn a living. Another friend from college,
Barbara Zimmerman, introduced him to Jason Epstein (her
future husband), who was starting up Anchor Books, the
trade paperback division of Doubleday. Gorey got a job in
the art department and was soon designing covers and writing his own books in his spare time. A photograph taken at
that time shows a clean-shaven young man in a white shirt
and seersucker suit wearing only one ring, on his right pinky.
But he soon grew his beard and began wearing jeans to the
office, and he decorated his workspace with skeletons, puppets, and small sculptures. Ten years later, finding himself
unemployed after a shakeup at Bobbs-Merrill, where he then
worked, he realized that he had enough freelance design
assignments that he could control his own time and use his
talent and imagination more freely.[13]

## Dividing His Time

When he began working at Doubleday, Gorey had moved into a second-floor studio apartment on East 38th Street in Manhattan, where he lived for thirty years. Once he began freelancing, though, he spent more than half the year in Barnstable, Massachusetts, in a house shared with an aunt, uncle, and cousins. In both places, his workspace was small and as free of distraction as possible. Otherwise, his life was very different in each home.

In New York, a house cleaner took care of his laundry and other domestic chores. Despite the small space, she had her work cut out for her. A visitor described the apartment: "All books, lined with them, crazy stacks of them rising from the floor. A drawing board. A bed. Two ancient Noguchi lanterns . . . Pictures revealing evil, enchanting monsters, a Francis Bacon postcard—and small, fascinating, rust-encrusted metal objects—scissors, old keys—cover the few unbooked vertical spaces. Dusty. Dim. Even the fireplace is stopped up with books. The kind of place in which only a fool would not feel comfortable. Home." And at least three cats. Also a mummy. He generally ate out, because the apartment was small and poorly ventilated, so that cooking smells lingered. Probably cat smells did too.[14]

Gorey spent a great deal of time at the New York City Ballet and became devoted to the work of George Balanchine: by 1958, he was attending every performance. He also took full advantage of the city's many cinemas and film festivals to indulge his love of movies. He recalled: "There was a period in New York when I would see a thousand movies a year . . . I would sit through anything." He sought out art films and foreign films—especially Japanese—but he also watched the latest Hollywood extravaganzas. He especially loved silent films: "I really do think movies made a terrible mistake when they started to talk, for the most part . . . The greatest single talent the movies ever produced was Charlie Chaplin. Not my favorite—my idol is Buster Keaton . . . [With silent films] our imagination is engaged, whereas movies today get more in your face by the moment."[15]

In Barnstable, Gorey's life was far more domestic. He lived in what one interviewer saw as "a quite ordinary-looking house, with painted floors, hooked rugs, summery furniture, a television set, piles of books, three resident cats, and New York City Ballet bath towels (after a design by Gorey)." Another saw "a writer's dream of an abode; rooms upon rooms decorated with Gorey's beanbag toys, antiques, and old bargain-basement chairs and couches. It is comfortable and cozy. The attic where he summers is filled with books piled from floor to ceiling. A draft blows in through the windows, making it quite cold in winter, but very pleasant in summer. In the tiny back room is a small, narrow bed where Gorey sleeps, accompanied at any given moment by at least three of his cats." His private space—bedroom and studio— was on the third floor, but he did all the cooking for the family, so the kitchen was another focus of his life there. He told an interviewer: "I have no social life down here at all, except in the summer, when all my relatives are here, and I do the cooking. I can cook almost anything, however complicated, so long as it doesn't have to look pretty when it's over with."[16]

His letters written in Barnstable are full of the tedium and futility of domesticity: "tomorrow I have to clean the house . . . rushed about today trying to make the house look presentable"; "both the washing machine and the dryer are making their curious noises, and will ultimately have to be emptied. Folding up sheets by oneself is extremely awkward and tedious. The dishwasher has been emptied after several

FIGURE 24. Edward Gorey and friend in Barnstable, 1964. *Courtesy of the photographer, Eleanor Garvey.*

days, but on the other hand it will sooner or later have to be activated with the results of those several days. What life would be like without these aids to domesticity I do not like to think, considering my general incompetence in the realm

of life, except for working." "I spent the morning cleaning
kitchen cupboards and so forth, and so on, and now there
are more ants than ever. Very mysterious. I have put ant cups
about in places where the cats can't get to them, though pre-
sumably the ants can. I am really more and more tolerant to
all insect life, as life goes on, but I think I'd better get the
ants out of here before I leave, and keep my fingers crossed
that they will stay away until the rest of the family gets here,
probably in June. They panic easily, even at a ladybug for
instance."[17]

Without Manhattan's theaters, he spent hours watching
television, and not just *Masterpiece Theater*. He admitted to
being "passionately devoted to reruns" and had watched all
of *Golden Girls* several times. *Buffy the Vampire Slayer*, *The
X-Files*, *Third Rock from the Sun*, *Frasier*, the *Mary Tyler Moore
Show*, and soap operas were among his favorites. Much of his
reading was highbrow; his television watching was not. He
had an extensive collection of classical music, with baroque
composers and the operas of Handel, Haydn, and Mozart at
the top of his list.[18]

In both homes, his work was central. It had to be. No
matter how talented, a freelance artist has little security. Even
after he had achieved a fair amount of success, he said he felt
financially tenuous: "I'm a little reluctant to take out a mortgage. Being free-lance, you never know." He took on nearly
every project he was offered, either because he did not like to
disappoint people or because he feared running out of paid
work. Gorey was not extravagant, but he did spend money
on ballet tickets, restaurant meals, and—above all—books.
When he received a check from *Playboy*, he rejoiced that he
could buy "one beautiful book on American tombstones and
two beautiful books on Japanese Art that I have been covet-
ing. Also pay my rent, eat, and so forth." Note that the books

came first. Gorey read constantly, usually finishing a book or two a day. In each of his books, he noted when he began reading it, when he finished it, and whether he reread it.[19]

Gorey always had more ideas than he could carry out, and—like many creative people—he found thinking and planning less taxing than writing and drawing. He told one visitor: "That cardboard box over there—that's full of scribblings of this, that, and the other thing that I'll never get around to doing. I keep having ideas, and I say to myself, 'You'd better get it done, kiddo. Work, for the night is coming.'" Although he claimed to be easily distracted and reluctant to sit down to work, he was astoundingly productive. By the end of his life, he had published more than a hundred books, illustrated many others, written or designed plays for actors and puppets, and designed countless book jackets and covers.[20]

None of his work was done quickly. Even at Doubleday, when he was designing paperback covers for other people's books, Barbara Zimmerman Epstein remembered that "he worked very slowly, with a tremendous perfectionism, and he would never let a drawing out of his hands if it was less than perfect." His work—done with pens dipped in ink—shows the attention to detail and time-consuming technique behind the complex images. His books were invariably hand lettered. He was a perfectionist who once sat in the Gotham Book Mart, with brush and watercolors, to get the right shade of lavender on the covers of 1,100 copies of *The Lavender Leotard*. True, the books are short and the drawings small, but it is nevertheless a remarkable body of work. Even when he was watching television, he kept his hands occupied with knitting, needlework, or stuffing Uncle Ben's rice into Figbash dolls (lizardlike creatures from his book *The Raging Tide*).[21]

Gorey's income was enhanced through the efforts of Andreas Brown, who owned the Gotham Book Mart in

New York. Gorey said that Brown had created a "cottage industry." He exhibited Gorey's work in the Gotham Gallery and sold the images on T-shirts and greeting cards. He also saw the market for anthologies of the small books that were out of print: the various *Amphigorey* volumes. The turning point in Gorey's finances came with the 1978 Broadway production of *Dracula*, starring Frank Langella, a project that Gorey said he would never have taken on "if they hadn't offered lots of money." He would have preferred designing a Gilbert and Sullivan operetta. The production also brought fame—articles in *US* and *People*, among other things. "I was beginning to be recognized a lot more. I was also making a lot more money." Gorey won a Tony Award for the costumes and a nomination for the set design. His royalties from the play and the broader popularity of his work gave him enough money to buy the house on Strawberry Lane.[22]

### "At Any Given Moment, the Floor May Open Up"

In 1979, Gorey told an interviewer that "life is intrinsically boring and dangerous at the same time. At any given moment, the floor may open up." He may have had a premonition about the house he would soon buy. Although the floors of Gorey's new house were quite sturdy, everything else needed attention. The oldest part—facing the street—was built in 1820 for Captain Edmund Hawes. It looked out on what was then a swamp and clay pit, later drained and filled to become the town green. Captain Hawes was lost at sea, and in 1830 the house was sold to Nathaniel Stone Simpkins, whose wife, Eliza Jane, belonged to the family that owned most of the surrounding land. The couple had six children, and Eliza died in 1836, soon after the youngest child, George, was born. Nathaniel enlarged the house and planted trees and shrubs. He was a Boston businessman, but he invested in Barnstable businesses as well, including a bookstore and newspaper, a wharf, and a business managing fishing boats. He was active in local politics and churches, a director of a local bank and the Cape Cod Railroad, and three times a member of the Massachusetts House of Representatives. When Nathaniel died in 1887, George became the owner of the house.[23]

George, though, was living in St. Louis, where he was treasurer and vice president of the Hydraulic Press Brick Company. His wife, Mary Louise Michael, was a St. Louis native and a founding member of the Missouri Woman Suffrage Association.[24] The house on Strawberry Lane became their summer home. With seven children, they needed a lot of space, and they added a section to the back of the house, creating a large kitchen, a new drive and porte cochere, and more rooms on the second and third floors. When they were finished, the house had seven bedrooms and three baths on the second floor, with third-floor rooms for servants. And they did have servants. The Simpkins family traveled from St. Louis to Cape Cod in style, often in a private railway car. They brought their cook, a coachman, and "sewing girls" from an orphanage.

George died in 1901, and Mary Louise followed eight years later. For many years the three Simpkins daughters—Louise (b. 1872), Olive (b. 1879), and Ethel (b. 1882)—continued to live on Strawberry Lane in the summers. Ethel married William Griffith McRee Jr. in 1909, and the couple wanted their own summer house, so they built one very similar to 8 Strawberry Lane behind the original. They later became year-round residents. Louise and Olive never married, and with money inherited from their father and an uncle in Colorado, they were able to maintain both the Yarmouth Port house and an apartment in a St. Louis hotel. Their comings and goings were duly noted in the society columns of the *Boston Sunday Post*.[25] Louise and Olive built a garage to the right of the barn for the car that Olive drove around the Cape and beyond. On an excursion to Virginia, they visited Mount Vernon and bought the southern magnolia tree, now enormous, that flourishes on the south side of the house.

After Louise died, in 1952, Olive spent her summers at the Colonial House Inn, and when she died ten years later, Ethel inherited the house. Except for occasional tea parties in the front parlor, Ethel didn't use it. The only occupants were a family of raccoons whose descendants remained in residence for a while after Gorey moved in. Her heirs put the house on the market when she died in 1976, and three years later Edward Gorey drove by. The house had been empty of human occupants for more than two decades. It was forlorn, overgrown, and obviously in need of rescue. Gorey fell in love, and the damsel in distress was soon his.

It took Gorey seven years to make the house habitable, largely because he kept running out of money. He began by removing walls to enlarge some of the rooms and making other internal changes. Then the contractor told him he needed a new roof, which he could not afford. At some point he installed central heating and had the original wide-plank floors refinished. In 1983—after losing the lease on his Manhattan apartment—Gorey moved in. There was still a great deal of work to do. The contractor told him that all the windows should be replaced. His neighbor Rick Jones, who had a great deal of experience with old houses, advised him that it would be better to restore the original windows. In the end, it was Jones who removed the windows one at a time, scraped off the old paint, primed and painted them, reglazed the panes, replaced the cords, and rehung them. It took him a year and a half, and during that time he was at the house every day. Work ended in the afternoon, when he joined Gorey and the cats for tea. Jones also fell victim to Gorey's Tom Sawyer approach in the garden. Gorey fell in love with black pansies and bought thirty flats, pots, and potting soil. He asked Jones to show him how to pot them. Rick demonstrated with one plant, and Gorey paid close attention. He asked him to show him again, which he did. Looking up from the second pot, Rick noticed that Gorey was nowhere to be seen. He had gone back into the house, leaving his friend to complete the job.[26]

The kitchen and bathrooms needed to be modernized. Gorey recognized the shape of an elephant in one of the toilets that was removed, so that became the base of a table. The new stove and kitchen cabinets, finished with white ceramic tile, were raised several inches to make cooking more comfortable for someone of Gorey's height. It also brought his beard closer to the gas flames, resulting in an occasional garnish of singed whiskers. This was the room where Gorey entertained visitors, who were rarely invited further into the house.

Gorey had shelves built in most of the rooms to house books and to display items he collected. His favorite finds were exhibited at his eye level. He removed closets, which he disliked, and stored clothing (and many other items) in old blanket chests. His large collection of jewelry was hung from wooden racks attached to the walls. No horizontal surface in the house—mantels, windowsills, door frames—was left empty.

The rooms in Gorey's books almost always have ornate wallpaper, patterned rugs, and heavily grained wood paneling. Sometimes paintings add to the clutter on the walls.

His fictional rooms are sparsely furnished, and the few pieces shown are carved, upholstered, fringed, and otherwise bedecked. Windows are at least partially covered with layers of draperies. There are few books or ornaments. Gorey decorated his real house with the opposite aesthetic. The walls were plain, except in the living room, where removing the wallpaper uncovered stencils dating back to the house's earliest days. The floors were bare. The furniture was antique, with simple lines. Most pieces were not upholstered, and those that were had been thoroughly shredded by the cats. The windows had no curtains or drapes, making the house light and airy.

The most striking difference was the overwhelming presence of books and *things*—there is really no more precise noun that covers them all. Books filled the shelves, piled up on tables, and towered to precarious heights in nearly every room, sometimes loose and sometimes in boxes. An organizing principle underlay their arrangement, but it was fallible. Soon after Gorey had ordered a book about Turgenev, he told an interviewer, "I looked down on the floor and there was another copy of it, and then a week ago I looked somewhere else and there was another copy, and I thought 'Do I really need three?'" The larger question was, Do I really need twenty-five thousand? Navigating the house was treacherous: "the paths between my drawing board and the bed tend to vary from week to week." The overflow went to the barn. His music collection—spanning technologies from LPs to CDs—was also housed in towering stacks, along with videotapes and DVDs. The visual line from the sofa to the television screen was clear, however.[27]

And the things. Antique shops were the source of much of his furniture and the more recognizable objects, but his scavenging ranged far afield. The barn now houses art bought at yard sales, the source of many other collections. He also hunted for appealing natural objects, including rocks whose shape or color interested him. These were displayed on the porch and front steps, as well as the kitchen counter and windowsills. Some of them—especially the round ones—joined other spherical artifacts (mostly balls of various kinds) and hemispherical containers (bowls, wooden and ceramic, nested and not) in the "ball room." Like the books, the rocks were organized in some way that was known only to Gorey and proved fallible. He told an interviewer: "I had a terrible trauma this week: I didn't know what had become of my favorite rock. And I thought, Oh my God, I can't live. Fortunately, it was found."[28]

Collections of other household objects, including an extensive array of graters, decorated many rooms. A tray with about fifty salt and pepper shakers sat on a table in the ball room, while sugar bowls were lined up beneath the windows. (The ball room also housed Gorey's exercise bicycle, complete with reading stand, which he acquired and used under doctor's orders.) The porch was decorated with a treadle sewing machine base and a collection of flatirons. The living room housed collections of wooden objects—darning eggs, pestles, rolling pins, finials, and churn paddles—as well as eggs of marble and other stones. The television room had a dozen mysterious metal objects with two round holes on either side of a triangular hole. These, with a little imagination, look like flattened skulls. A metal bowl held a half-dozen lead sinkers used in fishing. The light from many of the windows filtered through a variety of glass objects—sun catchers, blue bottles, purple bull's-eye windows, prisms, stained glass, sea glass, paperweights, prescription vials, and small decorative pieces.

Animal images abound. Frogs (metal and ceramic) inhabited the porch and TV room; one even sat on Gorey's drawing table. There were rabbits on the porch and in the living room and alcove. Elephants were everywhere—not just the toilet/table in the entrance room but also a piece of driftwood in the kitchen and other versions in the alcove and the relatively uncluttered bedroom. Elsewhere in the house you could find hippos, birds, and a mouse (reading a book). The images of cats may have been outnumbered by the real cats, unless you count stuffed animals. The TV room housed countless small stuffed animals; the alcove was home to the most ancient of those, and the bedroom had a chair full. Human animals were also present: several primitive wooden figures and skeletons lived in the ball room, the living room displayed representations of human heads, and the kitchen windowsill had a small figure that may well have been a beastly baby.

Visitors to the house sometimes felt that Gorey was fighting a losing battle against disorder and dilapidation.[29] Although he may have wished that a few more repairs had been done, he had made the house into the home he wanted. In his kitchen he could cook and chat with visitors without admitting them to the spaces he wished to keep private. Every room accommodated comfortable reading, and the television room provided endless video and audio entertainment. His beloved objects were visible in spaces that he felt suited them. His books were within reach whenever he wanted them. His studio was of the size and in the space that worked best for him. His cats were comfortable. It was the home of a man who could do what he liked, when and where he wanted to do it.

## "I Know What I'm Doing"

Gorey's wardrobe was, he said, "genuinely eccentric." Both those words are important. Certainly fur coats with sneakers and many, many rings is a nontraditional look, but it was not an affectation. He was quite clear that "I wouldn't do it if it wasn't the way I wanted to dress." That authenticity extended beyond his wardrobe to his work and life. He told an interviewer that "part of me is genuinely eccentric, part of me is a bit of a put-on. But I know what I'm doing. I don't think I do anything I don't want to do."[30] Gorey was a very private person, but rather than disguise his thoughts and feelings, he simply withheld them from others. His responses to interview questions were sometimes evasive or nonresponsive, but they were never dishonest.

His house helped to protect his privacy by letting him choose how far to admit visitors. When friends were coming to the house to go off somewhere with him, he often met them on the porch or on the green rather than asking them in. He socialized at Jack's Outback, a nearby restaurant where he ate many of his meals, and he sometimes conducted interviews there. Friends were invited to tea in the kitchen, and he occasionally invited people to dinner, but only a very few intimate friends entered other rooms. One space, now known as the "hidden room," was accessible only through a door at the back of the bedroom closet.[31]

Gorey wrote and drew as he wanted to. Whatever the sources of his style and inspiration, they were of his choosing. He received direction from others only when designing book covers or illustrating someone else's work, and even then the influence was minimal. His version of collaboration was different from that of most artists: he would work on the same project that others were working on, but he worked independently. John Wulp, who produced *Dracula*, said that "collaborating with Edward is not collaboration . . . He meets once with the director, evolves a ground plan for the entrances and exits, and then goes home and does his designs." The curator of an exhibit of Gorey's work understood his independence: "He has a very distinct style, aesthetic, and set of values and the extent to which he's made to compromise those, I think, dilutes the strength of his work. Edward is rather like chamber music. You can't turn him into a symphony."[32]

Especially in the early years, Gorey often had a hard time finding a publisher. His books were odd in content and format, and publishers are leery of taking risks on the unconventional. Rather than let any of his books languish, he published them himself through the Fantod Press. But he was keenly aware of the economics of authorship, and he knew that his art was the source of his income. His work may have puzzled many readers, but he was not deliberately obscure: "I've been receiving letters from people who have known my work for a long time. 'Oh Mr. Gorey, do keep yourself recherché.' And I think, 'That's all very well for you to talk.'"[33]

Some of the hallmarks of his art were both artistic and practical choices. Working only in black and white was an aesthetic decision, reinforced by his New York experience: he knew that it was much more difficult to get a publisher to take on a book that required expensive color printing. He developed his limited color palette when he was designing book covers. He learned at Doubleday that "you had to keep to three flat colors, plus black. I guess I could have picked bright reds or blues, but I've never been much for that. My palette seems to be sort of lavender, lemon-yellow, olive-green, and then a whole series of absolutely no colors at all." He hand-lettered his covers and books at first because he knew nothing about type—and then because everyone liked it. Underlying the apparent eccentricity of his work was a firm foundation in the physical demands of bookmaking. He said he was "very conscious of what constituted a book . . . I naturally think in terms of how many pages there will be, how the pages turn, and so forth."[34]

An author whose books sell in small numbers has to be very productive, but Gorey made no stylistic concessions to that pressure. The omnipresent cross-hatching and ornate wallpaper in his drawings were not efficient, but they were essential. As he said, "Nonsense really demands precision." Rather than compromise, he learned over time to draw very quickly. He found the tools—pen nibs, ink, and paper—that worked best and stuck with them. He simply became very, very good at what he did. "I'm intricate, but there are other people, I think, who spend a lot more time at their drawings than I do."[35]

It is certainly easier to work hard if you love what you are doing. Gorey did not dislike illustrating other people's books, but that was always second best. The financial success he enjoyed after *Dracula* allowed him to focus on his own work and to experiment with theater. "Just think—how marvelous to work only on my own projects. Well, now basically that's all I do." John Updike wrote that Gorey's "life was virtually all hobby."[36]

What was true of his work was also true of his life. What he didn't like—travel, large parties, formal occasions, intimacy—he didn't do. People would ask him, "Why don't you travel? Why don't you get a master's degree in . . . something? Why don't you try doing this, that, or the other? Well, you're probably not doing it because it's not right. Why worry about it?"[37]

He told a friend that he found it "not difficult, but impossible" to express his feelings directly, but the lack of intimacy did not mean that he was lonely. Despite his misgivings about children, he was close to his cousins in Barnstable. He had an active social life, attending dinner parties, playing cribbage, and enjoying the company of friends. One neighbor was embarrassed when she met him because she had not realized that he had designed the set and costumes for *Dracula*. She had seen the play, but all she remembered was Frank Langella, one of Broadway's sexiest vampires. But they became friends: he loved her brownies, and she loved hearing his "laugh that would rattle windows."[38]

The people he knew in Yarmouth Port—his neighbors, the folks at Jack's Outback, the actors and others who participated in local theater and his puppet shows—were fond of him and provided as much company as he wanted. In perhaps the ultimate test of his likability, the couple who cleaned his house adored him. Interviewers may not have been told everything they wanted to know, but they were treated with courtesy and good humor. He was always gracious to fans who visited and often invited them in for coffee. Given his imposing appearance, people were happily surprised to find him friendly and kind. Gorey may have avoided intimacy beyond friendship in part because he preferred not to be responsible for anyone else or compromise to accommodate others. He knew he was "very fortunate . . . I have done pretty much what I wanted to do . . . But only because I didn't really see any way of doing anything else."[39]

## From House to Museum

After Edward Gorey's death in 2000, the Highland Street Foundation bought the house on Strawberry Lane, which through the efforts of many people became a museum. Rick Jones, Gorey's close friend, is the director. The museum brings together the house, its owner, and his work in numerous creative ways that Gorey would have enjoyed.

The house is much tidier than it was in Gorey's lifetime. The most noticeable change is that the stacks of books are gone—housed at the library at San Diego State University. The cats, too, are gone, though they continued to live in the house for a month after Gorey's death. Ralph Menconi, a neighbor, adopted the cat that he had been sharing unknowingly with Gorey: neither of them knew that the other was feeding him. Rick Jones found homes for the others.[40] The museum honors both Gorey and the cats by promoting animal welfare, the cause to which the Edward Gorey Charitable Trust is dedicated.

The house still contains a television set, but it plays a video of the introduction that Gorey designed for *Mystery!* rather than *Golden Girls*. The kitchen is as he left it, and the shelves that he built continue to house his collections, though they are now protected by glass. The spaces that used to be full of boxes and books now house display cases that feature changing exhibits, including book covers, books Gorey illustrated for other authors, Fantod Press books, childhood memorabilia, and the drawings he made on envelopes. The museum has kept the tradition of "envelope art" alive by sponsoring an annual contest for artists of all ages. Other events include a summer festival, readings, story times, and parties. The Gashlycrumb Tinies meet their doom in a scavenger hunt: visitors search for the tiny bodies appropriately crushed, mauled, or otherwise done in throughout the house. (Their little tombstones decorate the garden.) Gorey's commercial side is present in the gift shop.

The museum honors Gorey's work and life, but it is more whimsical and less worshipful than most homes of famous authors that are open to the public. The changing exhibits illustrate and continue Gorey's creativity. The director and some of the docents knew Gorey personally, and they speak of him as a friend. (One of the docents is his cousin, Skee Morton.) They have created a museum that captures the genius, the whimsy, and the good nature of its owner along with his eccentricities. The house, the exhibits, and the staff tell visitors about Gorey's life and work without invading his privacy. As he would have wished.

## To Visit

The Edward Gorey House (www.edwardgoreyhouse.org) is open from April 15 to December 31; hours vary with the seasons. Check the website for details. The house is accessible.

Two other historic houses are nearby. The Captain Bangs Hallet House, the home of an early nineteenth-century sea captain, is right across the green. It is open in the afternoon, Friday–Sunday, from June to October 9. It is operated by the Historical Society of Old Yarmouth (www.hsoy.org). The Winslow Crocker House, ca. 1780, was moved to 250 Main Street in 1936. It has been altered considerably but displays a large collection of antique furniture and furnishings. Operated by Historic New England (www.historicnewengland.org), it is open on the second and fourth Saturdays of each month from June through September.

Other artists' houses and museums in Massachusetts include the Frelinghuysen-Morris House and Studio in Lenox, built in 1930 and 1941 by American abstract artists L. K. Morris and Suzy Frelinghuysen (www.Frelinghuysen.org); Chesterwood, the Stockbridge summer home of sculptor Daniel Chester French, built in 1820 (www.chesterwood.org); and the Whistler House Museum of Art in Lowell, the home of painter James McNeill Whistler.

## To Learn More

Karen Wilkin's edited collection of interviews, *Ascending Peculiarity: Edward Gorey on Edward Gorey*, brings together twenty-one interviews conducted between 1973 and 1999. The interviewers posed many of the questions that most of us would like to have asked, and the answers are very useful. Kevin McDermott's *Elephant House or, The Home of Edward Gorey* is a superb collection of photographs of the house taken immediately after Gorey's death. It documents the house very well and is a beautiful book. In *Floating Worlds: The Letters of Edward Gorey and Peter F. Neumeyer*, Peter Neumeyer offers a selection of his correspondence with Gorey in the late 1960s, when they were collaborating on three children's books. Some of the letters are very personal and reveal Gorey's emotional state far better than the interviews. The first full biography of Gorey was just published: Mark Dery, *Born to Be Posthumous: The Eccentric Life and Mysterious Genius of Edward Gorey* (Boston: Little, Brown, 2018).

Gorey's own work, of course, is essential. His early books long ago became collector's items, but some of them are being reprinted, beautifully, by Pomegranate.

Gorey's books are at the San Diego State University Library. The Harry Ransom Center at the University of Texas, Austin, has books, manuscripts, illustrations, and correspondence, mostly from Gorey's years at Harvard, as well as material related to *Dracula*.

# NOTES

## 1. Over the River and through the Woods

1. The children were baptized as follows: John, 1617/18; George, 1619; Mary, 1621/22; Susan (baptismal date unknown); Jonas, 1624/25; and Jonathan, 1628/29; see *Ye Fayerbanke Historial* 1, no. 1 (November 1903): 12. Lorenzo Sayles Fairbanks, *Genealogy of the Fairbanks Family in America, 1633–1897* (Boston: Printed for the author, 1897), 10–12, 23; Abbott Lowell Cummings, *The Fairbanks House: A History of the Oldest Timber-Frame Building in New England*, 2d ed. (Boston: Fairbanks Family in America and New England Historic Genealogical Society, 2002), 14; visit to Fairbanks House, conversation with curator Daniel Neff, July 8, 2016. The house was built according to a standard plan imported from England, probably by a housewright who had come to Dedham from Suffolk; see Keith N. Morgan, ed., *Buildings of Massachusetts: Metropolitan Boston* (Charlottesville: University of Virginia Press, 2009), 8, 537.
2. L. S. Fairbanks, *Genealogy*, 12, 23–25; the quotation about Jonathan comes from the Records of the First Church of Dedham, Dedham, Mass.
3. Cummings, *Fairbanks House*, 14–18. John will feature in a story in the companion volume to this book, for the western part of the state: In 1663, the town of Dedham sent him to examine land it had been offered in Pocumtuck, which it accepted and settled as Deerfield; "Biographical Memoir of the Rev. John Williams," appended to John Williams, *The Redeemed Captive Returning to Zion* (Northampton, Mass.: Hopkins, Bridgman, 1853), 97.
4. L. S. Fairbanks, *Genealogy*, 17, 35–40.
5. L. S. Fairbanks, *Genealogy*, 17, 35–40, 84–87; Cummings, *Fairbanks House*, 19–21.
6. Cummings, *Fairbanks House*, 8–9, 23–30, 37, 64, 73.

7. L. S. Fairbanks, *Genealogy*, 87, 157; Ebenezer Fairbanks Jr., *The Solemn Declaration of the Late Unfortunate Jason Fairbanks, . . . to Which Is Added Some Account of the Life and Character of Jason Fairbanks* (Dedham, Mass.: Minerva Press, 1801), 13, reprinted in *A Massachusetts Mystery: The 1801 Tragedy of Jason Fairbanks and Elizabeth Fales* (Carlisle, Mass.: Applewood Books, [2009]).

8. E. Fairbanks, *Solemn Declaration*, 14–17. The mercury probably caused nerve damage and atrophy of muscles.

9. E. Fairbanks, *Solemn Declaration*, 3–6.

10. E. Fairbanks, *Solemn Declaration*, 7–8.

11. *Report of the Trial of Jason Fairbanks on an Indictment for the Murder of Miss Elizabeth Fales*, 4th ed. (Boston: Russell and Cutler, 1801), 6–7, reprinted in *A Massachusetts Mystery*.

12. *Report of the Trial*, 12–13; Dale H. Freeman, "'Melancholy Catastrophe!': The Story of Jason Fairbanks and Elizabeth Fales in Public and Private Writings," www.fairbankshouse.org, 5; Nathaniel Ames, Diary, quoted in Freeman, "'Melancholy Catastrophe!,'" 6.

13. *Report*, 28; *Boston Gazette*, August 13, 1801, in Freeman, "'Melancholy Catastrophe!,'" 7; Daniel A. Cohen, "Martha Buck's Copybook: New England Tragedy Verse and the Scribal Lineage of the American Ballad Tradition," *Proceedings of the American Antiquarian Society* 114, pt. 1 (2004): 159; *Luzerne County Federalist* (Wilkes Barre, Pa.), August 31, 1801; *Sciotto Gazette* (Chillicothe, Ohio), August 10, 1801.

14. The defense arguments appear on pp. 37–65, and the prosecution's, on 65–80; *Report*.

15. *Report*, 43, 45.

16. *Report*, 67, 69.

17. *Report*, 83; Daniel A. Cohen, *Pillars of Salt, Monuments of Grace: New England Crime Literature and the Origins of American Popular Culture, 1674–1860* (Amherst: University of Massachusetts Press, 2006), 194; John Lowell biographical sketch, Guide to the Lowell Family Papers, Massachusetts Historical Society, Boston, Mass.

18. Freeman, "'Melancholy Catastrophe!,'" 15.

19. Freeman, "'Melancholy Catastrophe!,'" 20–23; *Connecticut Courant* (Hartford), September 7, 1801, quoted in Freeman, "'Melancholy Catastrophe!,'" 22.

20. *Columbian Centinel*, September 12, 1801, quoted in Freeman, "'Melancholy Catastrophe!,'" 26.

21. E. Fairbanks, *Solemn Declaration*, 8–9. There is some doubt that Jason was the author, or at least the sole author, of this letter.

22. Thomas Thacher, *The Danger of Despising the Divine Counsel: Exhibited in a Discourse, Delivered at Dedham, Third Precinct, September 13, 1801* (Dedham, Mass.: Herman Mann, 1802), 17–18, reprinted in *A Massachusetts Mystery*.

23. Thacher, *Danger*, 20; italics in original.

24. Thacher, *Danger*, 22.

25. Thacher, *Danger*, 23–24.

26. L. S. Fairbanks, *Genealogy*, 157.

27. Freeman, "'Melancholy Catastrophe!,'" 34–35; L. S. Fairbanks, *Genealogy*, 157.

28. Alvin Lincoln Jones, *Under Colonial Roofs* (Boston: C. B. Webster, 1894), 183, 187; visit, July 8, 2016.

29. Jones, *Under Colonial Roofs*, 189; "A Boston Newspaper, 1885," quoted in L. S. Fairbanks, *Genealogy*, 873. Mrs. George Young, their great niece, said that each sister took charge of the housekeeping every third day ("The Story of My Great Aunts," *Homestead Courier*, July 1977).

30. In L. S. Fairbanks, *Genealogy*, 873; visit to Fairbanks House, September 16, 2016. The scroll is in the Fairbanks archives. The poem, by Oliver Goldsmith, was included in his *Vicar of Wakefield* (1766).

31. Young, "Story of My Great Aunts."

32. L. S. Fairbanks, *Genealogy*, 869–70; Young, "Story of My Great Aunts."

33. *Dedham Transcript*, April 1, 1871; L. S. Fairbanks, *Genealogy*, 300–301; visit to Fairbanks House, August 13, 2016.

34. Frank Tripp, "Rebecca Sells Guns," *Ellensburg (Washington) Daily Record*, January 20, 1949. Tripp was a Fairbanks descendant.

35. Jonathan L. Fairbanks, "Thoughts on the Eve of the Homecoming of a Carved Oak and Pine Chest, Original to the Old Fairbanks Homestead," *Homestead Courier*, Reunion 2003.

36. *Boston Daily Globe*, July 15, 1892; Cummings, *Fairbanks House*, 40.

37. Cummings, *Fairbanks House*, 40–41; *Boston Sunday Globe*, November 1, 1896, April 17, 1898.

38. *Boston Evening Transcript*, April 3, 1897.

39. *Boston Evening Transcript*, April 8, 1897; *Boston Sunday Globe*, April 18, 1897.

40. Jones, *Under Colonial Roofs*, 183; John Wilder Fairbanks, "Family Secretary Explains the Alleged Eviction," *Boston Sunday Post*, November 13, 1904.

41. *Boston Daily Globe*, August 28, 1902; Cummings, *Fairbanks House*, 41; J. W. Fairbanks, "Family Secretary Explains."

42. *Boston Sunday Post*, November 13, 1904.

43. *Boston Sunday Post*, November 13, 1904; *Boston Evening Transcript*, June 1, 1909; *Boston Daily Globe*, March 30, 1911.

44. Wallace Nutting, *Massachusetts Beautiful* (Garden City, N.Y.: Garden City Publishing, 1935), 49, 53; James Michael Lindgren, *Preserving Historic New England: Preservation, Progressives, and the Remaking of Memory* (New York: Oxford University Press, 1995), 107.

45. Lindgren, *Preserving*, 108; Cummings, *Fairbanks House*, 42–43.

46. Jessica Neuwirth, Robert Paynter, Kevin Sweeney, Braden Paynter, and Abbott Lowell Cummings, "Abbott Lowell Cummings and the Preservation of New England," *Public Historian* 29, no. 4 (Fall 2007): 67; Max Page and Randall Mason, *Giving Preservation a History: Histories of Historic Preservation in the United States* (Sussex, Eng.: Psychology Press, 2004), 67. For more on Appleton and SPNEA, see chapter 3, "Decline and Rise."

47. Cummings, *Fairbanks House*, 43; *Boston Globe*, August 19, 20, 1964, July 5, 1967; *Homestead Courier*, 1965, 1968, October 1973, March 1980, April 1982.

48. Richard Longstreth, "Architectural History and the Practice of Historic Preservation in the United States," *Journal of the Society of Architectural Historians* 58, no. 3 (September 1999): 326; www.nps.gov/nhl/; *Boston Globe*, November 22, 1972; *Homestead Courier*, 1972, June 1973, April, September 1974; Cummings, *Fairbanks House*, 45–49.

49. *Homestead Courier*, Spring 2007.

50. *Homestead Courier*, Spring, Fall 2009, Spring 2010, Winter/Spring 2013.

51. *Ye Fayerbanke Historial* 1, no. 3 (November 1904): 18; *Boston Sunday Post*, July 23, 1905, August 17, 1913; *Boston Post*, December 21, 1906, August 3, 1907.

52. *Ye Fayerbanke Historial* 1, no. 1 (November 1903): 35, 43.

## 2. First Families

1. Kirsten Holder, James Bertolini, and Jaime R. Young, *Cultural Landscape Report for Adams Birthplaces, Adams National Historical Park, Quincy, Massachusetts* (Boston: Olmsted Center, National Park Service, 2014), 18–19, 26.

2. John Adams diary, 1758, and John Adams to John Wadsworth, October–November 1758, in John Adams, earliest diary, both in *Founding Families: Digital Editions of the Papers of the Winthrops and the Adamses*, ed. C. James Taylor (Boston: Massachusetts Historical Society, 2017), www.masshist.org/adams/adams-family-papers (hereafter *AFP*).

3. Holder, Bertolini, and Young, *Adams Birthplaces*, 27–29; www.abigailadamsbirthplace.com; David McCullough, *John Adams* (New York: Simon and Schuster, 2001), 54–56; "Introduction," Adams Family Correspondence, 1, *AFP*.

4. John Adams diary, February [April] 18, May 9, July 2, 1771, November 28 [27?], 1772, and John Adams autobiography, both in *AFP*; Adams Family Timeline, www.masshist.org/2012/adams/timeline.

5. John Adams diary, February 28, 1774, *AFP*.

6. Abigail to John, June 18, 1775, and note following, *AFP*.

7. Abigail to John, May 24, 1775, *AFP*.

8. Abigail to John, September 8, 16 [17], 1775, *AFP*.

9. Abigail and John's correspondence during this period, July 13–August 31, is in *AFP*.

10. Abigail to John, July 21, 1776, *AFP*.

11. Abigail to John, September 7, August 29, 1776, *AFP*.

12. Abigail to John, March 31, 1776, September 20, 1777 [1776], *AFP*.

13. John to Abigail, March 1777; Abigail to John, July 16, 1777; John to Abigail, July 28, 1777; *AFP*.

14. Abigail to John, August 1, 1781, *AFP*.

15. John to Abigail, ca. August 15, 1782; John Adams diary, November 26, 1778; John to Abigail, June 9, 1783; *AFP*.

16. Abigail to Mercy Otis Warren, September 1, 1780; Abigail to John, July 23, 1777; *AFP*.

17. James Warren to John Adams, April 27, 1777, *AFP*.

18. Abigail to John, June 20, 1783, *AFP*; Adams Family Timeline.
19. Abigail to John, October 8, 1782, *AFP*.
20. John to Abigail, October 16, 1782, *AFP*.
21. Abigail to John, June 20, 1783; John to Abigail, December 4, 1782, September 7, 1783; *AFP*.
22. Abigail Adams to Cotton Tufts, June 18, 1784; Abigail to John, January 3, February 11, May 25, 1784; Will of the Reverend William Smith, September 12, 1783; Abigail Adams, Journal, June 20, 1784; *AFP*.
23. John to Abigail, July 3, 1784; John Adams to William Smith, July 19, 1784; Abigail to John, July 23, 1784; John to Abigail, July 26, 1784; Abigail Adams to Mary Smith Cranch, September 5, 1784, *AFP*.
24. Abigail Adams to Mary Smith Cranch, May 25, 1786, *AFP*.
25. Abigail Adams to Mary Smith Cranch, September 5, 1784; Abigail Adams (daughter) to Elizabeth Cranch, September 4, December 10, 1784; *AFP*.
26. Abigail Adams to Mary Smith Cranch, February 20, 1785; Abigail Adams to Elizabeth Cranch, March 8, 1785; Abigail Adams (daughter) to Elizabeth Cranch, May 6, 1785; *AFP*.
27. Abigail Adams to Mary Smith Cranch, December 9, 1784; Abigail Adams to Thomas Jefferson, June 6, 1785; Abigail Adams (daughter) to Lucy Cranch, June 23, 1785; Abigail Adams to Mary Smith Cranch, June 24, 1785; quotation from Abigail Adams to Mercy Otis Warren, May 10, 1785; *AFP*.
28. Abigail Adams to Mary Smith Cranch, June 24, 1785; Abigail Adams to Mercy Otis Warren, May 14, 1787; Abigail Adams to Elizabeth Smith Shaw, November 21, 1786; *AFP*.
29. John Adams to Cotton Tufts and Richard Cranch, February 21, 1787; Abigail Adams to Mary Smith Cranch, March 8, 1787; Mary Smith Cranch to Abigail Adams, May 20, 1787; *AFP*.
30. Note 3 to Richard Cranch's letter to John Adams, January 18, 1780, *AFP*. This note provides a full history of the ownership of the house. A detailed account can also be found in M. C. Brown and others, *Cultural Landscapes Inventory, Peace Field, Adams National Historical Park* (National Park Service, 2012).
31. John to Abigail, January 22, 1783, Abigail to John Quincy Adams, June 13, 1786, *AFP*; Adams Biographical Sketches, www.masshist.org/2012/adams/biographies#AA2.
32. Cotton Tufts to John Adams, June 13, 1787, and note; Mary Smith Cranch to Abigail Adams, September 23, 1787; *AFP*.

33. Abigail Adams to Cotton Tufts, July 1, 1757 [1787]; Cotton Tufts to Abigail Adams, September 20, 1787; Mary Smith Cranch to Abigail Adams, September 30, 1787; *AFP*.

34. Abigail Adams to Cotton Tufts, November 6, 1787, *AFP*.

35. McCullough, *John Adams*, 390; Mary Smith Cranch to Abigail Adams, September 30, 1787, *AFP*.

36. Abigail Adams to Abigail Adams Smith, July 7, August 6, 1788, *AFP*.

37. National Park Service, *Cultural Landscapes Inventory, Peace Field*, 40–41. One of the rose bushes she planted still blooms in the garden.

38. John Adams to Cotton Tufts, August 27, 1787, *AFP*.

39. National Park Service, *Cultural Landscapes Inventory, Peace Field*, 41–42; John Adams diary, September 8, 1796, *AFP*.

40. John Quincy Adams diary 20, in *The Diaries of John Quincy Adams: A Digital Collection* (Boston: Massachusetts Historical Society, 2004), www.masshist.org/jqadiaries (hereafter *JQA Diaries*). June 3, 1795, 1–2; Adams Family Timeline.

41. Louisa Catherine Adams, "Record of a Life," in *Diary and Autobiographical Writings of Louisa Catherine Adams*, ed. Judith S. Graham, Beth Luey, Margaret A. Hogan, and C. James Taylor, 2 vols. (Cambridge, Mass.: Belknap Press of Harvard University Press, 2013), 1:21–22; for a full account of the couple's courtship, see Margery M. Heffron, *Louisa Catherine: The Other Mrs. Adams* (New Haven, Conn.: Yale University Press, 2014), chap. 4, quotation on 77.

42. Chronology, Louisa Catherine Adams, *Diary*, 2:779–80; John Quincy Adams diary 24, July 17, 1798, April 20, 1799, January 8, 1800, *JQA Diaries*.

43. Chronology, Louisa Catherine Adams, *Diary*, 2:780; John Quincy Adams diary 24, November 25, 1801, *JQA Diaries*; Louisa Catherine Adams, "The Adventures of a Nobody," in *Diary*, 1:164–65.

44. Louisa Catherine Adams, "Adventures," 1:186n192; Holder, Bertolini, and Young, *Adams Birthplaces*, 36–37.

45. Louisa Catherine Adams, "Adventures," 1:224–25; John Quincy Adams diary 27, April 8, 12, 18, 23, 1805, *JQA Diaries*, quotation from April 23.

46. Louisa Catherine Adams, "Adventures," 1:185–86, 225, 228.

47. Louisa Catherine Adams, "Adventures," 1:236, 238; John Quincy to Louisa, June 30, 1806, quoted in Louisa Catherine Adams, "Adventures," 1:236n262.

48. Louisa Catherine Adams, "Adventures," 1:241–42, 244–46.

49. John Quincy Adams diary 27, October 18, 1806, *JQA Diaries*; Louisa Catherine Adams, "Diary, 1819–1849," August 24, 1821, in *Diary*, 2:599.

50. Adams Biographical Sketches.

51. Adams Biographical Sketches; John Quincy Adams diary 35, January 25 1826, *JQA Diaries*.

52. Adams Biographical Sketches; John Quincy Adams to John Adams (son), July 26, 1834, quoted in Charles Francis Adams, *Diary of Charles Francis Adams*, ed. Marc Friedlaender and L. H. Butterfield, 8 vols. (Cambridge, Mass.: Belknap Press of Harvard University Press, 1964–86), 5:349.

53. Charles Francis Adams, *Diary*, May 31, June 2, October 31, 1824, 1:164, 167–68, 436.

54. Charles Francis Adams, *Diary*, April 6, 17, June 18, 1829, 2:364, 367, 391.

55. Adams Family Timeline; Charles Frances Adams, *Diary*, April 3, 1833, 5:61n66.

56. Charles Francis Adams, *Diary*, April 29, 1834, 5:303–4; August 19, 1835, 6:199.

57. Adams Family Timeline; Adams Biographical Sketches; Charles Francis Adams, *Diary*, May 21, 1832, 4:301; Louisa Catherine Adams to Charles Francis, May 26, 1832, quoted in note 2 to this entry.

58. Charles Francis Adams, *Diary*, November 6, 1832, 4:393; April 18, 1833, 5:70; October 1, 1835, 6:232; March 25, May 31, 1836, 6:358, 400.

59. Louisa Catherine to Charles Francis, July 30, 1828, quoted in his *Diary*, 2:264; Charles Francis Adams, *Diary*, June 19, 1830, 3:263–64; Adams Family Timeline.

60. Adams Biographical Sketches; National Park Service, *Cultural Landscapes Inventory, Peace Field*, 4–5.

## 3. Decline and Rise

1. Samuel Eliot Morison, *The Life and Letters of Harrison Gray Otis, Federalist, 1765–1848*, 2 vols. (Boston: Houghton Mifflin, 1913),

1:5, 35–36; Thomas H. Perkins, quoted in Samuel Eliot Morison, *Harrison Gray Otis, 1765–1848: The Urbane Federalist* (Boston: Houghton Mifflin, 1969), 6–7, 75; portraits at Otis House; Samuel A. Otis to Sally Foster, January 24, 1790, quoted in Morison, *Life and Letters*, 1:36.

2. Anne Grady and Linda Willett, *Harrison Gray Otis House Historic Structure Report* (Boston: SPNEA, 1998), 39; Morison, *Harrison Gray Otis*, 59, 75–79, 196.

3. Bioguide.congress.gov, s.v. Otis; H. G. Otis to S. F. Otis, December 3, 1797, quoted in Morison, *Life and Letters*, 1:235–36; visits to the Otis House, November 2, 2016, June 2, 2017.

4. Abigail Adams to John Quincy Adams, August 27, 1816; John Adams to John Quincy Adams, August 28[?], 1816; John Quincy Adams to John Adams, Oct. 29, 1816; all quoted in Morison, *Life and Letters*, 1:222, 223, 224.

5. Nancy S. Seasholes, *Gaining Ground: A History of Landmaking in Boston* (Cambridge, Mass.: MIT Press, 2003), 2–3, 44–48, 82, 107, 135–39, 141, 240–43; Jane Holtz Kay, *Lost Boston* (Boston: Houghton Mifflin, 1980), 94–96, 107.

6. Grady and Willett, *Otis House Historic Structure Report*, 39, 40; William A. Braverman, "The Emergence of a Unified Community, 1880–1917," in *The Jews of Boston*, ed. Jonathan D. Sarna, Ellen Smith, and Scott-Martin Kosofsky (New Haven, Conn.: Yale University Press, 2005), 67–69.

7. Grady and Willett, *Otis House Historic Structure Report*, 14, 65, 67, 78; Susan L. Porter, "Mrs. Mott: 'The Celebrated Female Physician,'" *Historic New England*, Winter/Spring 2005, 22–23. The full title was *The ladies' medical oracle, or, Mrs. Mott's advice to young females, wives, and mothers : being a non-medical commentary on the cause, prevention, and cure of the diseases of the female frame : together with an explanation of her system of European vegetable medicine for the cure of diseases, and the patent medicated champoo bath : to which is added an explanation of the gift, and an exposition of the numerous fabricated reports, "a weak invention of the enemy"* (Boston: Printed and published for the authoress, 1834).

8. Mary Roth Walsh, *"Doctors Wanted: No Women Need Apply": Sexual Barriers in the Medical Profession, 1835–1975* (New Haven, Conn.: Yale University Press, 1977), 22, 45; Porter, "Mrs. Mott," 22.

9. Harriot K. Hunt, M.D., *Glances and Glimpses, or Fifty Years Social, including Twenty Years Professional Life* (Boston: Jewett, 1856), 81, 110–13, 123, 160; Porter, "Mrs. Mott," 22–24.

10. Hunt, *Glances and Glimpses*, 215–16, 218, 265–70, 272; Ronald Takaki, "Aesculapius Was a White Man: Antebellum Racism and Male Chauvinism at Harvard Medical School, *Phylon* 39, no. 2 (Second Quarter 1978): 128–34.

11. Hunt, *Glances and Glimpses*, 170–71, 294–95.

12. Braverman, "Emergence of a Unified Community," 67–69; Gerald H. Gamm, "In Search of Suburbs: Boston's Jewish Districts, 1843–1994," in Sarna, Smith, and Kosofsky, *Jews of Boston*, 149.

13. Grady and Willett, *Otis House Historic Structure Report*, 35–36; Kelly H. L'Ecuyer, "From Gentility to Convenience: Boarders and Lodgers at the Otis House," *Historic New England*, Spring 2001, 10; www.mbta.com; Rosalie Warren, "Reminiscences of the Hill," *West Ender*, October 1992, quoted in Grady and Willett, *Otis House Historic Structure Report*, 41. On Boston boardinghouses, see Mark Peel, "On the Margins: Lodgers and Boarders in Boston, 1860–1900," *Journal of American History* 72, no. 4 (March 1986): 813–34.

14. L'Ecuyer, "From Gentility to Convenience," 10; William Sumner Appleton, quoted in Grady and Willett, *Otis House Historic Structure Report*, 36–37.

15. Grady and Willett, *Otis House Historic Structure Report*, 14, 73; Susan Ebert, "Community and Philanthropy," in Sarna, Smith, and Kosofsky, *Jews of Boston*, 225; "Lee M. Friedman," in Jacob Rader Marcus, *Concise Dictionary of American Jewish Biography*, 2 vols. (Brooklyn, N.Y.: Carlson, 1994), 1:182. The Sheltering Home moved instead to the corner of Cambridge and North Russell; *American Jewish Year Book* 24 (September 23, 1922–September 10, 1923): 270.

16. James M. Lindgren, "'A New Departure in Historic, Patriotic Work': Personalism, Professionalism, and Conflicting Concepts of Material Culture in the Late Nineteenth and Early Twentieth Centuries," *Public Historian* 18, no. 2 (Spring 1996): 41–55.

17. James M. Lindgren, "'A Constant Incentive to Patriotic Citizenship': Historic Preservation in Progressive-Era Massachusetts," *New England Quarterly* 64, no. 4 (December 1991): 594–608. The quotations are by Samuel Adams Drake, 594–95, and Charles Knowles Bolton, librarian of the Boston Athenaeum, 596–97.

18. Lindgren, "'Constant Incentive,'" 597–605.

19. William Sumner Appleton, "Annual Report of the Corresponding Secretary," *Old-Time New England*, ser. 24 (April 1921): 165; James M. Lindgren, "'A New Departure,'" 59.

20. Grady and Willett, *Otis House Historic Structure Report*, 20, 79; "Special Notice of Work Remaining to Be Done in Order to Complete the Dining Room, Parlor and Rear Stairway, *SPNEA Members' Newsletter*, [1917 or 1918], in Amy C. Shaffer, "The First Harrison Gray Otis House," documentation binder, 2 vols. (Boston: SPNEA, 1987), 2: n.p.

21. Appleton, "Annual Report," 165.

22. Grady and Willett, *Otis House Historic Structure Report*, 78.

23. "Its First Ride in 130 Years Just Ended," clipping in Shaffer, "First Harrison Gray Otis House," 1:n.p.

24. Grady and Willett, *Otis House Historic Structure Report*, 87; R. C. Nylander, "First Otis House," 620; Eleanor Early, *And This Is Boston!* (Boston: Houghton Mifflin, 1930), 60.

25. Grady and Willett, *Otis House Historic Structure Report*, 80.

26. Jane C. Nylander, "Henry Sargent's *Dinner Party* and *Tea Party*," *Antiques*, May 1982, 1173–84; Richard C. Nylander, "The First Harrison Gray Otis House, Boston, Massachusetts," *Antiques*, March 1986, 620; Shaffer, "First Harrison Gray Otis House," 2:n.p.

27. Nylander, "Otis House," 620–21. For a detailed explanation of the paint analysis, see Morgan W. Phillips, "Discoloration of Old House Paints: Restoration of Paint Colors at the Harrison Gray Otis House, Boston," *Bulletin of the Association for Preservation Technology* 3, no. 4 (1971): 40–47.

28. Visits, November 2, 2016, June 2, 2017. The booklet *Otis House* (Boston: Historic New England, 2011) has color photographs of most of the rooms, along with wallpaper samples and a brief history of the house.

29. Nylander, "Otis House," 621.

30. Thomas H. O'Connor, *Building a New Boston: Politics and Urban Renewal, 1950 to 1970* (Boston: Northeastern University Press, 1993), 125, 128–29, 133; unnamed residents and reporter Peter Anderson quoted on 128–29. Robert Campbell, "Phantom Pain: A Neighborhood Lives On after Its Destruction," *Architectural Record* 194, no. 4 (2006): 63.

31. O'Connor, *Building a New Boston*, 125–26, 129, 133.

32. Campbell, "Phantom Pain," 63; Lawrence W. Kennedy, *Planning the City upon a Hill: Boston since 1630* (Amherst: University of Massachusetts Press, 1992), 162–63.


## 4. Cousins


1. Emerson to Elizabeth Hoar, January 21, 1843, in *The Letters of Ralph Waldo Emerson*, ed. Ralph L. Rusk, 10 vols. (New York: Columbia University Press, 1939), 3:131.

2. Genealogical information is drawn from John M. Bullard, *The Rotches* (New Bedford, 1947); Charles Henry Jones, *Genealogy of the Rodman Family, 1620 to 1886* (Barbados: Allen, Lane & Scott, 1886); and Lydia Swain Mitchell Hinchman, *Early Settlers of Nantucket: Their Associates and Descendants* ([Philadelphia]: Ferris & Leach, 1901). The early life of Mary Borden Rodman is described in Barbara K. Wittman, *Thomas and Charity Rotch: The Quaker Experience of Settlement in Ohio in the Early Republic, 1800–1824* (Newcastle upon Tyne, U.K.: Cambridge Scholars Publishing, 2015), chaps. 1 and 2.

3. George Rogers Taylor, "Nantucket Oil Merchants and the American Revolution," *Massachusetts Review* 18, no. 3 (Autumn 1977): 581–606, quotation on 595; Lydia S. Hinchman, "William Rotch and the Neutrality of Nantucket during the Revolutionary War," *Bulletin of Friends' Historical Society of Philadelphia* 1, no. 2 (February 1907): 178–79. Taylor and Hinchman discuss the same events and evidence but come to very different conclusions about the Rotches' wartime activities.

4. Caroline Elizabeth Robinson, *The Hazard Family of Rhode Island, 1635–1894* (Boston: Merrymount, 1895), 76; Wittman, *Thomas and Charity Rotch*, 25.

5. Bullard, *The Rotches*, 74; Wittman, *Thomas and Charity Rotch*, 29–30; William and Elizabeth Rotch to Mary Rodman, April 21, 1790, and William Rotch to Samuel Rodman, March 17, 1790, box 1, Rotch Family Papers, New Bedford Whaling Museum, New Bedford, Mass.

6. Bullard, *The Rotches*, 74, 414–15.

7. Bullard, *The Rotches*, 409–10.

8. Bullard, *The Rotches*, 116–18, 443, quotation on 132.

9. *London Morning Chronicle*, October 29, 1817; William Rotch to Thomas Rotch, May 19, 1818, Rotch Family Papers; "Memorial of the Life of Elizabeth (Barker) Rotch, being the Recollections of a Mother by Her Daughter, Eliza Farrar" (Springfield, Mass., 1861), excerpted in Bullard, *The Rotches*, 348, quotation on 345; Morris Birkbeck, *Notes on a Journey to America* and *Letters from Illinois* (London: Ridgway, 1818). The advertising pamphlet for the auction of the house is in box 8, Rotch Family Papers. The date of the auction is crossed out, and a note has been added: "In One Lot, by Private Contract."

10. Jane Rodman, "The English Settlement in Southern Illinois, 1815–1825," *Indiana Magazine of History* 43, no. 4 (December 1947): 351; Charles W. Morgan, diary, December 1818, quoted in Peggi Medeiros, *New Bedford Mansions: Historic Tales of County Street* (Charleston, S.C.: History Press, 2015), 56; Benjamin Rotch to William, June 18, 1819, reprinted in Bullard, *The Rotches*, 353.

11. Francis Rotch to Thomas Rotch, February 10, 1819, Thomas and Charity Rotch Papers, Rotch-Wales Papers, Massillon Public Library, Massillon, Ohio.

12. Francis Rotch to Charles Morgan, February 12, 1819, reprinted in Bullard, *The Rotches*, 355–59.

13. Bullard, *The Rotches*, 25, 162.

14. September 19, 1835, *Diary of Charles Francis Adams*, ed. Mark Friedlaender and L. H. Butterfield, 8 vols. (Boston: Massachusetts Historical Society, 1974), 6:222.

15. Herman Melville, *Moby Dick* (New York: Oxford University Press, 1988), chap. 6, para. 5. Unless otherwise noted, the locations and descriptions of the houses in this section come from Bullard, *The Rotches*; *"Brave Houses and Flowery Gardens" of Old New Bedford* (S. Dartmouth, Mass.: Garden Club of Buzzards Bay, 1976), n.p.; Medeiros, *New Bedford Mansions*; "New Bedford Architecture: A Walking Tour: County Street" (New Bedford: New Bedford Preservation Society, n.d.); Daniel Ricketson, *New Bedford of the Past* (Boston: Houghton Mifflin, 1903), 40–41; Henry B. Worth, "The Patrician Homes of New Bedford," in *History of New Bedford*, ed. Zephaniah W. Pease (New York: Lewis Historical Publishing, 1918), 323–29; and visits by the author.

16. www.whalingmuseum.org/now-mariners-home-formerly-rotch -house/.

17. Illustration opposite p. 364 in Bullard, *The Rotches*. The archives at the Rotch-Jones-Duff House and Garden Museum, New Bedford, Mass., contain extensive documentation of purchases Joseph Rotch made for his home: collection 2017.5, box 7.

18. John Quincy Adams diary 44, 9 July 1843–31 December 1844, p. 85 (electronic edition), *The Diaries of John Quincy Adams: A Digital Collection* (Boston: Massachusetts Historical Society, 2004), www.masshist.org/jqadiaries.

19. James Arnold, will, box 12, Rotch Family Papers.

20. C. F. Adams, *Diary*, 6:223–24.; J. Q. Adams, diary 44, September 28, 1843; Lemuel Shaw to Lemuel Shaw Jr., July 6, 1852, quoted in Hershel Parker, *Herman Melville: A Biography*, 2 vols. (Baltimore, Md.: Johns Hopkins University Press, 1996), 2:113; Keith N. Morgan, ed. *Buildings of Massachusetts: Metropolitan Boston* (Charlottesville: University of Virginia Press, 2009), 267. See Hugh M. Raup, "The Genesis of the Arnold Arboretum," Arnold Arboretum, Harvard University, *Bulletin of Popular Information*, ser. 4, vol. 8 (April 26, 1940): 1–11.

21. The New Bedford Whaling Museum holds extensive business records from the Rotch and Rodman families.

22. Jane M. Clayton and Charles A. Clayton, *Shipowners Investing in the South Sea Whale Fishery from Britain: 1755–1815* (Hertfordshire, U.K.: Jane M. Clayton, 2014), 69, 83; Rundell Mudge to Benjamin Rotch, March 21, 1827, box 8, Rotch Family Papers; Bullard, *The Rotches*, 99, 100, 138, 452, 523.

23. Anne W. Rotch to Charles W. Morgan, September 8, 1840, in Bullard, *The Rotches*, 388.

24. Frederick B. Tolles, "The New-Light Quakers of Lynn and New Bedford," *New England Quarterly* 32, no. 3 (September 1959): 294, anonymous author quoted on 293.

25. Murray Gardner Hill, "'A Rill Struck Out from the Rock': Mary Rotch of New Bedford," *Bulletin of Friends Historical Association* 45, no. 1 (Spring 1956): 10–17, 19–22.

26. Eliza Rotch to Mrs. George Bond, September 2, 1828; Eliza Rotch Farrar, "Memorials of the Life of Elizabeth Rotch, being the Recollection of a Mother, by her daughter," 1861 (ms), both in box 11, Rotch Family Papers.

27. Higginson is quoted in Bullard, *The Rotches*, 130. On Eliza's life in Cambridge, see Elizabeth Bancroft Schlesinger, "Two Early

Harvard Wives: Eliza Farrar and Eliza Follen," *New England Quarterly* 38, no. 2 (June 1965): 147–67.

28. Bullard, *The Rotches*, 130. *A Young Lady's Friend* was published in Boston and London in several editions. The quotation is from the London edition (Parker, 1837), 2.

29. Tolles, "New-Light Quakers," 295–303, quotation on 300.

30. Tolles, "New-Light Quakers," 304; obituary in *New Bedford Mercury*, included in W. J. Potter, *A Tribute to the Memory of James Arnold* (New Bedford, Mass.: Fessenden & Baker, 1868); Elizabeth Rodman to William Logan Fisher (widower of Mary Rodman), May 28, 1820, quoted in Joseph L. McDevitt Jr., "The House of Rotch: Whaling Merchants of Massachusetts, 1734–1828" (Ph.D. diss., American University, 1978), 506. The dissertation was published in a facsimile edition by Garland in 1986 with the same title and pagination.

31. Tolles, "New-Light Quakers," 305–7, 311; Elizabeth Rodman to William Logan Fisher, January 4, March 30, 1823, in McDevitt, "House of Rotch," 508, 509; Moncure Daniel Conway, *Emerson at Home and Abroad* (London: Trübner, 1883), 69.

32. Tolles, "New-Light Quakers," 313, 314, 318; Samuel Rodman, journal, 2:86, 102–3, 139, box 6, Rodman Family Papers, New Bedford Whaling Museum, New Bedford, Mass.

33. S. Rodman, journal, 2:97–98, 109, 139. Sarah Morgan kept a journal recording the events of these meetings that is in the Alfred Rodman Hussey Manuscripts at Swarthmore College. The New Bedford Unitarian congregation was called the First Congregational Society until the 1950s, so that some sources call these early converts Congregationalists.

34. S. Rodman, journal, 12, quotation is on 147. The Massachusetts law was not changed until 1855: Appleton v. Hopkins, 71 Mass. (5 Gray) 530, 532 (Mass. 1855).

35. Bullard, *The Rotches,* 410; *Portsmouth Journal of Literature and Politics*, December 19, 1840. It must have been quite a feast, for there were only sixty prisoners.

36. Anne Rotch to Charles Morgan, September 8, 1840, reprinted in Bullard, *The Rotches*, 388–89.

37. Anne W. Morgan Rotch, journal/letters to her sisters, 1:1828, box 10, Rotch Family Papers, quotation from third letter.

38. Samuel Rodman to William Logan Fisher, September 15, 1819,

quoted in Kathryn Grover, *The Fugitive's Gibraltar: Escaping Slaves and Abolitionism in New Bedford, Massachusetts* (Amherst: University of Massachusetts Press, 2009), 102; Samuel Rodman to William Logan Fisher, June 28, August 15, 1819, quoted in McDevitt, "House of Rotch," 496.

39. Abner Forbes and J. W. Greene, *The Rich Men of Massachusetts* (Boston: Spencer, 1851), 190–91.

40. Bullard, *The Rotches*, 159–65. Most accounts use the terms *seduction*, *mistress*, and *affair*. Given the ages of Francis and Elizabeth and her feelings about the relationship, I find *molestation* and *abuse* more appropriate.

41. Letter quoted in Bullard, *The Rotches*, 163; S. Rodman, journal, 5:163.

42. Letter to Ann S. Rotch from one of her brothers, quoted in Bullard, *The Rotches*, 161; S. Rodman, journal, 5:162.

43. Megan Marshall, *The Peabody Sisters: Three Women Who Ignited American Romanticism* (Boston: Houghton Mifflin, 2005), 225–26; Louisa Catherine Adams to Mary Catherine Hellen Adams, November 26, 1830, Adams Family Papers, Massachusetts Historical Society, Boston, Mass.; C. F. Adams, *Diary*, 6:223. In 1830, Joseph Knapp asked his brother John to kill Captain Joseph White in a complicated plot to ensure that Joseph's wife would inherit White's estate. John hired Richard and George Crowninshield to commit the murder, which they did. The Crowninshields tried to blackmail the Knapps, and the plot was uncovered. Richard Crowninshield committed suicide in prison, and George was acquitted. Both Knapps were convicted. John was hanged on September 18, 1830; Joseph was hanged on December 31, 1830. Daniel Allen Hearn, *Legal Executions in New England: A Comprehensive Reference, 1623–1960* (Jefferson, N.C.: McFarland, 2007), 213–14.

44. Bullard, *The Rotches*, 125, 165; Anne W. Rotch to Charles W. Morgan, September 8, 1840, in Bullard, *The Rotches*, 389; S. Rodman, journal, 5:164.

45. Bullard, *The Rotches*, 409–10; Potter, *Tribute*, 9, 18. Elizabeth married Charles M. Tuttle. James did not approve of the marriage, and when Elizabeth died he paid Tuttle $30,000 to transfer to him "all the personal property, stocks, goods, estate, and effects of every kind which belonged to [Elizabeth]." That amount was equivalent to about $850,000 in 2018. Charles M.

Tuttle to James Arnold, 1860, collection 2017.5, box 6, Rotch-Jones-Duff House and Garden Museum.

## 5. Home and Family

1. F. B. Sanborn and William T. Harris, *A. Bronson Alcott: His Life and Philosophy*, 2 vols. (Boston: Roberts Brothers, 1893), 1:10, 17, 24, 29, 70, 73–74, 89, 102–4; Eve LaPlante, *Marmee and Louisa: The Untold Story of Louisa May Alcott and Her Mother* (New York: Free Press, 2012), 14–16.

2. Charles Strickland, "A Transcendentalist Father: The Child-Rearing Practices of Bronson Alcott," *History of Childhood Quarterly* 1, no. 1 (Summer 1973): 9–10.

3. Madelon Bedell, *The Alcotts: Biography of a Family* (New York: Clarkson Potter, 1980), 63, 66, 73, 120.

4. Bedell, *The Alcotts*, 73–75, 101–2; Bronson Alcott's journal, March 16, 1846, quoted in Charles Strickland, *Victorian Domesticity: Families in the Life and Art of Louisa May Alcott* (Tuscaloosa: University of Alabama Press, 2015), 28.

5. Bronson's journal quoted in Sanborn and Harris, *A. Bronson Alcott*, 1:176–78, quotation on 177; Bedell, *The Alcotts*, 93; John Matteson, *Eden's Outcasts: The Story of Louisa May Alcott and Her Father* (New York: Norton, 2007), 56. The building where Bronson taught was at the corner of Tremont Street and Temple Place and no longer exists. The building now known as the Tremont Temple is a Baptist church built in the early 1890s.

6. Bedell, *The Alcotts*, 123, 126–27, 129–33; Sanborn and Harris, *A. Bronson Alcott*, 1:214–27; Larry A. Carlson, "Bronson Alcott's 'Journal for 1837,'" pt. 1, *Studies in the American Renaissance* (1981), 28, 29, 77.

7. Bronson to his mother, December 28, 1839, and his 1835 journal, quoted in Sanborn and Harris, *A. Bronson Alcott*, 1:299, 204–5; Bedell, *The Alcotts*, 151; Abigail to Samuel May, Oct. 3, 1839, quoted in Eve LaPlante, ed., *My Heart Is Boundless* (New York: Free Press, 2012), 80.

8. Sanborn and Harris, *A. Bronson Alcott*, 1:249–50; Cyrus A. Bartol, *Amos Bronson Alcott: His Character, a Sermon* (Boston: Roberts Brothers, 1888), 11; James Russell Lowell, *A Fable for Critics: The*

*Original 1848 Satire* (Boston: Houghton Mifflin, 1848), 48. As editor of the *Atlantic Monthly*, Lowell was one of the first to publish Louisa's stories written in her own name.

9. Matteson, *Eden's Outcasts*, 93–95, Anna's journal quoted on 88; Sanborn and Harris, *A. Bronson Alcott*, 1:307–8, Bronson to Samuel May, April 6, 1840, quoted on 307.

10. Abigail to Samuel May, quoted in Sanborn and Harris, *A. Bronson Alcott*, 1:309; Abigail's journal, January 16, 1844, and March 6, 1843, in Odell Shepard, ed., *The Journals of Bronson Alcott* (Boston: Little Brown, 1938), 157, 152.

11. Sanborn and Harris, *A. Bronson Alcott*, 1:310–11, 320, 330; Bedell, *The Alcotts*, 175; Matteson, *Eden's Outcasts*, 104.

12. Bedell, *The Alcotts*, 175, 179–81, 187, 204; Abigail's journal, November 29, 1842, quoted in Susan Cheever, *Louisa May Alcott: A Personal Biography* (New York: Simon & Schuster, 2010), 56; LaPlante, *Marmee and Louisa*, 104–5, 115.

13. Richard Francis, *Fruitlands: The Alcott Family and Their Search for Utopia* (New Haven, Conn.: Yale University Press, 2010), 156, 195; Clara Endicott Sears, comp., *Bronson Alcott's Fruitlands* (Boston: Houghton Mifflin, 1915), 71, 84, 131; LaPlante, *Marmee and Louisa*, 114–15.

14. Matteson, *Eden's Outcasts*, 106; Lane quoted in Sears, *Alcott's Fruitlands*, 122; Abigail to Samuel May, January 6, 1844, in Cheever, *Louisa May Alcott*, 73; Louisa's journal, December 10, 1843, in Ednah D. Cheney, comp. and ed., *Louisa May Alcott: Life, Letters, and Journals* (New York: Gramercy Books, 1995), 22.

15. Bedell, *The Alcotts*, 227; Abigail to Samuel May, November 11, 1843, in Francis, *Fruitlands*, 240–41; Lane to Oldham, November 26, 1843, in Sears, *Alcott's Fruitlands*, 123.

16. Sanborn and Harris, *A. Bronson Alcott*, 2:386; Abigail's journal, February 17, 1844, in Bedell, *The Alcotts*, 232. Joseph Palmer bought the farm and lived there for twenty years, welcoming strangers and feeding them (Sears, *Alcott's Fruitlands*, 66, 137).

17. Bedell, *The Alcotts*, 234–35; Keith N. Morgan, *Buildings of Massachusetts: Metropolitan Boston* (Charlottesville: University of Virginia Press, 2009), 451.

18. Matteson, *Eden's Outcasts*, 173, 198; Shepard, *Journals*, xv; Sears, *Alcott's Fruitlands*, 104.

19. Abigail's journal, July 8, 1842, in LaPlante, *My Heart*, 114; Louisa to Abigail, 1845, in *The Selected Letters of Louisa May Alcott*, ed.

Joel Myerson and Daniel Shealy (Boston: Little Brown, 1987), 6; Louisa's journal, March 1846, in Cheney, *Louisa May Alcott*, 30; Matteson, *Eden's Outcasts*, 176.

20. Bronson to Junius, January 2, 1845, in *The Letters of A. Bronson Alcott*, ed. Richard L. Herrnstadt (Ames: Iowa State University Press, 1969), 117; Matteson, *Eden's Outcasts*, 167, 173.

21. Matteson, *Eden's Outcasts*, 171–72, 181; Sanborn and Harris, *A. Bronson Alcott*, 2:391, 429, 432; Abigail to Samuel May, February 8, 1847, in LaPlante, *My Heart*, 154.

22. Matteson, *Eden's Outcasts*, 197, 204, 208, 214, 220, 221, 227, quotation from Louisa's undated 1851 journal on 197; Bronson's journal, April 6, 1850, in Shepard, *Journals*, 231; LaPlante, *Marmee and Louisa*, 155, 178.

23. LaPlante, *Marmee and Louisa*, 180–81; Matteson, *Eden's Outcasts*, 231–33.

24. Louisa's journal, August 1858, in Cheney, *Louisa May Alcott*, 68; Matteson, *Eden's Outcasts*, 259, 266; Sanborn and Harris, *A. Bronson Alcott*, 2:502; LaPlante, *Marmee and Louisa*, 186–87.

25. Quoted in Sanborn and Harris, *A. Bronson Alcott*, 2:437.

26. March 13, September 18, 1858, October 19, 20, 21, 1865, August 6, 1869, in Shepard, *Journals*, 306, 309, 375, 399; Bronson to Abigail, April 24, 1863, in Herrnstadt, *Letters*, 338; visit, July 13, 2017.

27. Visit, July 13, 2017.

28. Matteson, *Eden's Outcasts*, 270, 281–82, 290, 292; LaPlante, *Marmee and Louisa*, 192–93, 223–28. The antiquarian booksellers and book historians Leona Rostenberg and Madeleine Stern identified Alcott as Barnard in 1975; see their *Old Books, Rare Friends: Two Literary Sleuths and Their Shared Passion* (New York: Doubleday, 1997).

29. Louisa's journal, December 1868, in Cheney, *Louisa May Alcott*, 141; LaPlante, *Marmee and Louisa*, 228–33.

30. Matteson, *Eden's Outcasts*, 371.

31. LaPlante, *Marmee and Louisa*, 250, 255.

32. LaPlante, *Marmee and Louisa*, 256–58.

33. Bronson's journal, June 10–14, 1878; Shepard, *Journals*, 490–91.

34. Louisa to Eden Conway, May 1, 1878, in Myerson and Shealy, *Selected Letters*, 230; Louisa's journal, May–June 1879, in Cheney, *Louisa May Alcott*, 231; Bronson to May, November 18, 1877, in Herrnstadt, *Letters*, 703; Matteson, *Eden's Outcasts*, 385; Sanborn and Harris, *A. Bronson Alcott*, 2:506, 531.

35. LaPlante, *Marmee and Louisa*, 266–68; May to her family, quoted on 263; May Alcott Nieriker, *Studying Art Abroad and How to Do It Cheaply* (Boston: Roberts Bros., 1879). After Louisa's death, Lulu returned to Switzerland to live with her father; she died in 1975: Harriet Reisin, *Louisa May Alcott: The Woman behind Little Women* (New York: Macmillan, 2010), 366–69.

36. LaPlante, *Marmee and Louisa*, 271, 273–74, 277–78.

37. Cyrus A. Bartol, *Amos Bronson Alcott*, 3, 5, 25–27, 31.

38. Visit, July 13, 2017; Cheever, *Louisa May Alcott*, 222.


## 6. A Room of Her Own

1. Gillian Gill, *Mary Baker Eddy* (Cambridge, Mass.: Perseus, 1998), 524–26. Except where otherwise noted, I have relied on Gill's excellent biography for the facts of Mrs. Eddy's life and noted page numbers for specific passages and quotations. I have used Mrs. Eddy's name as she would have at the time—Mary Baker, Mary Glover, Mary Patterson, and Mary Baker Eddy. Once her leadership of the church was established, "Mrs. Eddy"—as she was known except in formal references—seems the most appropriate form.

2. Mary Baker Eddy, *Science and Health*, facsimile ed. (Bedford, Mass.: Applewood, 2009), 136.

3. Irving Clinton Tomlinson, *Twelve Years with Mary Baker Eddy: Recollections and Experiences* (Boston: Christian Science Publishing, 1945), 7, 12, 17, © The Mary Baker Eddy Collection. Used by permission; Robert Peel, *Mary Baker Eddy*, 3 vols. (New York: Holt, Rinehart and Winston, 1966), 1:12–13.

4. Mary Baker Eddy, *Retrospection and Introspection* (Boston: Stewart, 1909), 5, 13.

5. Eddy, *Retrospection*, 2, 6–7, 10; Gill, *Mary Baker Eddy*, 30–36.

6. *Science and Health*, 1st ed., quoted in Gill, *Mary Baker Eddy*, 47. For a discussion of disputes over Mary's ability as a student, see Gill, *Mary Baker Eddy*, 36–38.

7. Abigail Baker to George Baker, April 24, 1836, quoted in Gill, *Mary Baker Eddy*, 29.

8. Eddy, *Retrospection*, 20; Gill, *Mary Baker Eddy*, 33, 35, 62–63.

9. Gill, *Mary Baker Eddy*, 69, 72–76, 84–89; Eddy, *Retrospection*, 20.

10. Tomlinson, *Twelve Years*, 19, © The Mary Baker Eddy Collection. Used by permission; Gill, *Mary Baker Eddy*, 102; Eddy, *Retrospection*, 20.

11. Eddy, *Retrospection*, 90, © The Mary Baker Eddy Collection. Used by permission.

12. Gill, *Mary Baker Eddy*, 102–10.

13. Gill, *Mary Baker Eddy*, 123–24.

14. Gill, *Mary Baker Eddy*, 125, 127, 131–33, quotation on 131.

15. George Quimby, in Horatio W. Dresser, ed., *The Quimby Manuscripts* (New York: Crowell, 1921), 438. Sarah Crosby to Allen A. Beauchamp, 1909, quoted in Gill, *Mary Baker Eddy*, 135.

16. Eddy, *Retrospection*, 24; Stephen Gottschalk, *The Emergence of Christian Science in American Religious Life* (Berkeley: University of California Press, 1973), 32.

17. John Modell and Tamara K. Hareven report that in 1885 fewer than 10 percent of female Massachusetts residents were living as boarders or lodgers: "Urbanization and the Malleable Household," *Journal of Marriage and the Family* 35, no. 3 (August 1973): 474. See also Mark Peel, "On the Margins: Lodgers and Boarders in Boston, 1860–1900," *Journal of American History* 72, no. 4 (March 1986): 813–34.

18. Peel, *Mary Baker Eddy*, 1:220; Eddy to Mary Ellis, October 7, 1872, and Eddy to Samuel Putnam Bancroft, December 15, 1874, both in "Selections from the Mary Baker Eddy Papers," marybakereddypapers.org; Daisette Stocking McKenzie, "Reminiscences," typescript, n.d., Mary Baker Eddy Library, Boston, Mass., 27–28. Letters and Reminiscences, © The Mary Baker Eddy Collection. Used by permission.

19. Peel, *Mary Baker Eddy*, 1:226, 276; Eddy to Sarah O. Bagley, December 13, 1872, marybakereddypapers.org, © The Mary Baker Eddy Collection. Used by permission.

20. Gill, *Mary Baker Eddy*, chap. 14.

21. Eddy, *Science and Health*, 468; Gottschalk, *Emergence*, viii.

22. Peel, *Mary Baker Eddy*, 2:153.

23. *London Times*, May 26, 1885; Gottschalk, *Emergence*, 84.

24. Eddy to James Ackland, January 21, 1880; Asa Gilbert Eddy to James Ackland, February 22, 1880; both in marybakereddypapers.org, © The Mary Baker Eddy Collection. Used by permission.

25. Eddy, *Retrospection*, 42; Gill, *Mary Baker Eddy*, 301.

26. Gill, *Mary Baker Eddy*, 302–3, 325, 339–40. Many of Mrs. Eddy's contributions to the journal can be found in her *Miscellaneous Writings, 1883–1896* (Boston: Stewart, 1896), and many subsequent editions.

27. The visitor was Mrs. Herbert H. Bangs, whose report of her visit is included in the Reverend Irving C. Tomlinson, "Mary Baker Eddy: The Woman and the Revelator," typescript, 1932, 4 vols., Mary Baker Eddy Library, 4:776.

28. Gill, *Mary Baker Eddy*, 312–17, 358; Gottschalk, *Emergence*, 176.

29. Tomlinson, *Twelve Years*, 117; John G. Salchow, "Reminiscences," typescript, n.d., Mary Baker Eddy Library, p. 12, © The Mary Baker Eddy Collection. Used by permission; Gill, *Mary Baker Eddy*, 388–90.

30. Gill, *Mary Baker Eddy*, 402. Claudia Stokes analyzes Mrs. Eddy's insistence upon good housekeeping in "The Mother Church: Mary Baker Eddy and the Practice of Sentimentalism," *New England Quarterly* 81, no. 3 (September 2008): 456–58.

31. Gill, *Mary Baker Eddy*, chap. 23; [Frederick Peabody], "True Origin of Christian Science; Documentary Evidence Refuting Mrs. Eddy's Claim That Her System Was Revealed to Her by God," *New York Times*, July 10, 1904.

32. Mark Twain to Frederick Peabody, December 5, 1902, quoted in Gill, *Mary Baker Eddy*, 454; Gill, *Mary Baker Eddy*, 458. The articles appeared in *Cosmopolitan* and the *North American Review* and were revised as a book titled *Christian Science*, published in 1907.

33. Gill, *Mary Baker Eddy*, 471–76. The *McClure's* articles appeared in book form in 1909 as *The Life of Mary Baker Eddy and the History of Christian Science*, credited to Georgine Milmine but in fact largely written by Ida Tarbell and Willa Cather. See Ashley Squires, "The Standard Oil Treatment: Willa Cather, 'The Life of Mary Baker G. Eddy,' and Early Twentieth-Century Collaborative Authorship," *Studies in the Novel* 45, no. 3 (Fall 2013): 328–48, and David Stouck, introduction to *The Life of Mary Baker G. Eddy and the History of Christian Science* (Lincoln: University of Nebraska Press, 1993).

34. Letter from Mary Baker Eddy to James Ackland, January 21, 1880, L10638, ©The Mary Baker Eddy Collection. Used by permission. Also in Gill, *Mary Baker Eddy*, chap. 25, quotation on 519.

35. Salchow, "Reminiscences," 93; Calvin C. Hill, "Reminiscences," typescript, n.d., Mary Baker Eddy Library, Boston, Mass. 183–85,

190; Adelaide M. Still, "Reminiscences of the Times I Spent in Mrs. Eddy's Home, May, 1907, to December, 1910," typescript, n.d., Mary Baker Eddy Library, 26–29, © The Mary Baker Eddy Collection. Used by permission.

36. Salchow, "Reminiscences," 94; Tomlinson, "Mary Baker Eddy," 4:775; both © The Mary Baker Eddy Collection. Used by permission. Salchow noted that Mrs. Eddy's declaration that Pleasant View was her home had favorable tax consequences: New Hampshire had a lower estate tax rate than Massachusetts.

## 7. Greater Than the Sum of Its Parts

1. Joseph E. Garland, *Eastern Point: A Nautical, Rustical, and Social Chronicle of Gloucester's Outer Shield and Inner Sanctum, 1606–1950* (Peterborough, N.H.: Noone House, 1971), 245, 249; *Boston Sunday Globe*, September 18, 1921. Red Roof was mostly demolished in 2012.

2. *New York Times*, March 17, 1911; www.historicnewengland/org; "Ex-Secretary Whitney," *Baltimore Sun*, March 15, 1895; "Whitney's Household," *Dallas Morning News*, November 22, 1895; Garland, *Eastern Point*, 243; David Randall-MacIver, *Joanna Randall-MacIver—A Memoir* (Oxford: Oxford University Press, 1932), 14.

3. Tara Leigh Tappert, "Choices—The Life and Career of Cecilia Beaux: A Professional Biography" (Ph.D. diss., George Washington University, 1990), 399–402, 410; Garland, *Eastern Point*, 245; Tara Leigh Tappert, "Aimée Ernesta and Eliza Cecilia: Two Sisters, Two Choices," *Pennsylvania Magazine of History and Biography* 124, no. 3 (July 2000): 287, 290; Cecilia Beaux to Piatt Andrew, 1904 and undated, Cecilia Beaux Papers, 1863–1968, Archives of American Art, Smithsonian Institution, Washington, D.C.

4. David W. Dangremond, "The Highlands: The Country Seat of Anthony Morris" (M.A. thesis, University of Delaware, 1981), 31–32; www.historicnewengland.org; Garland, *Eastern Point*, 261. Wrong Roof burned down in 2001.

5. Henry Sleeper to Helen Andrew Patch, July 8, 1918, in Philip Hayden, "The Sleeper-McCann House: Beauport" (Boston:

Society for the Preservation of New England Antiquities, January 1986), not paginated, vol. 7, Historic New England Library and Archives, Boston; Garland, *Eastern Point*, 262; Henry James to Isabella Stewart Gardner, October 1911, quoted in Garland, *Eastern Point*, 280.

6. Kevin D. Murphy, "'Secure from All Intrusion': Heterotopia, Queer Space, and the Turn-of-the-Twentieth-Century American Resort," *Winterthur Portfolio* 43, no. 2/3 (Summer/Autumn 2009): 224; www.historicnewengland.org.

7. Louise Hall Tharp, *Mrs. Jack: A Biography of Isabella Stewart Gardner* (Boston: Little Brown, 1965), 276, 280; Joseph E. Garland, "Dabsville," in Nancy Curtis and Richard C. Nylander, *Beauport: The Sleeper-McCann House* (Boston: Godine, 1991), 16. A portrait of Andrew by Anders Zorn, dated about 1911, hangs on the south wall of the Blue Room at the Gardner Museum, Boston (visit to Gardner Museum, September 4, 2016).

8. Isabella Stewart Gardner to Caroline Sinkler, March 17, December 17, 23, 1919, Beauport, Sleeper-McCann House Collection (MS036), Historic New England Library and Archives.

9. Historical and Biographical Note; Halfdan Hanson to Sleeper, March 8, 1921, November 7, 1922; Sleeper to Hanson, March 18, 1921, January 8, 1925, Halfdan M. Hanson Architectural Collection, 1884–1952 (AR010), Historic New England Library and Archives.

10. Sleeper to Hanson, January 8, 1925, September 13, 1921, Hanson Architectural Collection.

11. Tappert, "Aimée Ernesta," 280, 288–89; Tharp, *Mrs. Jack*, 277, 279; Linda Shoemaker, "Backstage at Beauport," *Historic New England Magazine*, Summer 2004, www.historicnewengland.org.

12. Shoemaker, "Backstage"; visit to Beauport, September 9, 2016; Andrew's diary, April 6, 1912, quoted in E. Parker Hayden Jr., and Andrew L. Gray, *Beauport Chronicle: The Letters of Henry Davis Sleeper to Abram Piatt Andrew, Jr., 1906–1915* (Boston: Historic New England, 2005), 21, 22, 65n. Mary Wonson became the first guide when the house was opened for tours.

13. Shoemaker, "Backstage"; visit, September 9, 2016.

14. Murphy, "'Secure from All Intrusion,'" 190.

15. Gray quoted in Garland, *Eastern Point*, 283–84; Sleeper to Mrs. Buswell (Leslie's mother), July 22, 1915, Beauport Collection, Historic New England Library and Archives.

16. Alan Axelrod, ed., *The Colonial Revival in America* (New York: Norton, 1985), 3, 10; James M. Lindgren, "'A Constant Incentive to Patriotic Citizenship': Historic Preservation in Progressive-Era Massachusetts," *New England Quarterly* 64, no. 4 (December 1991): 594–608. Historic Deerfield (www.historic-deerfield.org/) is a product of the Colonial Revival movement, with restored houses of various periods and an outstanding collection of furniture, household artifacts, and art.

17. Douglas Shand-Tucci, *Ralph Adams Cram: Life and Architecture*, 2 vols. (Amherst: University of Massachusetts Press, 1996), 1:88; David D. Doyle, Jr., "A Very Proper Bostonian": Rediscovering Ogden Codman and His Late-Nineteenth-Century Queer World," *Journal of the History of Sexuality* 13, no. 4 (October 2004): 446–76; Will Fellows, *A Passion to Preserve: Gay Men as Keepers of Culture* (Madison: University of Wisconsin Press, 2004); Murphy, "'Secure from All Intrusion,'" 185–228, esp. 213–26.

18. *New England Interiors*, quoted in Walter Knight Sturges, "Arthur Little and the Colonial Revival," *Journal of the Society of Architectural Historians* 32, no. 2 (May 1973): 149, 159; Curtis and Nylander, *Beauport*, 8.

19. Historical and Biographical Note; Sleeper to Hanson, December 25, 1917, Hanson Architectural Collection; Sleeper to Andrew, September 8, 1908, in Hayden and Gray, *Beauport Chronicle*, 41.

20. Hayden and Gray, *Beauport Chronicle*, 38; National Historic Landmark Nomination, NPS Form 10–900, Beauport (Sleeper-McCann House), U.S. Department of the Interior, National Park Service, 7; Robert A. M. Stern, *Pride of Place: Building the American Dream* (Boston: Houghton Mifflin, 1986), 94; www.historicnewengland.org. I have described most of the rooms in the house thematically. An excellent chronological narrative can be found in Paul Hollister, "The Building of Beauport, 1907–1924," *American Art Journal* 13, no. 1 (Winter 1981): 69–89. The National Historic Landmark application is another source for thorough descriptions of the rooms.

21. Stern, *Pride of Place*, 96.

22. Hollister, *Beauport at Gloucester: The Most Fascinating House in America* (New York: Hastings House, 1951), 5, 9; visit, September 9, 2016.

23. Garland, *Eastern Point*, 280–81; visit, September 9, 2016.

24. Andrew to Gardner, February 10, 1914, Isabella Stewart Gardner Papers, Gardner Museum, Boston; Sleeper to Andrew, March 4, 26, 30, 1915, in Hayden and Gray, *Beauport Chronicle*, 76, 81–83; Andrew to Gardner, November 19, 1920; July 15, 25, 1922, Gardner Papers; "Our Lady of Good Voyage Church," pamphlet, Gloucester, n.d., Beauport Collection.

25. Hollister, "The Building of Beauport," 74; *Boston Globe*, June 13, 1961; visit, September 9, 2016.

26. Visit, September 9, 2016.

27. Sleeper to Andrew, March 7, 1915, in Hayden and Gray, *Beauport Chronicle*, 78; *New York Times*, March 22, 1911.

28. A. Piatt Andrew biography, www.federalreservehistory.org/People/DetailView/253; Tharp, *Mrs. Jack*, 278–79. Closets at Beauport contain many of the costumes worn at the frequent parties (visit, September 9, 2016). On Sleeper's caretaking, see, for example, Sleeper to Andrew, August 4, September 1, 27, 1908, in Hayden and Gray, *Beauport Chronicle*, 18, 39, 53.

29. Andrew to Gardner, October 3, 1909, Gardner Papers; A. Piatt Andrew biography, www.federalreservehistory.org/People/Detail View/253.

30. Curtis and Nylander, *Beauport*, 8, 9, 108.

31. A. Piatt Andrew, introduction to *History of the American Field Service in France*, 3 vols. (Boston: Houghton Mifflin, 1920), 1:18–19; December 3, 1914, in A. Piatt Andrew, *Letters Written Home from France in the First Half of 1915* (N.p.: Privately printed, 1916), 1; Andrew to Mother and Father, December 19, 20, 1914, March 2, 1915, *Letters*, 4, 7, 52.

32. Andrew, introduction, 1:19–20; Sleeper, introduction, 1:48, in *History of the American Field Service*. The full text of the treaty can be found in *History*, 1:21–23.

33. Sleeper to Andrew, March 4, 26, June 10 or 11, July 1, 18, 1915, in Hayden and Gray, *Beauport Chronicle*, 75–76, 81, 98, 99, 100–102; Andrew to Gardner, October 24, November 13, December 19, 1915, and April 7, July 24, 1916, Gardner Papers.

34. Sleeper to Andrew, July 22, August 15, 1915, in Hayden and Gray, *Beauport Chronicle*, 103–5; Andrew, introduction, 1:9, 24; Sleeper, introduction, 1:49–50.

35. Sleeper, introduction," 1:42, 44–45, 47.

36. Charles A. Fenton, "Ambulance Drivers in France and Italy: 1914–1918," *American Quarterly* 3, no. 4 (Winter 1951): 337–38.

37. Sleeper, introduction, 1:51; Andrew, introduction, 1:6, 11, 16n1.

38. Andrew, introduction, 1:27; Sleeper to Gardner, n.d., November 7, 27, 1918, Gardner Papers.

39. Robert A. Donaldson, "Rue Raynouard and Mr. Sleeper," *AFS Bulletin*, April 16, 1919.

40. Sleeper to Gardner, October 4, November 7, 1918; n.d. [1920s?], Gardner Papers; Gardner to Caroline Sinkler, December 17, 1919, Beauport Collection.

41. Andrew, introduction, 1:6, 8.

42. Sleeper, introduction, 1:56–57.

43. Andrew to Gardner, February 1, 1920, July 21, 1921, with drafted response, Gardner Papers; *Boston Post*, September 14, 28, 1921; *Biographical Directory of the U.S. Congress*, s.v. Gardner, Lufkin, and Andrew; Douglas Shand-Tucci, *The Art of Scandal: The Life and Times of Isabella Stewart Gardner* (New York: Harper Collins, 1997), 315; www.federalreservehistory.org. For examples of visiting French dignitaries, see *Boston Globe*, July 17, 1929, and June 21, 1930.

44. Visit, September 9, 2016.

45. Sleeper's town house at 90 and 90A Chestnut Street is described in Alice Van Leer Carrick, "One House That Is Really Two," *Country Life*, April 1930, 34–39. On The Highlands, see Roger W. Moss and Tom Crane, *Historic Houses of Philadelphia* (Philadelphia: University of Pennsylvania Press, 1998), 188–91. Jacqueline Kennedy used the same wallpaper in the Diplomatic Reception Room in the White House in 1962 (Robert P. Emlen, "Imagining America in 1834: Zuber's Scenic Wallpaper 'Vues d'Amérique du Nord,'" *Winterthur Portfolio* 32, no. 2/3 [Summer–Autumn 1997]: 190, 209).

46. Curtis and Nylander, *Beauport*, 109; Hayden, "The Sleeper-McCann House," vol. 12, "Commissions."

47. Hayden, "The Sleeper-McCann House," vol. 12; museumblog.winterthur.org.

48. *New York Times*, July 25, 1926; Sergeant Mission House, National Historic Landmark application, U.S. Park Service.

49. Hayden, "The Sleeper-McCann House," vol. 12; James Reginato, "Michael S. Smith Renovates a Glamorous Beverly Hills Mansion," *Architectural Digest*, June 30, 2012; Arthur Kelley, "A New Old-World House," *Country Life*, November 1931. Nine Gables has been remodeled twice since it was built, so the rest of Sleeper's

design is unknown. The Fredric March house is described in the *Chicago Sunday Tribune*, March 31, 1935, and in *House Beautiful*, 1936.

50. Bucks County Community College, video tour of Tyler estate, www.bucks.edu/discover/history/estate/; Sophie Yarnall, "The Tyler Pewter Collection," *Country Life*, May 1934.

51. www.historicnewengland.org.

52. *Biographical Directory of the U.S. Congress*, s.v. Andrew.

53. Andrew to Gardner, September 9, 1923, May 9, 1924, and Sleeper to Gardner, August 26, 1918, both in Gardner Papers; Sleeper to Andrew, August 17, 1908, in Hayden and Gray, *Beauport Chronicle*, 29.

54. Sleeper to Andrew, August 14, September 1, 1908, in Hayden and Gray, *Beauport Chronicle*, 27, 39; visit, September 9, 2016.

55. Beaux to Andrew, January 17, 1904, [December 1906], Cecilia Beaux Papers, Archives of American Art, www.aaa.si.edu; Sleeper to Andrew, December 31, 1907, in Hayden and Gray, *Beauport Chronicle*, 15.

56. Sleeper to Andrew, December 23, 31, 1907, December 26, 1911, in Hayden and Gray, *Beauport Chronicle*, 11–12, 15, 63. For the bears, see *Beauport Chronicle*, 19n., Sleeper to Andrew, September 27, 1908, 53–54.

57. Sleeper to Andrew, June 10 or 11, July 18, [1915], in Hayden and Gray, *Beauport Chronicle*, 97, 101; Andrew to Mother and Father, January 30, 1915, in Andrew, *Letters*, 39. Sleeper later arranged to have these letters published in an edition of 250 copies.

58. Sleeper to Andrew, May 5, 1912, in Hayden and Gray, *Beauport Chronicle*, 65.

59. Curtis and Nylander, *Beauport*, 35; Shax Riegler, "The Legacy of Henry Davis Sleeper," *Antiques*, December 2009; Hollister, *Beauport at Gloucester*, 10.

60. Hollister, "Beauport," in Curtis and Nylander, *Beauport*, 25.

61. Abigail Carroll, "Of Kettles and Cranes: Colonial Revival Kitchens and the Performance of National Identity," *Winterthur Portfolio* 43, no. 4 (Winter 2009): 335–64; Curtis and Nylander, *Beauport*, 31, 52.

62. Visit, September 9, 2016; e-mail from Martha Van Koevering, site manager, Beauport, September 29, 2016; worldcat.org.

## 8. A Book by Its Cover

1. Robert Dahlin, "Conversations with Writers: Edward Gorey," in *Ascending Peculiarity: Edward Gorey on Edward Gorey*, ed. Karen Wilkin (New York: Harcourt, 2001), 49.

2. John Updike, foreword to Kevin McDermott, *Elephant House or, The Home of Edward Gorey* (San Francisco, Calif: Pomegranate, 2003), unpaginated.

3. Alison Lurie, "Of Curious, Beastly, and Doubtful Days: Alison Lurie on Edward 'Ted' Gorey," October 4, 2008, Yarmouth Port, Mass., www.goreyography.com/north/north.htm; Ogdred Weary [Edward Gorey], *The Beastly Baby* (New York: Peter Weed Books, 1962), not paginated; Edward Gorey, *The Gashlycrumb Tinies, or After the Outing* (New York: Peter Weed Books, 1963), not paginated; Stephen Schiff, "Edward Gorey and the Tao of Nonsense," in Wilkin, *Ascending Peculiarity*, 145.

4. Lisa Solod, "Edward Gorey," 96; Richard Dyer, "The Poison Penman," 112; Schiff, "Tao of Nonsense," 151; Simon Henwood, "Edward Gorey," 166, all in Wilkin, *Ascending Peculiarity*; conversation with Rick Jones, director of the Edward Gorey Museum, June 10, 2016.

5. Polly Root Collier to Mrs. Helen Garvey Gorey, November 11, 1942, April 5, 1940, on exhibit at the Gorey Museum, summer 2016; Carol Stevens, "An American Original," in Wilkin, *Ascending Peculiarity*, 129; Dyer, "Poison Penman," 112.

6. Dahlin, "Conversations," 46; Stevens, "American Original," 129; Dyer, "Poison Penman," 113; conversation with Rick Jones, June 10, 2016.

7. Solod, "Edward Gorey," 100; James Sullivan, "From the Cape: A View of Edward Gorey," *Boston Globe*, February 6, 2011; Jane Merrill Filstrup, "An Interview with Edward St. John Gorey at the Gotham Book Mart," in Wilkin, *Ascending Peculiarity*, 78–79.

8. Dyer, "Poison Penman," 113.

9. Brad Gooch, *City Poet: The Life and Times of Frank O'Hara* (New York: Harper Perennial, 2014), 115–17.

10. Dick Cavett, "The Dick Cavett Show with Edward Gorey," in Wilkin, *Ascending Peculiarity*, 58; Gooch, *City Poet*, 118; Schiff, "Tao of Nonsense," 152.

11. Dyer, "Poison Penman," 113–15; Filstrup, "Interview with Edward St. John Gorey," 82; Gooch, *City Poet*, 119.

12. www.poetstheatre.org/our-history/; Dyer, "Poison Penman," 116; Lurie, "Of Curious, Beastly and Doubtful Days."

13. Schiff, "Tao of Nonsense," 155; photo in Wilkin, *Ascending Peculiarity*, 114; Stevens, "American Original," 130.

14. Tobi Tobias, "Balletgorey," in Wilkin, *Ascending Peculiarity*, 14; www.departures.com/art-culture/culture-watch/inside-homes -famous-authors; Filstrup, "Interview with Edward St. John Gorey," 75.

15. Tobias, "Balletgorey," 15; Annie Nocenti, "Writing 'The Black Doll': A Talk with Edward Gorey," in Wilkin, *Ascending Peculiarity*, 197–200, 207–15; Henwood, "Edward Gorey," 167–68. The Gorey House in 2017 exhibited his vast collection of ticket stubs: visit, May 19, 2017.

16. Dyer, "Poison Penman," 110, 119; Solod, "Edward Gorey," 94.

17. Edward Gorey to Peter Neumeyer, October 7, 18, 1968, April 8, 1969, in *Floating Worlds: The Letters of Edward Gorey and Peter F. Neumeyer*, ed. Peter F. Neumeyer (San Francisco, Calif.: Pomegranate, 2011), 48, 50, 76, 210.

18. Schiff, "Tao of Nonsense," 138; Christopher Lydon, "The Connection," in Wilkin, *Ascending Peculiarity*, 218; McDermott, *Elephant House*.

19. Schiff, "Tao of Nonsense," 150; Stevens, "American Original," 129; Gorey to Neumeyer, Oct. 14, [1968?], in Neumeyer, *Floating Worlds*, 67; conversation with Rick Jones, June 10, 2016; Sullivan, "From the Cape."

20. Dyer, "Poison Penman," 123.

21. Barbara Epstein, quoted in Schiff, "Tao of Nonsense," 155; Jan Hodenfield, "And 'G' Is for Gorey Who Here Tells His Story," in Wilkin, *Ascending Peculiarity*, 2; conversation with Jean Martin, docent at the Gorey Museum, June 10, 2016.

22. Stevens, "American Original," 131–32; Dahlin, "Conversations," 34; Solod, "Edward Gorey," 107–8; conversation with Rick Jones, June 10, 2016.

23. Linda Winer, "Gorey Story behind the Dracula Settings," *Chicago Tribune*, February 4, 1979. Information about the history of the house comes from a typescript by Skee Morton, Gorey's cousin, "Before It Was the Gorey House," a copy of which was

kindly given to me by Gregory Hischak, curator of the Gorey House.

24. William Hyde and Howard Louis Conard, *Encyclopedia of the History of St. Louis* (St. Louis, Mo.: Southern History, 1899), 2530.

25. See, for example, *Boston Sunday Post*, August 4, August 25, September 15, 1912; October 24, 1915; August 6, 1916; September 23, 1917.

26. Conversation with Rick Jones, June 10, 2016. Descriptions of the house come from three sources. Rick Jones provided information about work Gorey did on the house. My visit allowed me to see the details of the house, while Rick Jones, Curator Greg Hischak, and Docent Jean Martin told me what had been changed. Kevin McDermott's *Elephant House* documents the house as it looked at the time of Gorey's death.

27. David Streitfeld, "The Gorey Details," in Wilkin, *Ascending Peculiarity*, 177; "Miscellaneous Quotes," in Wilkin, *Ascending Peculiarity*, 241; Schiff, "Tao of Nonsense," 148; McDermott, *Elephant House.*

28. Conversation with Jean Martin, June 10, 2016; Schiff, "Tao of Nonsense," 149.

29. For example, see Streitfeld, "The Gorey Details," 176–77.

30. Solod, "Edward Gorey," 96.

31. Conversation with Rick Jones, June 10, 2016. On Jack's Outback, see Marc Parry, "Customers Swallow Hard as Jack Loses Jack's Outback," *Cape Cod Times*, March 16, 2004.

32. John Wulp and Clifford Ross, quoted in Stevens, "American Original," 133–34.

33. Filstrup, "Interview with Edward St. John Gorey," 74.

34. Filstrup, "At the Gotham Book Mart," 76; Dahlin, "Conversations," 36; Steven Heller, "Edward Gorey's Cover Story," in Wilkin, *Ascending Peculiarity*, 233–35.

35. Schiff, "Tao of Nonsense," 147; Jean Martin, "The Mind's Eye: Writers Who Draw," in Wilkin, *Ascending Peculiarity*, 86–88; Dahlin, "Conversations," 32.

36. Dahlin, "Conversations," 34; Updike, foreword.

37. Schiff, "Tao of Nonsense," 157.

38. Gorey to Neumeyer, October 2, 1968, in Neumeyer, *Floating Worlds*, 37; conversations with Jean Martin and Rick Jones, June 10, 2016.

39. Dyer, "Poison Penman," 119; Cavett, "The Dick Cavett Show," 60.

40. The San Diego State University Library acquired the books in 2009 because of two personal connections: Gorey's friend and collaborator Peter Neumeyer was on the faculty, and Andreas Brown, the bookseller who had promoted Gorey's career, was an alumnus. E-mail from Gregory Hischak, June 27, 2016.

# INDEX

**Beth Luey** was born in Columbus, Ohio, and attended Radcliffe College and Harvard University. She is a past president of the Association for Documentary Editing and the Society for the History of Authorship, Reading, and Publishing. She was the director of the Scholarly Publishing Program at Arizona State University from 1980 until she retired in 2006, and an editor at the Adams Family Papers from 2008 to 2013. She lives in Fairhaven, Massachusetts.